THE
COMPLETE
TRAVEL GUIDE
TO CUBA

THE COMPLETE TRAVEL GUIDE TO CUBA

BY PAULA DiPERNA

with the assistance of the
Center for Cuban Studies and
the Cuban National Tourism Institute

ST. MARTIN'S PRESS • NEW YORK

917.29
D596c

Library of Congress Cataloging in Publication Data

DiPerna, Paula.
    The complete travel guide to Cuba.

    Includes index.
    1. Cuba—Description and travel—1951—Guide-books. I. Title.
F1754.7.D56   917.291′04′64   78-19436
ISBN 0-312-15862-9
ISBN 0-312-15863-7 pbk.

All photos are by the author, unless otherwise noted.

Maps by Donald T. Pitcher

Photo processing by Lexington Labs, Inc., New York City

Designed by Ruth Kolbert Smerechniak   79-3600

Manufactured in the United States of America

*This guide is dedicated to the hope
that the goodwill between people affirmed
by travelers can outlive the enmity
nurtured by governments.*

CONTENTS

ACKNOWLEDGMENTS

Any book of this nature is indebted to the assistance of many people. There is no practical way to thank, for example, the hundreds of Cubans I met during my travels, whose goodwill, hospitality, and graciousness inspired me to continue.

I am also indebted to Joaquin Gongora, president of the Cuban National Institute of Tourism, who first approved the project; and to Jesus Jimenez, director of Cubatur, who set it in motion. There are many others to thank: Iraido Cartaya and Ernesto Marcel of Cubatur's U.S. department, and Roberto Salas, for riding the ups and downs with me. All these people facilitated my extensive Cuban travels. I must mention too, Caridad Hernandez, Cubatur's guide extraordinaire, and Sylvestre Rodriguez, and Pedro Pablo Alberto for their long hours on the road; the staff of Havana's Capri Hotel for making me a home; Roberto Segre, Pedro Pérez Sarduy, Jean Stubbs, Reynaldo Gonzalez, Pablo Armando and Maruja Fernández, and Raúl Martínez—whose love of Cuba fed my own; and finally, the countless officials, historians, museum directors, and hotel managers who received me and shared their knowledge. Without all these people, there would be no book.

In the United States, I wish to thank Sandra Levinson and the staff of the Center for Cuban Studies especially Nani Martinez and Jerome Nickel, for initial encouragement and continued assistance; my family, especially my mother, brother, and sister, who have never let me down; Shirley L. Hulsart and Lois E. Wright of Bellinger Davis Co. who taught me everything I know about the travel business and provided the most professional environment possible in which to learn; Victor S. Navasky, who helped me when he had nothing to gain by doing so; Joy Gould Boyum, whose creative and critical energies trained mine; and my personal friends—all, but especially Susan and Denis Giblin, Walter Earl Haraway, Ellen Lee Ferguson, Vincent Fitzgerald, Zahre Partovi, Donna Voss, and Melinda S. Jones—without whose advice, assistance, creative suggestions, moral support, free meals, and enduring patience the book could never have been finished.

Finally, I am grateful to Eric Kampmann, who befriended my idea; to Paul De Angelis, Joanne Michaels and Leslie Pockell, who saw it through; and to my publisher, especially the editorial, art and production personnel, whose understanding, combined efforts and sustained support have made this book a work of which I am very proud.

PREFACE

In Cuba, the older houses have long wooden doors, often brightly painted, which open sweepingly into the main living room. In each door, there is a small opening—sometimes rectangular, sometimes square or oval—called a *postigo,* through which the house may be ventilated and from which visitors may be sized up before they are admitted. *Postigos* afford protected points from which to view the street outside, and many a portrait could be painted of the Cuban, with folded arms resting on the open *postigo* rim, interestedly, but reservedly, watching the day's activities. Opening the *postigos* is a kind of prelude to action.

As far as U.S. tourism in Cuba is concerned, it is definitely the *postigos* which have opened. Developments are unfolding with the same mixture of hospitality and caution which characterizes the behavior of anyone who is about to open his or her house to a visitor for the first time.

The new Cuba, which is after all just 20 years old, began receiving American tourists again as of March, 1977, when the United States lifted the travel ban on its citizens. Although some time has passed since then, it might as well have been yesterday when one considers the number of years during which travel to Cuba was forbidden to Americans. Since the thaw, some 8,000 U.S. citizens—all with diverse interests—have visited Cuba, but probably every American who has visited has had at least a passing curiosity about Cuban life since the Revolution.

Developing tourism sensibly requires a kind of high-wire balance, and Cuba is immersed in somewhat ambivalent feelings. Tourism anywhere is inherently a contradictory enterprise. On the one hand, it provides a country with hard-currency income, creates jobs, stimulates investment, and generates development. On the other, it jolts the local culture, consumes resources and products which may be scarce for local inhabitants, often spoils the natural environment, and creates a dependence which is socially and economically dangerous.

In Cuba, these contradictions are magnified. As a Caribbean island, it is a natural destination for the hordes of North Americans whose desperation to escape winter has generated a multimillion-dollar tourism industry. But to capture even a fraction of this business, Cuba must compete fiercely with Puerto Rico, the Virgin Islands, Jamaica, Haiti, the Dominican Republic, the Bahamas—islands which offer some of the world's finest and most sophisticated hotels and have gained reputations for the very things that Cuba's Revolution eliminated—gambling, hot night life, chic, and subservient attentiveness to the tourist.

Yet Cuba's climate and wonderful beaches are resources which Fidel Castro himself has said must be employed for economic development. How can this be done without compromise? How can Cuba stimulate the potential benefits of tourism while insulating itself from the potential ravages? This is one of the fascinating challenges of tourism there today.

Writing about tourism in contemporary Cuba is like attempting to describe the shape of a wave that is beginning to crest: the motion is constant, the parameters dynamic. To be definitive about the description, one would have to stop the wave.

Changes in the Cuban tourist industry—not just to suit the renewed U.S. market but as part of a national effort to expand the industry for all visitors—occur almost daily. Therefore, any guide to Cuba is by definition a work in progress, a process the reader is invited to join by using the blank note pages provided. (see pages 275–276).

Every recommendation herein is based on personal experience and inspection of facilities. I covered thousands of kilometers in several trips, visited every hotel in Cuba currently in use or under construction, had access to areas that probably no U.S. citizen has visited since 1961, talked with tourism personnel at every level and with tourists on holiday. I have ferreted, observed, discovered, sampled, and lived all the experiences likely to be encountered by the visitor. The picture presented is as complete as is possible at this time.

My historical comments are based on interviews with Cuban historians and corroborated by extensive readings, including fascinating 18th- and 19th-century travelogues, current histories, and the numerous publications of the Center for Cuban Studies and the Cuba Resource Center, both in New York.

My travel agency experience has enabled me to anticipate most of the interests and concerns of the visitor, though I first went to Cuba with no preconceptions. But I left Cuba fired by its optimism, moved by its spirit, and swept up by the Cuban sense of *adelante*—forward momentum.

The people of Cuba have seduced me with their goodwill and with the beauty of their island. I hope here to transmit my enthusiasm, and trust that visitors to Cuba will come to share it.

A WORD ABOUT THE CUBAN PEOPLE

Imprecision plagues any description of the marvelous Cubans, who embody a host of characteristics at once, a variety of races, an array of attitudes.

As hosts, Cubans are supremely gracious and solicitous. Even the rural farmer generously offers coffee (a genuine Cuban love which is tightly rationed) to a guest, despite the sacrifice. With visitors, Cubans are highly tolerant. They give directions gladly and wait patiently while well-meaning tourists bludgeon Spanish trying to order a ham sandwich. Despite what may be expected, Cubans are not at all anti-American, believing that the actions of the U.S. government are not the actions of its citizenry. In fact, Cubans often go to extra lengths for

Americans in an effort to play a small part in effecting a rapprochement.

Cubans also are unusually candid with tourists. They recognize that the eyes of the world are fixed on their island, and they are extremely proud of the interest foreigners take in their way of life. Cubans are loquacious, yet their elegant reserve emits unmistakable signals when the tourist has breached the bounds of good taste. A Cuban glance can be piercingly eloquent.

Cubans and music are synonymous. There is music everywhere, too loud and too early in the day for some, but for most foreigners, irresistible. Dancing is a national pastime, and occasionally waiters or waitresses can be seen balancing trays of glasses and meals to a steady Cuban rhythm.

The Cuban sense of humor is indomitable, sparklingly dry, and witty. Cubans have an enviable ability to laugh at problems—not to make light of them, but because they have learned from experience that sooner or later they will arrive at a solution. They wryly satirize all life's minor irritations—everything from the elusive taxi driver to broken video tapes on TV.

Many Cubans are also admirers of good food and fine clothes. Though most Cubans before the Revolution lived in miserable poverty, their personality is the antithesis of Spartan, and even the rural *campesinos* can now indulge what seems to be a Cuban love of the splurge. The heart philosophy of city dweller and *campesino* alike seems to be that life should be a balance of work for the common good and good times to reward the work of the common man.

WHY VISIT CUBA?

It's there. While U.S. citizens have been prevented from visiting, Cuba has been undergoing tremendous changes. It's a challenging, exciting environment that few Americans have ever seen.

Its beaches are among the best in the world. Certainly the ten miles of soft, white, perfect sand at famous Varadero rank it among the world's top five beaches, and Cuba offers countless others—all among the Caribbean's last "unspoiled." Scuba, fishing, swimming, and snorkeling are excellent in Cuba's transparent waters, and the weather is worth escaping to.

It's fun. No one can help reacting to Cuban music, the rum, or the *joie de vivre* of the Cubans themselves.

It's cheaper. Considering that most vacations to Cuba include all meals, round-trip airfare, sightseeing, and the best available hotel accommodations, the daily rate in Cuba undercuts many other winter destinations.

SECTION **1**

PRACTICAL INFORMATION

It is with infinite reluctance that the temporary sojourner in Cuba leaves her delicious shores, and takes his farewell look at their enchanting features. A brief residence in the island passes like a midsummer night's dream, and it requires a strenuous effort of the mind to arrive at the conviction that the memories one brings away with him are not delusive sports of the imagination. . . . The vexations incident to all travel, and meted out in no stinted measure to the visitor at Cuba, are amply repaid by the spectacle it presents.

MATURIN M. BALLOU,
HISTORY OF CUBA, 1854

BACKGROUND

Location: Caribbean Sea, 90 miles south of Key West, Florida; 48 miles west of Haiti; 87 miles north of Jamaica; 130 miles east of the Yucatán peninsula of Mexico.

Area: 44,218 square miles. Cuba is the largest island in the Caribbean, covering an area equal to half the remaining West Indies land area. It is approximately 760 miles long and 22–124 miles wide. It is surrounded by hundreds of small cays; depending on which ones are included, the coastline is 3,500–5,000 miles long. There are some 137 beaches.

Population: 9 million as of 1977. Male to female ratio is approximately 1:1; urban to rural, 3:2.

Climate: tropical gulf. November–April is the vacation season, with temperatures averaging 80° F. May–October is the rainy season, with occasional tropical showers and changeable skies. The hurricane season is early fall. June–August is the

3

summer, with temperatures averaging 90° F, especially in the eastern part of the island.

The sea temperature is 75° F in winter, 80° in summer. Average annual rainfall is 50 inches in coastal areas, 60 inches in the interior.

Topography: 4 main mountain ranges—the Sierra de los Órganos and Sierra del Rosario in the west, 2,300 feet; the Escambray Mountains in the south, 3,700 feet; and the Sierra Maestra in the east, the highest point of which is Pico Turquino, 6,500 feet.

The national flag: a red equilateral triangle with a 5-pointed star in the center for a field, and 5 stripes—3 blue and 2 white. Formally adopted in 1869.

THE GOVERNMENT OF CUBA

Head of state. Since 1959, Dr. Fidel Castro Ruz, whose other titles are commander in chief of the armed forces, first secretary of the Communist party, and president of the Council of State and the Council of Ministers, has been the head of state.

The constitution. The 1976 constitution proclaims Cuba a "socialist state of workers and peasants and all other manual and intellectual workers."

The Communist party. The party is the nation's major policy organ, composed of exemplary citizens from all walks of life. Membership in the party is via nomination. The central committee of the party is the ultimate decision-making body.

People's Power. Poder Popular ("People's Power") refers to the elective units in which candidates stand for office every 3 months. There are both provisional and national levels, and the first National Assembly was held in 1976. Eventually, all state operations will be converted to Poder Popular control.

Geopolitical organization. Cuba is divided into 14 administrative provinces: Pinar del Río, City of Havana, Havana province (including the special municipality of the Isle of Pines), Matanzas, Villa Clara, Cienfuegos, Sancti Spíritus, Ciego de Ávila, Camagüey, Las Tunas, Holguín, Granma, Guantánamo, and Santiago de Cuba.

LANGUAGE

Spanish is Cuba's official language. In hotels and tourist centers, English, French, German, Italian, Russian, and other languages are spoken, all in varying degrees of fluency. Intensive foreign-language study is presently under way.

Life is infinitely simpler for the traveler who learns a few words of Spanish, especially the rudiments of ordering meals, asking directions, and using money. Trying to speak the language will go a long way toward breaking the ice with Cubans, who are genuinely pleased when a foreigner makes that extra effort. (See phrasebook in appendix.)

WHO CAN GO AND HOW

IMMIGRATION REGULATIONS

U.S. tourists. American-born U.S. citizens who hold valid passports may visit Cuba as tourists provided they have an entry visa.* Cuban-born U.S. citizens may not visit Cuba as tourists at this time, though exceptions are sometimes made on a case-by-case basis.

The entry visa is, as of this writing, granted *only* to members of bona fide tours, *unless you have been invited individually by a Cuban ministry or other governmental agency*. If you have such an invitation, your Cuban sponsor (*responsable*) will initiate your visa request and handle formalities.

*The Ministry of Immigration usually holds passports for two to three days after tourists arrive. This is a formality, and the passports are returned to the tourist's hotel when immigration procedures are completed.

The visa granted to tour members covers only the areas and cities in Cuba which are included in the tour package. Therefore you may not deviate from your preplanned itinerary without the express permission of the Ministry of Immigration in Cuba. This does not mean that you may not move freely during the tour—it simply means that if you take a tour that provides eight days' accommodation in Havana, you may not desert the tour on arrival and spend eight days somewhere else. (Some critics have alleged that these restrictions are enforced so tourists can be monitored. Actually, the regulations are designed to keep individual tourists out of difficulty, as Cuban tourist facilities—hotels, transportation, foreign language services—cannot yet handle large numbers of visitors.)

Since 1977, the United States has maintained an "Interests Section" in Cuba attached to the Swiss embassy, though housed in the old U.S. embassy building. (When the building was opened for the first time since 1961, a Coke machine—the bright red, round-shouldered kind—was still operative, stocked with eight-ounce Coca-Cola bottles for a dime!)

The office was established to handle all matters affecting U.S. citizens or interests in Cuba. Its address is Malecón and N, Vedado, Havana (tel. 320551 or -2).

Non-U.S. citizens. Holders of other than U.S. passports should check with their local Cuban consulate, embassy, or representative for up-to-date information. However, as of this writing, citizens of the following nations *do not* require visas and are free to enter Cuba as individual tourists: Canada, Denmark, France, Sweden, Switzerland, and Italy as well as the Soviet Union, Poland, Czechoslovakia.

Should the need arise, citizens of Canada may contact the Embassy of Canada, Calle 30, #518, Miramar, Havana (tel. 26421 or –22 or –23). Nations which maintain diplomatic relations with Cuba have embassies or consular offices in Havana. Check with the state department of your home country before leaving, or with your Cuban sponsor.

Citizens of the United Kingdom, Australia, Mexico, Spain, and West Germany, to name a few, are subject to the same visa restrictions as U.S. citizens.

Members of the press. Members of the press who wish to visit individually as journalists must secure special press visa applications from the nearest Cuban embassy or representative. These applications provide full instructions. Members of the press who enter Cuba with tourist groups and tourist visas *usually cannot* have their status changed to "accredited press" once they arrive in Cuba. It is wisest to start out with a press visa if you plan to do any extensive or official interviews. Free-lance writers are, as usual, in limbo. If you have a specific assignment and there is time to wait, hold out for a press visa. If you are going as a tourist and hope to drum something up, don't count on having the doors opened to you.

Special cases. All visa requests other than tourist requests, which must be routed through tour operators for U.S. citizens, should be directed to: Cuba Interests Section of Czechoslovak Embassy, 2639 16th St., NW, Washington, DC 20009 (tel. 202-363-6315).

CUBAN CUSTOMS REGULATIONS

You may enter Cuba with a *reasonable supply* of any items required for personal use during your stay on the island. This includes liquor for personal consumption, cosmetics, and medicines. (If you travel with large quantities of pills, carry your prescriptions to verify that the medicines are for your own use.)

On arrival in Cuba, your baggage may be inspected and a declaration required for all electrical appliances and articles of special value. Cuba's drug laws are strict, and even the smallest amount of marijuana or any hallucinogen will lead to serious problems with the immigration authorities. Violation of drug laws can lead to imprisonment.

You may not take any archaeological artifacts out of Cuba without appropriate permits. You also won't be allowed to bring any plants or animals from Cuba into the United States.

OTHER REGULATIONS

Vaccinations. For U.S. citizens, no special vaccinations are required to enter Cuba unless you are coming from an area infected with smallpox, cholera, or yellow fever, in which case the appropriate shot is required.

Weight allowance. International airline regulations permit each passenger two pieces of checked baggage, the first not to exceed 62 inches in total dimensions, the second not to exceed 55 inches. One piece of carry-on baggage is permitted, not to exceed 45 inches in total dimension. Overweight to Cuba must be booked in advance. Check with your airline for charges.

If you are traveling via charter flight, different regulations apply, so consult your tour operator for specific instructions.

TOURS TO CUBA

REGULAR TOURS

Most regular tours to Cuba emphasize the straightforward tourist attractions—beaches, museums, nightclubs, and shops. They do not usually include visits to schools, hospitals, or work centers, although sometimes a combination of tourist and sociocultural attractions is offered. Regular tours are the most frequently scheduled, but special tours for divers, fishermen, and bird watchers have also been organized.

As a member of a regular tourist group, you are not permitted to simply drop in to an office, factory, or school without previous authorization. While this may seem obvious, Cubans have been genuinely astonished by the number of U.S. tourists who have turned up unannounced at various facilities, expecting to be given guided tours or, at the least, to be allowed just to stroll around.

SPECIAL INTEREST TOURS

Visitors who have specific interests in Cuba are better advised to visit on a special interest tour rather than on a regular one. These tours are usually assembled by Cuba-U.S. friendship groups, universities, or professional associations. They focus on sociocultural aspects of Cuban life but are less frequently available than regular tours. Those interested in special interest tours should consult their local professional association to find out if one is planned or can be arranged.

TOUR OPERATORS

Tours vary, depending on the tour operator organizing the trip. Some use regularly scheduled airlines, others use charter flights. Some fly directly from the United States, others via Canada, Mexico, and Jamaica. All operators handle visa formalities, and tours should be booked at least a month in advance. A one-week tour to Cuba, all-inclusive, costs approximately $600 per person, but be sure to ask for current rates, as some tours are even less expensive.

All tour operators organize tours from cities other than their own home office, so contact all of them before making definite plans. The following operators have organized tours to Cuba:

Anniversary Tours, 250 W. 57th St., New York, NY 10019 (tel. 212-245-7501), specializing in youth and college tours.
Caribbean Holidays, 711 Third Ave., New York, NY 10017 (tel. 212-573-8900).
CubaTours, USA, P.O. Box 60144, Houston, TX 77205 (tel. 800-231-0641), specializing in diving, fishing, hunting and bird-watching.
Orbitair, International, Ltd., 20 E. 46th St., New York, NY 10017 (tel. 212-986-1500).
Sunflight Holidays, Ltd., 3000 Marcus Ave., Lake Success,

NY 11040 (tel. 516-354-3300 or, for travel agents only, 800-521-4044) or 1470 Don Mills Rd., Don Mills, Toronto, Ontario, M3B2X9 (tel. 416-445-0110). *Unitours, Ltd.*, 1255 Philips Square, Rm. 307, Montreal, PQ H3B3G1 (tel. 514-871-8686).

For more information about special interest tours contact: *The Center for Cuban Studies*, 220 E. 23rd St., New York, NY 10010 (tel. 212-685-9038); *The Venceremos Brigade*, G.P.O. 3169, New York, NY 10001. *U.S./Cuba Health Exchange*, Box 342, Planetarium Station, New York, NY 10024; *Cuba Resource Center*, Box 206 Cathedral Station, New York, NY 10025; *National Lawyers Guild*, 853 Broadway, New York, NY. These organizations occasionally sponsor group trips to Cuba.

CUBATUR—EVERYONE'S RESPONSIBLE

The visa sponsor for all tourists is Cubatur, an agency of the National Institute of Tourism (INIT), through which all travel arrangements and information are secured. Foreign tour operators and other visitors book through Cubatur. The agency handles hotel reservations, sightseeing excursions, car hire, special-permission educational visits, tickets for sports and cultural events, etc. Cubatur operates offices in all major Cuban cities, and in small towns there is at least an INIT reservations bureau. The tourist's best link to Cubatur is either the guide assigned to each group or the information desks located in each hotel.

Here are some local tourist center offices for easy reference:

Havana—Calle 23, #156 between N and O Sts., Vedado (tel. 324521).

Santiago de Cuba—Plaza Céspedes, beneath the Casa Grande Hotel (tel. 7278).

Isle of Pines, Nueva Gerona—Calle 39, between 22nd and 24th Sts. (tel. 2200).

Varadero Beach—Via Blanca at the Darsenas Boat Basin (tel. 061-580 or 2506).

WHEN TO GO

For the beach and sun, January–May are ideal months. Autumn can be cool, and June–September often extremely hot. However, Carnival is a big summer attraction, and for those who are interested in Cuba's political life, visiting during a national holiday may provide a glimpse of Fidel Castro giving a speech in Revolution Square.

The sugarcane harvest, December–July, livens up the countryside and is also a fascinating time to go.

NATIONAL HOLIDAYS

Carnival in Cuba. The national holiday season culminates in the celebration of July 26, an exotic, gay, and buoyant time commemorating both the end of the sugarcane harvest and the anniversary of the Moncada attack, the first battle of the Revolution in 1953. In every city, town, and village, the streets ring with music—Afro, Latin, rock; floats parade with Carnival stars (estrellas); street vendors sell noisemakers of every conceivable type; food and drink abound. Masqueraders carrying decorated poles called *farolas* wind through the streets conga fashion, so absorbing their audience that sometimes an entire town is drawn into the dance.

The last week in July is the height of the season, although there are celebrations throughout the month and into August, the national vacation period, when many hotels are devoted to the exclusive use of Cuban citizens.

The Remedios *parrandas* take place at Carnival (see "Remedios" in the City-by-City Guide), and the Santiago de Cuba Carnival is probably the most electric, although in Cuba anywhere is a fine place to be during Carnival. (Consult Cubatur or the Ministry of Culture for special Carnival events.)

Other holidays. In addition to Carnival, there are many other celebrations and commemorations throughout the year.

NATIONAL HOLIDAYS

January 1	Anniversary of the triumph of the Revolution
January 2	Day of Victory celebration
May 1	International Workers Day
July 26	Anniversary of the Moncada attack
December 7	Anniversary of the death of Antonio Maceo

OTHER COMMEMORATIONS

January 28	Birthday of José Martí
February 24	Anniversary of beginning of 1895 revolution
March 13	Anniversary of attack on presidential palace
April 19	Anniversary of victory at Bay of Pigs
July 30	Day of the Martyrs of the Revolution
October 8	Anniversary of death of Che Guevara
October 10	Anniversary of beginning of 1868 revolution
November 27	Anniversary of Student Mourning (8 medical students shot by the Spanish during independence struggles)

Offices and some museums are closed on the national holidays but not on the other commemorative days. Special exhibits, poster issues and speeches accompany all national holidays in Cuba. Fidel Castro often speaks on the first of January, the 26th of July and at numerous times during the year. His speeches are printed in the newspapers the next day and translated in the foreign-language weeklies.

THE CUBAN SCHEDULE

Office hours: 8 a.m.–5 p.m. usually, with lunch between noon and 2 p.m. Depending on the size of the staff, some offices close completely for an hour; others stagger the lunch breaks. *Merienda* is the Cuban equivalent of a coffee break—one is taken in most offices in the morning around 10 a.m. and the afternoon around 3 p.m.

Shopping hours: 12:30 p.m.–7:30 p.m. in most places. Hotel shops are open on Sundays; others are not, except for selected pharmacies. (Hotel reception desks have lists of these drugstores.)

Mealtimes. Cubans never dine before 7 p.m., and usually dine even later. Hotels serve breakfast generally between 7 a.m. and 10 a.m.; lunch between noon and 3 p.m.; dinner between 7 p.m. and 10 p.m.

WHAT TO BRING

Note that no U.S. products, and virtually no Western European ones, are available in Cuba due to the U.S. imposed trade blockade. Therefore, it is wise to bring an ample supply of any items you consider indispensable. In most hotel shops, Cuban toothpaste, shampoo, cologne, and soap can be purchased. Most medicines are available under their generic names in pharmacies. Film from either the Soviet Union or the German Democratic Republic is the *only kind* available in Cuba, and cannot usually be processed in the U.S.

Recommended to bring with you: cosmetic supplies; sun lotion; mosquito repellent; sanitary napkins or tampons; personal medicines; photographic equipment, including ample film, flashbulbs, and lens cleaners; extra tapes for tape recorders if you are using one; extra batteries for all battery-operated appliances.

If you plan to take notes or do written work, carry extra stationery supplies, including pens. Typewriters cannot be rented, so those with extensive writing projects might wish to carry a portable.

Large beach towels are a must—they cannot be obtained at hotels. Flashlights are useful to have for those staying in national parks or in very rural areas. A Spanish dictionary should be carried by everyone. During the May–October season, a folding umbrella will come in handy for brief shower periods. It is wise to bring one along, just in case, no matter when you go.

WHAT TO WEAR

DRESSING FOR COMFORT

Unless there is freakish weather, summer-weight clothes are appropriate all year. In late fall and early winter you may need a light jacket or sweater, expecially in the evening and in restaurants where the air conditioning is often set at maximum.

DRESSING RIGHT

Cubans are extremely careful about their appearance and usually don't go out for the evening without having changed into fresh clothes. The overall atmosphere, however, is casual. Saturday evening tends to be the night "to dress up a little."

For men, sports jackets are always acceptable in the evening but never required except in deluxe restaurants. Ties are rarely worn. For women, pants, skirts, and sports clothes are always acceptable. Long dresses and skirts are rarely worn except at diplomatic functions, and even then, not by everyone. T-shirts are not permitted in deluxe or first-class restaurants.

Shorts are uncommon in Cuba and will always draw raised eyebrows. They are never acceptable in hotel restaurants. Bathing suits, even in resort areas, are never worn in hotel restaurants or lobbies.

Jeans are popular, though Cubans do not usually wear them in hotel dining rooms, restaurants, or nightclubs.

MONEY

CURRENCY AND MONEY EXCHANGE

The Cuban peso, represented by a symbol that resembles the dollar sign, is the Cuban unit of currency; it is divided into 100 centavos. Prices in Cuba are quoted only in pesos.

At the current rate of exchange, 1 Cuban peso equals approximately $1.25.

CHANGING MONEY

Where to change. Banks and hotel foreign cashier windows are the only recognized and legal sources of currency in Cuba.

In banks, you must present your passport to change money. They are usually open from 9 a.m. to 5 p.m. Monday through Friday, and 9 to 1, Saturday morning, but check again locally. Since Immigration often holds passports for two days after tourists arrive, the first currency exchange is most conveniently made in your hotel.

In hotels, you will need to present your hotel identification card, which will be issued upon check-in and which establishes your credit line at the hotel. Cashiers are on duty from 9 a.m. to 5 p.m., and the major hotels have 24-hour cash service.

Changing cash. As explained above, cash can be changed only in banks or at hotel foreign cashier windows. As on any trip, it is wise not to travel with large amounts of cash. You are not allowed to bring pesos into Cuba from any source.

Changing traveler's checks. Traveler's checks are readily cashed in banks and hotels at the foreign cashier window. Shops, however, even in hotels, cannot cash traveler's checks and will accept only pesos. All well-known types of checks (American Express, Barclay's, First National City, etc.) are accepted in Cuba. Cuban procedures require that you *do not fill in the payee or the date* when cashing a traveler's check. Just sign your name.

SPENDING MONEY

Currency control. Wherever you change your money, you will be issued a white currency control slip for the amount changed. This slip will be required when you purchase items in the tourist shops in the hotels, and the amount of your purchase will be deducted from the total on the slip. This currency record will also be required at the airport when you leave Cuba if you want to change residual pesos back to your home currency. (This can only be done at the airport on departure; it cannot be done outside of Cuba.) In other words, if you have $100 worth of pesos, but only $50 worth of slips, you can reconvert only $50. Although the reconversion desk at the airport has been known to accept peso coins, usually only peso bills can be changed back into home currency.

It is wise to carry some small-denomination traveler's checks for last-minute expenses and avoid having to reconvert large amounts of pesos on departure. The reconversion desk is usually swamped.

Credit Cards. As of this writing, *no* American credit cards are accepted anywhere in Cuba. Non-Cuban airlines operating out of Cuba do not accept credit cards either. Therefore, do not plan on charging return tickets or overweight. (This situation is presently being negotiated, but play it safe and carry cash or traveler's checks.)

Tipping. Tipping is no longer the custom in Cuba and is officially discouraged, the idea being that pride in work ought to be the incentive. The no-tipping policy extends to waiters and waitresses, elevator operators, maids, guides, porters, and taxi drivers. However, if you wish to show your appreciation to someone who has been especially helpful, a small gift—a book, a bottle of rum, flowers, etc.—would be more appropriate than a cash tip.

What to buy. All hotels have shops which carry a complete line of souvenir items—cigars, rum, records, Cuban T-shirts, ceramics, woven items, papier-mâché, *diablito* dolls, books, and posters. Prices are moderate but not cheap, and a price restructuring is currently in progress for tourist items. Your currency control slip is required for every purchase made in a hotel tourist shop.

With the exception of records and books, most tourist items are not available outside the hotel shops. Records and books purchased elsewhere are higher priced than those in the hotels. Political posters are usually not for sale, except in certain bookstores. The best selection is available in the Varadero Beach Exposition Gallery, and the Habana Libre Hotel.

If you are looking for a specific item, go to several shops. Selection and quality vary from hotel to hotel, and often small, unpretentious hotels have some unusual items. In Havana, the most complete selections can be found at the Riviera, the Habana Libre and the Hotel Nacional. In Santiago de Cuba, the Versalles Motel has unique gifts; at Varadero, try the Kawama and the International. For other shopping tips, see the City-by-City Guide.

The *guayabera* is a cotton jacket-shirt—starched, impeccably pressed, four-pocketed, double-pleated, acceptable anywhere—the exact origins of which appear to be unknown. An excellent souvenir of Cuba, it's been worn since the early 1900s and may have found its way to Cuba via Andalucian bullfighters. For men and women, available in a variety of colors, it comes with long or short sleeves and is ideally suited to the climate. Most tourist shops sell *guayaberas*, but lately some (and not necessarily less expensive) polyester versions have slipped onto the market. If you don't mind ironing hold out for the original cotton model with the Criolla label saying "Hecho en Cuba"—it's about 15 pesos.

Duty allowance. The usual $100 worth of items—jewelry, clothing, souvenirs, etc.—is permitted duty-free into the United States. There is an airport shop for last-minute purchases. Note that Cuban cigars are permitted to enter the United States *only if purchased in Cuba*, so make sure to get a receipt to show where you bought your cigars. Returning U.S. residents are allowed one quart of liquor duty-free.

COMMUNICATION FROM/TO/ WITHIN CUBA

MAIL

All mail to Cuba should be registered. Allow one month for delivery to or from the United States.

TELEPHONE

Calls within Cuba. Local calls can be dialed without an operator, though calls from hotels require switchboard assistance, and it is helpful if you can give the operator the number in Spanish. Long-distance calls within Cuba all require operator assistance and sometimes advance booking. A nationwide automatic phone system is currently being planned.

International calls. Rates depend on the time of day and whether the call is person-to-person or station-to-station. The average charge is $5 for 3 minutes, $1.50 per minute thereafter.

Calls to Cuba from the United States must be handled by the international operator for Cuba. There may be delays of up to six hours during the business day. Book the call in advance. Collect calls are not possible.

Calls to the United States from Cuba are handled by the international operator for the United States, with long delays.

Formerly, all calls had to be collect, but now you can pay for the call locally, at least in Havana. (Check policy in each city.) Book the call in advance and avoid daytime hours. When the appointment time arrives, call the operator and ask that your call be "reclaimed," (reclamada).

TELEGRAMS AND TELEX

Telegrams and cables may be sent from/to/within Cuba in the usual manner. Normal rates apply, and there is a cable desk in most hotels.

Telex calls to Cuba from the United States are routed via the international operator. As with the telephone, the efficacy of this method is determined by the demand at any given time.

GETTING AROUND

CITY BUSES

Extremely comprehensive systems exist in all Cuban cities. The fare is 5 centavos within the city and 20 centavos to the suburbs, payable in exact coin.

There are bus stops about every four blocks but sometimes farther. Drivers are usually very cooperative and will point out your stop if you ask for it when you enter. Stops are marked by *Pare* signs which list the numbers of the buses using that particular stop. Therefore, bus numbers are crucial when asking directions. (Bus maps are not yet available.)

Avoid using buses during rush hours. At each stop, usually two lines form—one for those waiting for seats, the other for those willing to stand.

Be aware that Cubans would generally rather take a bus than walk. Therefore, always check to see how far a given destination actually is before waiting for a bus. Often you find that things are closer than Cubans indicate.

TAXIS

Taxis in Cuba, especially Havana, are quasi-affectionately called *los incapturables*, a term which reflects the exquisite Cuban sense of humor, as well as justified frustration.

To ensure an equitable distribution of taxi services, taxis are assigned bases (airports, hotels, rail stations, main plazas) to which they must return on completion of a trip. Empty taxis that do not stop when flagged are not necessarily just being independent. They are not *libre* (free)—you'll see lights up on top of the cab when they are—to pick up street passengers, although occasionally they will stop to see if by chance you are heading in the direction of their base.

How to get a taxi. The best way is to go to a hotel, preferably your own, and give your destination to the dispatcher, who assigns the taxis as they return on a first come, first served basis.

In the evenings, during rush hours, and especially on Saturday evenings after the dinner hour, be prepared to spend a long time—often an hour or so—waiting for a taxi. (Seasoned Cuban travelers are never without something to read, and schedule appointments loosely.)

Taxis for special excursions or airport service can be reserved in advance through your hotel to avoid delays.

Costs of taxis. All trips are metered, and taxi drivers are scrupulously honest. In Havana, the run from Vedado to old Havana is about 1 peso; from Vedado to Miramar about 2.5 pesos; from Santa Maria Beach to Havana (10 miles) about 8 pesos.

CAR HIRE

Self-drive cars. As of this writing, self-drive cars are not available in Cuba. However, by winter of 1978 Cubatur hopes to have a limited fleet of cars in service.

Car and driver. Every major city in Cuba has a *Servicio Especial*, a car and driver service that provides automobile transport for official delegations and government officials. However, travelers may also rent cars with drivers. Rates are high. For 8 hours in Havana, the cost is approximately $60; rates double for out-of-town runs. Consult Cubatur or your sponsor for details. *Servicio Especial* must be booked at least 24 hours in advance.

For your convenience, following are *Servicio Especial* numbers in major cities:

Havana	32-0034/328243
Varadero	2642
Santa Clara	2490
Camaguey	8411
Santiago de Cuba	4328

INTERCITY BUSES

Many brand-new, gleaming white Japanese Hino buses will be seen along the highways—the Cubans have nicknamed them *colmillos blancos*, meaning "eyeteeth." However, bus reservations must be made well in advance through Cubatur, and there is usually a few days' delay in securing a seat. Therefore, travelers may find the service inconvenient.

Sample fares: Havana–Varadero, 6 pesos; Havana–Santiago, 12 pesos. Trips are long; the bus trip to Santiago from Havana, allowing for all stops, is about 18 hours.

INTERCITY TRAINS

The train system in Cuba offers very basic amenities and is generally inferior to the bus system. Sample fares: Havana—Santiago, 19 pesos (express night train, 12 hours, no sleeping accommodation) or 17 pesos (non-express train, 18 hours). Reservations must be made well in advance, also through Cubatur.

AIR TRANSPORTATION

National. Cuba's national carrier, Cubana, offers regular flights between all major Cuban cities. Sample fares: Havana to Santiago, 50 pesos (1 hour 20 minutes); Havana to Nueva Gerona, Isle of Pines, 25 pesos (50 minutes). Reservations should be made through Cubatur well in advance. A Cubana desk is located in the Cubatur office on Calle 23.

Havana's airport is José Martí, located about 25 minutes from the center of Havana. Both national and international flights use this airport. Other cities with airports are Pinar del Río, Santa Clara, Camagüey, Holguín, Santiago de Cuba, Baracoa, and Guantánamo, with other service projected.

International. In addition to Cubana regular flights to Europe and Canada, Cuba is served by a number of other airlines, including Iberia, Aeroflot, CSA (the airline of Czechoslovakia), Air Angola, Mexicana, Air Jamaica, Air Panama and LOT (the airline of Poland). Air Canada has the most frequent and convenient service for U.S. citizens—from Montreal and Toronto direct to Havana. (Air Canada, Calle 23 and P Street, Tel. 74-911.)

Thus far, flights from U.S. cities have been charter flights only, although several U.S. carriers are considering beginning direct, regularly scheduled flights within the next two years. Before leaving home, ask for the address and phone number of your air carrier's Havana reservation office. Individual tourists in Cuba must reconfirm their departure flights at least two days in advance.

SHIPS

There are limited passenger ships operating between Canada and Cuba, though Havana is now being included in Caribbean cruises of some U.S.-based companies.

TIPS FOR TOURISTS

TAKING PHOTOGRAPHS

Except for military and industrial installations, airports, and soldiers in uniform, photography is permitted almost anywhere in Cuba. Some museums, however, do not permit cameras, so it is wise to check the policy at each place you visit.

As in any country of the world, tact and discretion should govern photography in Cuba. Usually Cubans enjoy having their photos taken and will give permission, but they do appreciate being asked first. On tours to institutions like hospitals and schools, always ask before taking photos of the facilities.

VISITING CHURCHES

For churches of special historical or architectural interest, hours are listed in the city index of Section III. However, in general, all religious buildings may be visited during the regular service hours. Some are also open in the early evening for meditation, depending upon the size of the congregation.

TRAVELING WITH CHILDREN

Cuba is a fine destination for family vacations, with the resorts of Varadero Beach, Santa Maria del Mar (outside of Havana), and Guardalavaca offering appropriate accommodation and a variety of diversions. Most beaches in Cuba have perfectly graduated sea floors that make swimming very safe, and waters are usually calm. Baby-sitting can be arranged through Cubatur, with advance notice, in any hotel. Medical attention in emergencies is readily available. Children are revered in Cuba—nationals and foreigners alike.

PERSONAL SAFETY IN CUBA

Street crime is virtually nonexistent in Cuba. Tourists can walk the streets of any Cuban city without fear, although late-night solos on the Malecón in Havana may tempt fate. Travelers should take the usual precautions with valuables in hotels, although Cuba's are among the most secure in the world.

Women traveling alone in Cuba should be aware that the street compliment, or *piropo*, as much directed at Cuban women as at foreigners and delivered with admirable poetic flair and sincerity, remains very much alive in Cuba. Naturally, every woman has her own level of tolerance, but if one were to assign the thoroughly cathectic Piazza di Spagna in Rome a bothersomeness index of 10, and Constitution Square in Athens an 8, La Rampa in Havana (Calle 23, especially the corner of L) would score a 4.

However, the street action in Cuba is much less aggressive than in other Latin countries—one is never pinched or followed, and women alone outside the tourist centers generally go unnoticed.

One often sees foreign women alone or in groups in restaurants and bars, but rarely Cuban women, except at lunch. There is not a "singles scene" in the American sense of the word, although there are often single people on tours to Cuba.

ILLNESS

Gastroenteritis, common in other tropical areas, is uncommon in Cuba. However, should you become ill from any cause, you will be entitled to the same free health care as Cuban citizens so long as you are on Cuban territory. This means all hospital and physician services, with the exception of medicine for outpatients, will be provided at no charge.

If you require medical attention, Cubatur or a member of the hotel staff will assist you.

LOSS OF VALUABLES

Report any loss to Cubatur or your sponsor immediately.

Lost passport. If you lose your passport, contact the American Interests Section of the Swiss Embassy in Havana, Malecón (tel. 320551 or –52).

Lost money. If you lose your money, the American Interests Section may be able to assist you by wiring your bank for authority to advance you funds.

Lost travelers checks. Report the loss as soon as possible to the office where you purchased the checks. (When purchasing the checks, ask for the "loss report" phone number if you wish to report the loss from Cuba.) Since new checks cannot be issued in Cuba at this time, refunds will be processed and issued when you return to the United States.

Emergency transfer of funds. As this procedure is very complicated, it is best to exhaust all local remedies first. However, if absolutely necessary, money can now be transferred to Cuba from the United States in the following manner, *only* through the Royal Bank of Canada (tel. 212-363-8315, as of this writing).

A *relative* in the United States must make the request for a funds transfer. It is easiest if this relative has the same name as you do; otherwise documentation has to be provided to prove the family connection. Any amount up to $500 can be wired and collected at the Royal Bank of Canada on Calle 23 in Havana.

This process under ideal communication conditions takes a minimum of 24 hours. Since it is unlikely that ideal conditions will exist, a money transfer from the United States will probably take a few days.

Note: It is very likely that if what you lost carries identification, and is found by a Cuban, the items and/or money will be returned to you.

HOTELS IN CUBA

Before the Revolution, Cuba had a thriving tourist industry, but one which was based on gambling, flashy neon, and high-style living. Most tourists came from the United States, and tourism was concentrated in Havana or Varadero Beach. The rest of Cuba rarely saw foreigners and had no new hotels.

The pre-1959 hotels have continued to operate ever since—minus the gambling and prostitution—but redecoration and restoration have never been a priority. Consequently, many hotels seem frozen in 1950s decor. Plans have been developed to revitalize Cuba's hotels, but this will take time. The tourist will find adequate facilities most everywhere, but there is no hotel in Cuba at this moment comparable to the grand deluxe hotels in some other nations.

Since the Revolution, many new hotels have been built throughout the country, mainly to accommodate Cuban workers, who receive extensive annual vacation time. These hotels have the very latest amenities, including enormous swimming pools, several bars, cabarets, and sports facilities.

Most, but not all, hotels in Cuba have hot water. Cubatur steers tourists to those that do, unless there is no choice. The better hotels offer laundry service, barber shops, beauty salons, room service, and the usual hotel trappings. Service is not always fast, but making requests in Spanish speeds matters considerably.

HOTEL COSTS

Group travelers to Cuba will not be concerned with hotel bills, since all accommodation is prepaid. Individual tourists should know that the best hotels cost $20–$30 per day for a single room with bath, $30–50 per day for a twin or double. Less expensive accommodation—a single for about $10 and a twin for $15—can be secured in hotels with considerably fewer amenities. Individual tourists must pay their hotel bills in advance, in full. Reservations should be made through Cubatur before your arrival in a city.

Individual hotel descriptions and specific rates will be found in the alphabetical city-by-city guide in Section III.

ELECTRICITY

Cuban hotels have 2-prong, 110-volt a.c. outlets, the same as in the United States, so hairdryers, electric razors, etc. can easily be used. By 1980, however, Cuba expects to convert to 220 volts, and American appliances will require the use of a transformer.

HOTEL IDENTIFICATION

At each hotel, you will be issued a *tarjeta de huésped*, which identifies you as a hotel guest and establishes your line of credit. The card must be presented when ordering and signing for drinks or meals, and when changing money. It is a time-consuming process to have the card replaced should it be lost.

GUESTS IN ROOMS

Because of Cuba's past experiences with prostitution, and to discourage illicit marketeers, visitors are not permitted in hotel rooms without special permission of the management. Elevator operators usually ask to see an entrance pass for non-hotel guests. If you invite someone to join you for dinner or in your room, the reception desk must issue a pass and will do so only if your guest presents a passport or at least his/her own *tarjeta de huésped*.

CUBAN CUISINE

EATING OUT

Reservations. Most tours to Cuba include all meals on a pre-paid reserved basis, though many travelers venture off the meal plan to try different restaurants. Refunds are not made for uneaten prepaid meals. Dining out in Cuba is an extremely pleasant and rewarding experience, but reservations in well-known restaurants are recommended, and essential on Saturday nights. In hotels, guests are given preference. Reservations can be made either directly with the hotel or restaurant, or via Cubatur.

Prices. Cuba abounds in snack bars and cafeterias, which offer meals for as little as 2 pesos. Even hotel cafeterias are priced as low as 4 pesos for a 3-course meal. In moderately priced restaurants, entrées average 3–5 pesos; in first-class restaurants, 5–7 pesos; in deluxe restaurants, 7–15 pesos. Wine (usually Bulgarian, Soviet, or Portuguese) is at least 9 pesos per bottle in restaurants, although the tourist receives a 40% reduction. The average dinner will be about 10 dollars per person, slightly less for lunch, including beer or wine.

Details on specific restaurants are listed in the City-by-City guide in Section III.

CUBAN CUISINE

The Cuban diet has undergone a tremendous transformation since the Revolution, with new emphasis on fish, dairy, and meat products. The fishing industry in particular has been primed, and seafood, almost never eaten by Cubans 20 years ago (partly because of a lack of refrigeration facilities) has become a staple.

Food is plentiful for the tourist. There is often a choice of three or four different kinds of fish on the menu, plus abundant shrimp, lobster, and crab in season. A variety of meat dishes is also available in most restaurants.

The *mesa sueca* ("Swedish table") buffet has become very popular in Cuban hotels. The selection and variety are extremely impressive—long attractive tables set with various salads, fish, meat, and fruit. Ultra-gourmets may find Cuban hotel food a bit repetitious, but few travelers complain about the quality or freshness.

Especially worthwhile are the seafood buffets common in hotels one night a week, or the *Noche Cubana* ("Cuban Night"), during which traditional Cuban foods are served.

Menu selections. Traditional Cuban foods are: *cerdo asado con frijoles negras* ("roast succulent pork with black beans"); *picadillo* (a kind of spiced ground beef); *arroz con pollo* ("chicken with rice"); fried bananas (platanos) and banana chips; *natilla* (a delicious custard pudding); steak with onions; and *ajiaco* (a rice stew).

On the menu, too, one can always find roast chicken, grilled chops, and occasionally roast beef. Continental items can be ordered in the deluxe and first-class restaurants.

Rice and sweet potatoes (*boniato*) are staple side dishes, along with yucca and malanga, root vegetables which date to pre-Columbian cultivation. Certain spices and styles can be traced to the African elements in Cuban cooking.

Vegetables are not common, although lettuce and green beans in season are crisp and delicious. Tomatoes are usually served green, beets raw as a salad.

Bread is always baked locally and often served in buttery stick twists or small rolls. Each hotel seems to have its own type of bread.

Dessert is usually caramel custard (*flan*), marmalade with cheese, or French-style pastries. Not to be missed, however, is the famous Cuban ice cream, (helado), served in hotels and restaurants and just about everywhere—it is simply excellent.

> It is perhaps in the sherbets that the Havana confectioners will be found by visitors from abroad to excel. All the native fruits that can possibly be adapted to the purpose are put in requisition and in their infinite variety the most fastidious palate will not fail to find something to please.
>
> C. D. Tyng, *Handbook for Havana*, 1868

Coppelia is the Revolution's contribution to Havana's sherbet tradition. New dairy production enables Cuba to produce some of the world's best ice cream—countless fresh, creamy flavors—and it has become something of a national food.

It is served either at Coppelia ice cream parlors or street stands, or in a soft variety called "frozen" and served at Coppelita (little Coppelia) stands. You are never very far from ice cream. You can also order yogurt, a new product in Cuba since the Revolution, or try some Cuban fast food—pizza, Pio-Pio (fried chicken), or Pio Cuac (fried duck).

Drinks. *Alcoholic beverages* include Cuban beer (*cerveza*), excellent and readily available, and imported wine, usually from Bulgaria, the Soviet Union, or Portugal, which can be ordered by the glass or bottle in most first-class and deluxe restaurants. Rum drinks are the most common cocktails—mojitos, daiquiris, rum collinses, cuba libres (rum and cola). (The mojito—a Cuban signature drink immortalized by Ernest Hemingway—is lovely: rum, lime juice, crushed ice, and a minty sprig called *yerbabuena*, or "good grass". The daiquiri also owes its fame to Hemingway. Both drinks were invented in Cuba.) Havana Club rum is reputed to be the world's best.

Hard liquor is available in Cuba but is rather expensive. (Scotch and water at a first-class bar is 3 pesos before discount.)

Holders of foreign passports paying for drinks with foreign currency are entitled to a 40%–50% reduction on all liquor consumed—40% on rum drinks, 50% on wine and hard liquor. This discount applies in all first-class restaurants and bars and is granted upon presentation of your currency control slip, so remember to carry it with you.

Soft drinks, including fruit juice and fresh lemonade, are available in hotels—the larger the hotel, the greater the variety. There are Cuban versions of cola and ginger ale, both quite good.

Water is safe to drink everywhere in Cuba, but mineral water is always available.

Cuban coffee is thick and strong, like espresso. It is usually served in small cups, presweetened and without milk, unless you request otherwise. In the morning, *café con leche* ("coffee with hot milk'') is served. *Café americano* (''American coffee'') is served in major hotels, but it is basically Cuban coffee with more water added. The Cuban-style coffee is excellent, however, and well worth becoming accustomed to.

Some Cuban fruits. *The plátano*, or banana, is eaten raw, fried, crisped, boiled, and baked and is ubiquitous, as are the pineapple, orange, grapefruit, guava, mango, and papaya (called *fruta bomba* in Havana only). All of the latter are squeezed fresh daily in most hotels for pure luxuriant juice.

The aguacate (avocado) is common as a salad, and quite delicious, if less exotic than other Cuban fruits.

The guanábana is a thick-skinned, irregularly shaped fruit covered with briars. The fruit pulp is white, somewhat soupy yet sweet, and a bit like eating vanilla ice cream in a shell.

The mamey colorado is a chocolate brown, oval fruit that, when served raw and fresh, has the texture of very rich pudding.

The zapote is a very sweet granular fruit, ovular or circular, resembling a dark potato, but with coarser skin. It yields a delicious juice and is most common in Oriente, the eastern part of Cuba.

THE LANDSCAPE OF CUBA

The varied topography of the island gives Cuba the Caribbean's most interesting and varied landscape, with wide, flat plains interrupted by rolling hills and clusters of lush tropical vegetation. The coasts are pressed with white, wide beaches and touched by crystal blue sea. In Oriente, the island's easternmost region, the Sierra Maestra mountains reach into the sea with craggy fingers, and on the Farola, or en route to Gran Piedra National Park, the land undulates with every conceivable shade of green. After a rain, the water runs off plants and trees in streams, and the dark brown earth goes warm and steamy and sensual. In the central plains area, Cuban cowboys (*vaqueros*) often playfully try to keep pace with your car, and the rows and rows of cane in sugar areas distort your sense of distance.

The rural towns, strung out along the roads, are much the same everywhere—interesting focal points where remarkable economic progress encounters traditions that have not changed in a hundred years. The front patios are often full of people rocking gently through the heat of the day, taking in the Sunday of the afternoon. Superimposed on such scenes are the Revolution's images—the factories, schools, new housing projects, posters of heroes, and slogans.

For interested eyes, there is no rest in Cuba.

ECOLOGY IN CUBA

In 1978, legislation was in progress to create the National Committee for the Protection and Conservation of Natural Resources and Environment. This agency will be responsible for monitoring the new industries in Cuba, modifying the old ones where possible, and controlling air and water pollution and the depletion of resources. The committee will also supervise wildlife management and maintain the necessary liaison between the fishing and forestation industries and tourism. (Interestingly, solar energy is being studied in Cuba and is already used in some new housing projects. However, it is not yet considered a viable energy alternative, although the climate would seem to be ideal.)

THE NATIONAL PARKS SYSTEM

In 1963, the Cuban Academy of Sciences created 6 national parks within which hunting and deforestation are completely prohibited. These parks account for 4% of the national territory. New legislation proposes to establish an additional 110 reserves.

Penalties for violating reserve wildlife rules are stiff—fines, jail, or both—and they are advertised by Cuban newspapers, TV, and radio. Tourists are not exempt from the rules or the penalties.

ENJOYING THE NATURAL
ABUNDANCE OF CUBA

The Sierra Rosario parks—Soroa and LaGuira—offer accommodation, as do Pinares de Mayari, Zapata peninsula, Gran Piedra, and Topes de Collantes (see each in Section III). Camping is permitted at Jibacoa outside Havana, but nowhere else except with express permission.

Several tour operators have organized tours specifically for nature-loving visitors with bird-watching, fishing and other interests.

Flora. Cuba is a veritable garden island, with an estimated 8,000 varieties of plants, flowers, and trees. Some 2,000 are observable at the National Botanic Garden in Soledad near Cienfuegos, which also has 40 of the 65 species of Cuban palm (see "Soledad").

The stately *palma real* (royal palm) is a national resource protected by legislation from excessive cutting. Its straight trunk, the color and texture of new cement, rises 60–80 feet in the air and explodes into a top of green palm fronds. The *palma real* provides not only landscape elegance but a multitude of products. The fronds (*pencas*) are used for thatching and are secured to the trunk by thick green bases called *yaguas*, which are elastic and waterproof and are used for siding and roofing, sometimes affording better and tougher construction than wood. The palm heart, or *palmito*, makes a delicious salad. Bees gather palm honey, and the seeds (*palmiche*) are used for pig feed. The wood of the trunk itself, covered with milky fibers when cut, dries into a tough board with innumerable uses. Romantics might be pleased to know that the royal palm grows new *pencas* and *yaguas* with each new moon.

Other palms you may notice are the *barrigona*, or belly palm, whose trunk bulges where it collects water; the *licuala*, a dark green, fan-shaped leave; and the coconut palm, short, feathery, yellowish, and umbrellalike.

The fragrant white *mariposa* is the national flower, and the *yagruma* (a deciduous tree with a two-tone leaf looking as though snow had just fallen on it) is the national tree. Today, about 8% of the territory is covered with forests of precious and semiprecious wood, including mahogany, cedar, and ebony. During the colonial period, some 60% was forested, but the trees were cut for fuel and to clear land for sugarcane growing, as well as for wood products. Reforestation is currently a national priority (see "Las Terrazas").

Fauna. In wooded areas, there are deer, boars, and other woodland animals, the most common being the *jutía*, an edible forest rodent which is currently on the endangered-species list. There are 8 species and 3 subspecies, all of which have been overhunted.

The *almiqui* (*Solenodon cubanus*) is an extremely rare insectivorous mammal. When one was spotted several years ago in Oriente, the habitat was immediately declared a reserve. A pair was matched but never mated. Only the female remains alive, and no males have been seen lately.

The sea *manatí*, which Columbus's men described as "a large fish with tough skin all around except for a soft pig-like nose," is virtually extinct and has been completely protected from hunting. Jail sentences are mandatory for violations. The flat-nosed *manjuari* enjoys similar protections. Both species may very occasionally be seen in the Zapata Swamp near the Hatiguanico River.

Colorful land snails called polymites are unique to Cuba, and may be found especially around the city of Baracoa in Cuba's eastern extreme.

Fishing. The Caribbean waters around Cuba are excellent fishing grounds, especially for bonefish and tarpon. At Treasure Lake, reputed to be the best bass (Cubans call lake bass, "trout") lake in the world, anglers in groups of 25 or 30 have been known to catch 2,000–3,500 fish in 3 days, ranging from 3 to 14 pounds each. (The fish are returned to the lake, except for one trophy fish per person.) Special fishing excursions have been arranged to the lake resort of Guama, especially by CubaTours, USA.

Bird watching. Bird watchers comment that the woods of Cuba are teeming—of the total 388 species, 85 have been sighted in a day by a professional bird watcher, and 102 in a day and a half. Of the 21 endemic species, 12 have been sighted in a day.

Some of the species which can be seen are the trogon (the Cuban national bird), the tody, the pygmy owl, the Cuban grassquit, the solitaire, and the blue-headed quail dove. And bird watchers have commented that Cuba is an excellent place to expand one's "life list," since half the birds to be seen in Cuba cannot be seen elsewhere in North America.

On the endangered list are the *carpintero real* (billed woodpecker), the Cuban parrot, the *ferminia*, the *zunzuncito* (bee hummingbird—the smallest bird in the world), the *grilla*, and the *gavilancito*, among others.

Special bird-watching tours have been organized to visit the habitats of Soroa, LaGuira, and Zapata Swamps, with the Isle of Pines and Viñales valley projected. Tours will begin in the winter of 1978 (see "Tour Operators").

Scuba diving. Cuba has recently begun hosting diving clubs for what is regarded as some of the best scuba in the Caribbean. There are Spanish, English, and pirate shipwrecks, rare black coral trees, underwater aquatic life, and drop-offs—all barely explored by divers. Plans call for an underwater refuge at Varadero, as well as diving safaris between the Isle of Pines and Cayo Largo. Present diving centers are the Isle of Pines, Casilda (near Trinidad), Varadero Beach, and the north coast shelf. Cayo Largo is in development. French equipment may be rented at most resorts in Cuba, and instructor/guides are provided.

Gulf of Mexico

Yucatan Channel

La Esperanza
Viñoles
Sierra de los Organas
Peninsula de Guanahacabibes
C. de Guaniguanico
Pinar del Rio

Cabañas
Soroa
LA GUIRA
S. del Rosario
HAVANA
Artemisa
Golfo de Batabano

Jaruco
Matanzas
Varadero
Cardenas

Pen. de Hicacos
Archipier

Laguna del Tesoro
Guama
L. Hanabanilla
Manicarage
Cienfuegos
Sierra Esca

Golfo de Cazones

Isla de la Juventud

Cayo Largo

Trinida Casil

CUBA

| 0 | 100 | 200 | 300 | 400 Mi. |

| 0 | 200 | 400 Km. |

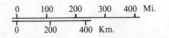

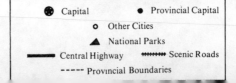

● Capital   ● Provincial Capital
○ Other Cities
▲ National Parks
━━ Central Highway   ╫╫╫ Scenic Roads
----- Provincial Boundaries

BACKGROUND ON CUBA

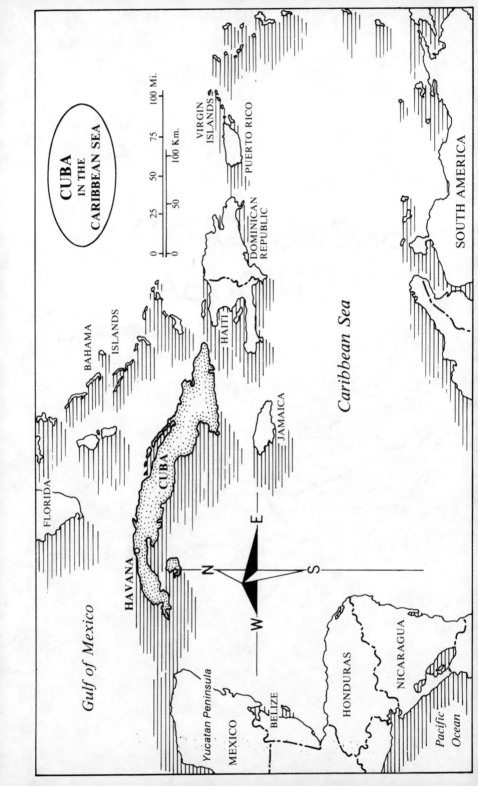

CUBA
IN THE
CARIBBEAN SEA

HISTORY OF CUBA

Discovery. When Christopher Columbus sailed through the Caribbean possessed by the idea of discovering the Orient, he found Indians who spoke of "Colba," a large island that took many canoe days to sail around. The navigator Columbus assumed they were directing him to Chipangu, or Japan, and he plotted a course that brought him to the north coast of Colba, or Cuba, on October 27, 1492.

It is difficult to say exactly what Columbus's first Cuban port of call was, but the general consensus is that he landed at Bariay Bay in what is today Holguín province, exploring the coast as far west as Gibara and as far east as Baracoa before leaving Cuba on December 5, 1492.

In letters home, Columbus wrote that the lands and rivers of Cuba were lush, fertile, and magnificent beyond his ability to describe them. He named the island Juana, after the daughter of Ferdinand and Isabella.

The first Cubans. Carbon testing of flint knives suggests that Cuba was inhabited as early as 3500 B.C. The present archaeological nomenclature divides the civilization into the

Pre-Ceramic (3500 B.C.–A.D. 1200) and the Ceramic (A.D. 1100—A.D. 1600). Of the Pre-Ceramic groups, the Ciboney and Guanahacabibes tribes, little is known, though it is clear that they were coastal cave dwellers dispersed throughout the island.

The Ceramic group, the Taino, emigrated from South America in two waves, the latest of which was about A.D. 1450, and seems to have lived mainly in eastern Cuba. The first descriptions of these people were provided by two emissaries Columbus sent inland to bring good tidings to the Japanese emperor. The expedition instead discovered a village of about 50 rounded huts with palm-frond roofs, inhabited by a tall and peaceful people—hunters, farmers, and fishermen who slept in *hamacs* (hence the word *hammock*) and who played *batos*, which was perhaps the antecedent of the baseball so popular in Cuba today.

They were artistic people who decorated their bodies and their implements with simple but bold designs. They were clever in basic matters, using the guaican fish, equipped with a sucking mechanism, to hook and catch other fish; and curious in metaphysical ones—their elaborate astronomical chart plotting the path of the sun and moon can still be seen in the Punta del Este cave on the Isle of Pines. They cultivated crops which persist in Cuba today—manioc and yucca—and their smoking habit triggered an industry that put Cuba on the map economically.

In the Indian pantheon, there were no gods as mighty as the Spanish, riding on horseback, sailing in giant boats, shooting with gunpowder, speaking with authority. No statement, however, is more eloquent on the Indian attitude than a speech made to Columbus on his second voyage by a chief, translated by an Indian who had learned Spanish.

> Whether you are divinities or mortal men, we know not. You have come into these countries with a force against which were we inclined to resist, it would be folly. We are all therefore at your mercy; but if you are men, subject to mortality like ourselves, you cannot be inapprised that after this life there is another, where a very different portion is allotted to good and bad men. If therefore you expect to die, and believe with us that everyone is to be rewarded in a future state according to his conduct in the present, you will do no hurt to those who do none to you.

But conquerors could hardly be expected to respond to such elevated reasoning. No one really knows how many Indians this chief spoke for, but the most generally accepted estimate of the population in 1512 is 100,000. By 1540 the figure had dropped to 40,000. This depletion was accompanied by rebellion, notably by the chief Hatuey, who was burned at the stake. When asked to at least embrace the Christian god so that he could go to heaven, Hatuey declined defiantly, saying that if the likes of the cruel Spanish went there, he'd be happier outside the gates.

By 1570, the Taino Indians had disappeared as a race, mainly the victims of outright murder and ongoing cruelty, but also prey to disease, overwork, and cultural domination. At least their name for the island—Cuba—survived.

Colonization. The expeditionary Diego de Velázquez received authority to colonize Cuba on behalf of Spain and to distribute land and Indian labor among Spanish nobles. He established the first city at Baracoa in 1512, and by 1515 seven cities— Baracoa, Bayamo, Sancti Spíritus, Trinidad, Puerto Principe (now Camagüey), Santiago de Cuba and Batabanó (now Havana)—had been founded. But ambition bred ambition, and the interloper lieutenant Hernán Cortés secured separate authority to explore Mexico, in the process depleting Cuba of leadership, manpower, ships, and money. What he conquered in the golden Aztec halls of Mexico City, and what other Cuban settlers captured in the Yucatán, irrevocably altered the history of the Western Hemisphere.

Gold production in Cuba was never significant, and after the Mexican conquests, Cuba was cast in the role of service station to the Spanish fleet, which was busy whisking between the mother country and the Caribbean, South American, and Central American colonies. Piracy, smuggling, and tawdry adventure thrived.

Slavery and the never-setting British sun. In Cuba, with the extinction of the Indians, the need for cheap labor spawned a lucrative slave trade. England and France too were deep in slave trading to supply their respective colonies, Jamaica and Haiti—the Caribbean's main sugar producers during the 16th and 17th centuries. Cuba, during that period, had been concentrating on cattle production, timber, and tobacco. But slavery and sugar fed each other, and both markets were growing constantly. By 1750, Cuba had enormous economic potential that was rigidly monopolized by Spain, although smuggling was rampant.

England, to say the least, was not satisfied with clandestine trade. She was out for the lion's share, of the slave trade especially, and captured Havana in 1762, injecting the island with mercantilism such as it had never seen before. Historians report that in the one year England held Cuba, some 700 merchant ships entered Havana, whereas under Spain, 15 a year might be expected. And, of course, the English trade included the 13 colonies to the north. A northward trading tendency, begun with the conquest of Mexico, was thus solidified by the English conquest of Cuba.

Sugar fever. After eleven months, Cuba was ceded back to Spain by England in exchange for other trading rights, but mainly because of political influence exerted in London by Jamaican sugar planters who realized all too well that a Cuba buoyed by the powerful English presence would be formidable sugar competition. But when the black slaves revolted in Haiti in 1791, collapsing Haitian sugar production and stimulating waves of French white landowner migration to Cuba, it became clear that Cuba would become the Caribbean sugar king.

Planting expertise from Haiti allowed more cane growth just as world demand was heightening. Slave merchants, recognizing the value of their product to the sugar cycle, loaned Cuban planters money to expand farms and make capital improvements. Steam engines were introduced; more land was cleared. In 1762, half of Cuba was wooded, but eventually 60% of the forests were cleared for cane—and always, more slaves. Cuba's slave population in 1774 has been variously estimated at 30,000–45,000. By 1860, it had jumped to 470,000, and some have suggested a total as high as 1.5 million. Sugar slavery was especially brutal. Cutting, hacking, carrying, and boiling, the slaves were the foundation of the sugar business, and by 1800 sugar was the foundation of Cuba's economy.

Slaves had been rebelling in Cuba since 1533 and continued to do so throughout the 16th and 17th centuries. Legislation passed by Spain in 1789 weakly attempted to improve slave conditions but was largely ignored. Even after abolition, black sugar workers were less than human in the eyes of the owners. Samuel Hazard, an American who visited the "nursery" of a friend's sugar mill, remarked in 1871: "It is very amusing to enter one of these nurseries when the children are being fed. . . . they all appear jolly and happy and make as much noise and have as much fun as would satisfy any 'radical' in the States. Poor things, they happily know nothing of the hard lot in store for them."

U.S. involvement and the rumblings of revolution. By 1848, 40% of Cuban sugar was being sold in the U.S. market, and both Cuban sellers and U.S. buyers were eager for expanded trade, thus deepening the relationship virtually preordained by proximity.

In the meantime, the inequities of Spanish rule in Cuba persisted. The governors were scandalously inefficient and repressive, demanding loyalty but refusing the Cubans, who by the time of the sugar boom had developed a strong sense of nationhood, any form of self-determination. Yet when Spain's South American colonies revolted under the leadership of Bolívar, Cuba's planters for the most part withheld their support, hoping thereby to avoid economic disruption through civil war as well as to maintain slavery. In addition, American policy statements by Henry Clay and others declared that U.S. interests were better served by a Cuba dependent upon Spain. So the Cuban gentry looked to the United States, where slavery was thriving prior to 1860, to stabilize their situation and insulate Cuba from the abolitionist tendencies that were becoming popular in Europe.

The route to this protection appeared to be U.S. annexation of Cuba, an idea that caught the imagination of Americans, especially Southern landowners. The notion had been on the back burners for a long time. Jefferson had toyed with it as early as 1808, and Polk actually sent an emissary to Madrid in 1848 to seal the purchase, but the deal was never consummated. The pro-annexation position was boldly expressed by Senator Singleton of Mississippi: "Nature has written upon Cuba, in legible characters, a destiny far above that of a subjugated province of a rotten European dynasty. Her home is in the bosom of the North American confederacy."

For the next ten years, through other attempts by the United States to purchase or take Cuba by force, the island was uneasily poised between continued Spanish control and absorption into the United States. But when the American Civil War ended slavery, it was no longer possible for Cuba to maintain it. The constant agitation in Cuba erupted in 1868. Landowners rebelled in Oriente. They were led by Carlos Manuel de Céspedes, who freed his slaves and armed them for battle. Other leaders were Máximo Gómez and Antonio Maceo, considered brilliant generals. The fighting continued through the 1870s, and though the United States ostensibly sided with the rebels on democratic principle, it withheld recognition of the state of belligerency, thus ensuring that Spain would be bound by international law to protect U.S. property during the fighting.

In February, 1878, the Cubans signed an armistice with Spain called the Treaty of Zanjón, which did not provide for independence. In the protest of Baragua, Maceo and his followers refused to sign (Céspedes was dead by then). Fighting was renewed briefly, and Maceo left Cuba. Between 1878 and 1895, revolutionary activities like the *Guerra Chiquita* ("Little War") interrupted an uneasy peace. Slavery was eventually abolished in 1886, without compensation to the owners.

The years 1880–1890 saw tremendous U.S. investment in Cuba. The island needed capital and technical advances to compete with cheaper beet sugar production, which was proliferating in Europe. The United States built railroads and large mills, creating the famous "centrals"—self-contained sugar cities. In 1890, there was a general reduction in the U.S.-Cuba tariff, and Cuba was providing the United States with 10% of its total imports. By 1895, the United States had some $30 million invested in Cuba, including public works and railroads. It was a U.S.-controlled Monopoly board.

Meanwhile, corruption persisted, as did sugar dependence. Poverty was rampant. In 1885, Maturin Murray Ballou described it: "Saturday is the harvest day for beggars in the Cuban cities, on which occasion they go about by scores from door to door carrying a large canvas bag" for gathering rolls. "These mixed with vegetables, bits of fish, and sometimes meat and bones when they can be procured are boiled into a soup, thus keeping soul and body together in the poor creatures during the week.''

In addition, hundreds of Chinese workers, illiterate and some blind, were imported to Cuba to supplement the slave labor force. Their lives were as miserable after abolition as before.

José Martı and the second Cuban revolution. No traveler to Cuba will leave without having seen a bust or heard the name of José Martí, considered Cuba's ''Apostle'' and the ''intellectual author'' of the 1959 Revolution. The fiercely patriotic Martí, born in 1853, had been jailed for seditious tendencies against Spain by the time he was 18. He was a poet, newspaperman, and political thinker who was eventually exiled. Martí worked in the United States as a reporter, arguing strongly that U.S. domination of the Cuban scene was ultimately as dangerous to the island as Spanish domination had been.

In 1895, Martí banded together with the Maceo brothers and returned to Cuba, landing by boat in April on the southern tip of Oriente to begin the second Cuban revolution. The rebels secured help from the landowners, blacks, workers, and peasants—the Mambisas (an African word meaning ''children of vultures,'' used by the Spanish to refer to the rebels, and connoting ''the dregs'').

Martí himself was killed in 1895, and his death effectively left Cuba without a leader of sufficient stature to negotiate with Spain or the United States. Around the same time, American expansionist forces were observing the Cuban scene with great interest. Many statesmen declared it the destiny of the United States to own Cuba, though most of the U.S. press and some supporters had favored Martí's effort. There is little doubt that, in the end, the economics of the situation determined U.S. policy.

U.S. intervention. In 1895, Theodore Roosevelt clearly had the ear of President Cleveland, and neither of them were pacifists. The Hearst newspapers fanned war fever, with William Randolph himself directing the campaign. A famous cable exchange between Hearst and the artist Frederic Remington exemplifies the Hearst arrogance on the war. Remington, who was covering the war in Cuba for Hearst's chain, could not get to the front and wired Hearst, "There will be no war. I wish to return." Hearst shot back, "Please remain. You furnish the pictures and I'll furnish the war."

Hearst's interest was not least to boost circulation with stories—admittedly not always exaggerated—of Spanish atrocities against the Cubans. The infamous General Weyler had established concentration camps around the island, herding rural people together to defuse the rebel movement. However, despite such activities and the humanitarian concerns they aroused, the question of belligerent rights returned to the forefront, and the United States continued to withhold recognition of the rebels. In addition to the material considerations, many U.S. statesmen feared that too much support of Cuba would produce a black republic there, given the Haitian experience and the formidable presence of Antonio Maceo, the black Cuban general. By then, some 75% of the rebel army was black, as well.

In mid-1896 Weyler banned exports from Cuba in an attempt to ruin Cuban businessmen abroad who were supporting the rebels. A depression in the United States at the time influenced McKinley, then campaigning for the presidency, to present himself as not being "indifferent" to war.

Meantime, the battles in Cuba raged, and Maceo, "the Bronze Titan," was finally killed in late 1896. Theodore Roosevelt again strongly urged U.S. intervention. By 1897–98, however, a new political administration in Spain seemed resigned to independence for Cuba. Weyler resigned in protest against Cuban autonomy. McKinley, who'd been elected, ordered a "watch and wait" policy, but rumors of continued danger to U.S. citizens in Cuba prompted the dispatch of the U.S. ship *Maine* to Havana harbor.

On February 15, 1898, the *Maine* mysteriously blew up. Theories persist that the blast was deliberately set, either by U.S. interests attempting to force entry into the war or by Cubans anxious to draw the United States into the conflict. Whatever the reason, hysteria followed, and McKinley, in a last gesture to avert battle, offered to buy Cuba for $300 million. For unknown reasons, his message to Spain crossed wires, and the U.S. Congress peremptorily declared war on Spain on April 25,

1898, some 40 years after the first Cuban rebellion.

The last gasp of war. Most Americans are familiar with the legends of the Spanish-American War (called by the Cubans "the U.S. intervention"), replete with glorious charges up San Juan Hill by Teddy Roosevelt's Rough Riders. In truth, the war was inglorious in the extreme; men died of malaria and yellow fever by the thousands; some 500 were killed in actual battle. Press interest in the war waned, and finally, on July 17, 1898, Spain surrendered.

The victory was bitterly hollow for the Cuban army. They had been fighting Spain since 1868 and were denied permission by the United States to attend the surrender ceremony. Calixto García, the commanding Cuban officer, was invited as a "guest" of the United States to the formal exit of Spain. When the war ended, it was the American flag, not Cuba's, which was run up. The end of the war found Cuba's condition more than sorry.

The population was then about 1.5 million, and it appears that about 10% of the people died during the war years. Some 60% of the population were illiterate; only 90,000 of the school-age population of 550,000 were in school. Poverty and disease were rampant, and half the cultivated land had been ravaged. In effect, Cuba had become an occupied territory, and citizens were asked to sign declarations renouncing the king of Spain and to "solemnly swear that I will bear true faith and allegiance to the U.S.A. and recognize its supremacy until a stable government is established upon the Island of Cuba."

The transition and the Republic. The United States immediately established a temporary government, insisting that the Cubans did not really want full-scale separation from the United States. Congress passed the Platt Amendment, which provided that the United States "reserve and retain the right of intervention for the preservation of Cuban independence and the maintenance of stable government," as well as hold title to Cuban land where necessary to carry out its obligations. Thus, the period now known in Cuba as the "pseudo-republic" was ushered in.

On May 20, 1902, the Cuban flag was finally raised, and Estrada Palma became the first president. The U.S. governor withdrew, leaving behind some $100 million invested by the United States in sugar, tobacco, railroads, schools, and utilities.

Those interested in political intrigue, scandal, brutality, and corruption will find a mother lode in the history of Republican Cuba. One need not be a Marxist to acknowledge that between 1902 and 1959, the Cuban presidency was entered through a revolving door controlled by the United States. Ineptitude and indifference characterized Cuban leadership. Fortunes were made and lost in sugar, but no improvement took place in the life of the average person. The infamous Gerardo Machado, elected in 1925 on a relatively liberal platform, received $0.5 million in campaign expenses from a U.S.-owned electric company. He extended his term of office from four to six years and terrorized his political enemies. Protests mounted; so did the repression. A vocal Communist student leader, Julio Antonio Mella, was assassinated; other enemies were dropped to the sharks in Havana harbor. Demonstrations were brutally squelched, and always the U.S. Marine Corps was on hand "to preserve order." In the meantime, U.S. investments continued to mount, and Cuba grew more dependent on sugar and on the U.S. purchase quota. When sugar prices dropped and Cuba attempted to limit production and diversify its economy, U.S. pressure in the form of withheld loans forced the Cubans to maintain production to favor American purchase prices. By 1936, the United States owned 56% of the sugar production facilities in Cuba at the same time that the rural minimum wage was only 80¢ a day, $1 per day in the cities.

Fulgencio Batista, an army sergeant who had led a revolt of officers against Machado in 1933 actually held the reins of presidential power. Batista had endeared himself to U.S. ambassador Sumner Welles for taking staunch anti-Communist positions and continuing to favor U.S. investments. He too resorted to assassination of enemies who were too troublesome. With U.S. support Batista ran for president in 1944 and was very surprised when his opponent won. Batista retired to Florida, leaving Cuba to her own devices for awhile. Sensing that his hour had come at last, Batista returned to Cuba in 1952, staged a coup d'état, suspended the constitution, and headed an unprecedented, brutal regime.

Fidel Castro and the Moncada attack. What is rarely realized in the United States about the Cuban Revolution is that Fidel Castro did not just drop from the sky with talk of rebellion. He merely culminated—with a unique charisma and intelligence—a long series of insurrections, protests, and disorders.

The dynamic Fidel, as he is fondly referred to by all Cubans, was born in Oriente in 1927 into a comfortable agricultural family. He was educated in private schools and studied law at the University of Havana. Castro became a political activist early, demonstrating and striking at the university against the inequities of Cuban society. Just a few weeks after the 1952 coup, he presented a petition condemning Batista's actions.

The Revolution really began on July 26, 1953, with the attack on the Moncada barracks in Santiago de Cuba. Castro had gathered a group of young people—he himself was only 26— with the express purpose of overthrowing Batista. An elaborate plot to attack the barracks was planned for Carnival, when it was believed the officers would be too drunk or tired to resist. But the plan went awry, and 68 attackers were rounded up and imprisoned. Fidel Castro and some others escaped but were captured a week later.

The torture and brutality inflicted on the prisoners has been well documented. Haydée Santamaría, now head of the Casa de las Americas, was expected to divulge the secrets of the group when she was presented with the gouged eye of her brother, Abel. When she refused, the testicles of her fiancé were offered. Still she refused. The public was outraged by the army's behavior but powerless. At his trial after the attack, Fidel Castro delivered his famous "History Will Absolve Me" speech, in which he exposed the violence to international scrutiny as well as delineated the deficiencies of Cuban society. No visitor to Cuba should attempt to analyze the Revolution without reading this speech. (It is available in book form, both in Cuba and the United States.)

Exile and the Granma. The United States, for its part, had supported Batista since his salad days in the '30s and continued to back him during the early years of Castro's rebellion.

Castro and his followers were imprisoned on the Isle of Pines until 1955, when a general amnesty released them. Most left for Mexico, where Castro met Ernesto "Che" Guevara, the Argentine doctor, whose role in the Cuban Revolution was pivotal. Together they trained a guerrilla force and planned to return to Cuba.

They raised funds however possible, including through U.S. supporters, and eventually were able to outfit the leaky yacht *Granma* and sail for Cuba in heavy seas, with 83 men in a boat suited for 10. They were sick, scared, and inexperienced. Then, when they landed, the *Granma* got stuck in mud and missed the beachhead, and the men had to abandon supplies on the boat. To add to their problems, Batista's men had been alerted and launched an attack. Of the original group of rebels, some 15 survived, and with this core, Cuba made a revolution.

1959. The dissatisfaction of the Cuban people with Batista actually ensured Castro's eventual success. He was able to rely on the peasants, the farmers, and even the middle class to hide and feed him and aid the rebels. Soon the 15 were thousands, ill trained and rag-tag, but dedicated.

Batista's response was heightened brutality. Torture became the rule, murder accepted practice. But the rebel army gradually won control of more and more territory, in the process gaining widespread popular support. When Batista realized that he could no longer hold on, he fled Cuba, and on January 1, 1959, the guerrilla army marched victoriously into Cuban cities. Batista died in exile in 1973. The fronts and battles of the Revolution are described in detail in Havana's Museum of the Revolution.

The leaders, the Revolution, the end of U.S. presence. The amazing and most inspiring quality of the Revolution was its youth. The leaders were idealistic, intelligent, humane, but none had any experience running a government. All they knew was that they had promised that the Revolution would provide the basic necessities of life for everyone. Just how, was the problem. Despite its inexperience, the new government moved immediately to implement the program Castro had outlined in 1953.

The Revolutionary government also punished the members of Batista's army who had been responsible for violence against innocent Cubans. Many were executed after popular tribunals found them guilty. When criticized for their actions, today's leaders reply that they were obliged to rid Cuba of Batista's henchmen, who had committed heinous crimes and deserved punishment.

On March 6, 1959, all rents in Cuba were reduced by 50%, and on March 17, all beaches were declared open to the public. Under the First Agrarian Reform land that had been owned by Batista supporters was confiscated, and private land ownership fixed at a maximum of 1,000 acres. These socialist rumblings naturally alarmed the well-to-do, many of whom had supported Castro but were unwilling to surrender lucrative lands or rental incomes. The flight of the upper classes began.

In the meantime, Che Guevara, the new minister of industry, signed trade agreements with Egypt, India, Pakistan, Indonesia, Japan, and finally with the Soviet Union for oil at preferential prices. U.S. fear of Cuban Communism peaked. The refineries owned by Standard Oil and Shell refused to refine Soviet petroleum. Sabotage began, and in March 1960, a French ship exploded in Havana killing 20 people. CIA involvement was suspected.

In July, after Cuba and the Soviet Union had reestablished relations, which had been severed under Batista, the United Stated reduced Cuba's sugar quota, eventually refusing to purchase any at all. This was a potentially devastating blow, considering how dependent Cuba was on the U.S. market, but the Soviet Union agreed to take up the slack.

The new government also began to nationalize U.S. properties—the refineries, factories, and utilities. At the First Declaration of Havana, a million Cubans assembled to denounce the United States for "open intervention for more than a century in the affairs of Latin America." More nationalization, including Cuban-owned large businesses, preceded the suspension of diplomatic relations between the United States and Cuba in 1960.

Simultaneously, exiled Cubans were plotting ways to return and upset the Revolution. There was nighttime strafing of

Cuban cities and airports by planes that had observable U.S. military markings. Counter-Revolutionary activity burst out sporadically, even against the young literacy workers who were teaching peasants in the mountains to read.

On April 17, 1961, after President John F. Kennedy had publicly and repeatedly denied the existence of such a plan, some 1,500 U.S.-trained mercenaries and exiled Cubans landed at Playa Girón on the south coast of Cuba at the mouth of the Bay of Pigs. The troops expected to enjoy the support of the Cuban population, but instead local militia groups coalesced, Fidel Castro arrived on the scene, and the invasion was repelled in 72 hours.

On April 25, 1961, the United States declared a total embargo on all trade with Cuba, and on December 2, Fidel Castro publicly declared himself a Marxist-Leninist. In 1962, the situation deteriorated further when the United States protested the Soviet deployment of missiles, which the Cubans claim were defensive in nature. An international crisis followed when the United States imposed a military blockade on the island. After enormous tension and uncertainty, the missiles were withdrawn, but by then, U.S.-Cuba relations had reached a nadir. Americans were forbidden to travel to Cuba, and for most U.S. citizens the curtain fell on the Revolution.

The Cuban exile community continued its attempts to overthrow Castro, with various forms of U.S. support, but for the most part, Cuba ceased to exist for the average American. To sift the reality from 17 years of mystery and mythology is part of the reason to travel to Cuba today. The balance of this guide attempts to inform as well as facilitate that exploration.

SOCIAL PROFILE

Sociocultural aspects of Cuban life have drawn increasing attention from U.S. tourists, although regular tours do not include visits to schools, factories, health facilities, etc. The following section provides some very basic information about Cuban life and answers many commonly asked questions.

AFRICA IN CUBA

Although slaves were brought to Cuba from all over Africa, West Africans (Yorubas, Congos, and Carabali tribal people) predominated. In addition, there were Cuban free blacks— escaped slaves and those who had purchased their freedom or gained it as descendants of a match between a free black and a slave. The free blacks, who were segregated from the mainstream of Cuban life, held their own carnivals and maintained clubs called *cabildos*. These separate facilities protected customs which might otherwise have been lost. In 1960, racial discrimination was officially banned in Cuba, and today anyone will tell you that "we are all a little black."

Santeria is an Afro-Caribbean religion practiced today in some parts of Cuba, which amalgamates African beliefs and Catholicism. Two other cults, the Abakua and the Buyeria, were common in Cuba during slavery but have virtually disappeared. Though no longer encouraged as religions, the cults spawned many of the dances, rhythms, colors, and musical instruments used today as well as myths and archetypal patterns that have filtered into Cuban poetry and literature. The folklore Museum at Guanabacoa (see City-by-City Guide) is a must for tourists interested in the role played by Africa in Cuba.

MASS ORGANIZATIONS

The Federation of Cuban Women (FMC). A 19th century traveler to Cuba remarked that the shoes of wealthy women were made of the finest satin, light and supple, not meant for touching ground. The ladies traveled only by carriage, and goods were brought to the street for their perusal, lest the shoppers should have to alight. Ladies tended their complexions with *cascarilla*, an egg-white-based mixture, to create a porcelain finish. Reportedly there were "no strong-minded among them." Poorer women were usually either slaves or domestic servants. All women had the boundaries of their behavior drawn by that most Latin of male characteristics, *machismo*.

On August 23, 1960, the Federation of Cuban Women was established for the express purpose of incorporating women into the social, political, and economic life of the country. The

FMC set up the Ana Betancourt Schools for Peasant Girls, other Schools for the Advancement of Domestic Servants, and some 34,000 women participated in these programs. The FMC also sponsored the first day-care centers and was instrumental in securing passage of the Family Code and the exemplary laws governing maternity leave. The code, the first such law in the world, decrees that both marriage partners must participate in the running of the home, sharing household tasks.

Today there are approximately 600,000 working women, representing 28% of the total work force.

Committees for the Defense of the Revolution (CDR). The visitor will notice CDR bulletin boards on virtually every corner. The CDRs were organized for internal defense purposes shortly after the Revolution. However, these "block associations" also sponsor parties and cleanups, collect material for recycling, organize blood-donor campaigns, and raise money for special events. They constitute the first level of civic organization.

The Pioneers (Los Pioneros). Youngsters wearing blue and white scarves over their school uniforms are members of the Pioneers, an extracurricular organization that provides primary-school children with recreational opportunities, builds vocational interests, and introduces Marxist-Leninist theory. Tourists staying at Santa Maria del Mar will notice a nearby lagoon with cable cars strung across it. This is a typical Pioneer summer camp, as is the Camilo Cienfuegos Camp in Camagüey. Special interest tours often include Pioneer centers in preplanned itineraries, but visits usually cannot be arranged otherwise.

Young Communist League (UJC). The UJC is a transitional organization for Cuban youth who fall between the ages of the Pioneers and full-fledged Communist party membership.

HOUSING

The New Communities. In the countryside, one will often pass modern towns which seem to have sprung from the hills. One of the most interesting initiatives of the Cuban Revolution has been the construction of new towns in rural areas, usually around collective farms or dairy cooperatives. They are completely self-contained, with apartments, schools, pharmacies, day-care centers, and clinics. Typical of them is La YaYa in Villa Clara province, often visited by special interest tours. The most unusual new town is Las Terrazas, built around a reforestation plan in western Cuba. (See City-by-City Guide for details.)

If you have free time and the inclination, you can easily visit Alamar or Havana del Este, two large housing projects just outside Havana, built shortly after the Revolution on land cleared of slums. These communities can be reached by the #62 or #162 bus systems from Central Park, or via taxi for a few pesos. You are free to walk around the complexes just as in any other residential area, but schools, day-care centers, etc., may not be visited.

Minibrigade (microbrigada) housing units. All over the island, the visitor cannot help but notice the new housing construction, most of which is the work of minibrigades. This ingenious system employs and trains workers who have no previous building experience. Minibrigade buildings generally house employees of a specific work center.

At each place of employment—office, factory, etc.—approximately 30 people volunteer to join a construction unit. These workers actually build houses under the supervision of government architects and trained builders. While the minibrigade volunteers are out building, co-workers keep up productivity, but the volunteers continue to draw their regular salaries. Finished apartments are allotted to employees on the basis of need and work record, and the builders do not necessarily have priority. In each housing unit, usually one apartment is set aside for Latin-American exiles who emigrate to Cuba. Minibrigade buildings are usually prefabricated and brightly painted, and almost all apartments have balconies.

Cuba has long been plagued by a housing shortage. Prior to 1959, some 2 million Cubans lived in unsanitary, dilapidated dwellings without electricity and plumbing, and providing adequate housing has been one of the primary goals of the revolutionary regime. The activities of the minibrigades have gone a long way toward realizing that goal.

EDUCATION

Cuba's system has been internationally recognized as the finest in Latin America. Prior to the Revolution, 45% of the peasant population had never been to school, and of those who had, 90% had not gone past 3rd grade. Only 44% of the primary-school and junior-high-school age groups, and 10% of the secondary-school age group, attended school; a mere 1% went on to university. The percentages were significantly lower among blacks and in remote rural areas. The turnaround in Cuban education has been overwhelming.

At present, education is compulsory up to the 6th grade, with 12th grade the 1982 goal. The government spends 15 times the prerevolutionary education budget and has built 70% of the existing school buildings. It provides all materials, uniforms, and room and board free of charge. Scholarship students also receive living stipends.

The work-study concept. At vocational schools scattered around the island—there are 4 presently, and eventually there will be 14—students attend grades 7–13, sampling trades and vocations and selecting a specialty. During the school day, students turn out real products, dividing their time between factory and classroom work. Attendance is restricted to students with the highest academic averages, and the schools offer full recreation and academic facilities. The Lenin School in Havana province and the Guevara school in Santa Clara are often visited by U.S. special interest groups, by previous appointment only.

Agricultural training also receives priority attention. Under the Schools in the Countryside program begun in 1971, students live in boarding schools, dividing their time between agricultural work (three hours per day) and regular classroom study (four hours per day). Visitors will note the distinctive school buildings—double H-shaped constructions with dormitory, study, and cafeteria areas joined by wide open-air walkways. Each school is attached to a 1,250-acre plot of land, usually in citrus, coffee, or dairy areas. On the Isle of Pines, work done by agricultural students has literally transformed the island's economy.

In both the vocational and agricultural schools, the students' productive work is a serious matter inasmuch as it is intended to offset—but not cover completely—the operating costs of the school and to develop respect for all forms of labor.

The literacy campaign. One of the new government's first acts after the Revolution was to mount an all-out national campaign, from December, 1960 to December 1961, to eliminate illiteracy. Cuba's illiteracy rate dropped from approximately 25% to 3.9%, which today includes non-Spanish speaking immigrants and those with learning disabilities. The rate is the lowest in Latin America.

During the campaign, those who could read and write taught those who could not. Literacy workers called *brigadistas* worked with the people, often in isolated mountainous areas where books, pens, and pencils had been as familiar as silk pajamas. The UNESCO review of the campaign reported it as one of the most important events in the history of education.

The Literacy Museum of Havana, Ciudad Libertad, Marianao, Havana (tel. 208054). This small museum in Ciudad Libertad, a school city converted from the Batista central barracks, contains letters written by former illiterates and many other documents, including samples of materials used by the *brigadistas*. It is a must for educators. Admission is by appointment only, and Cubatur can make arrangements. Buses #22, #28, #98, and #198 serve Ciudad Libertad from Vedada. Open Mon.–Fri. only, 8 a.m.–5 p.m.

PUBLIC HEALTH

Prior to 1959 in some areas of Cuba, the most sophisticated health facility was a first-aid box stocked with gauze and fixed to the wooden wall of a mountain *bohío*. Today, the public health network is the most advanced in Latin America—all services, with the exception of medicine to outpatients, are completely free of charge. As of 1975, 58 rural hospitals, 109 clinics, and 21 blood banks were dispersed throughout the island. The number of hospital beds had risen since 1959 from 28,536 to 46,025 by 1975.

The gains in health care have been remarkable, considering that approximately 3,000 doctors—all but 14 of the 100 teaching doctors at Havana Medical School—left Cuba after the Revolution. There is now 1 doctor for every 850 persons, 5 schools of medicine, and 2 of dentistry. Life expectancy has risen from 55 years to 70 years, and the gastroenteritis, polio, diptheria, and parasitic infections which plagued Cuba have been entirely eliminated. The Havana Mental Hospital is an internationally recognized prototype of a humane and progressive facility.

COMMUNICATIONS AND MEDIA

Newspapers. Cuba has two main daily newspapers—*Granma*, the official organ of the Communist party, which publishes a weekly resumé issue on Saturdays in English, French, and German; and *Juventud Rebelde*, the Young Communist League afternoon paper. Outside Havana, there are other local dailies.

Television. All hotel lobbies have TVs, and some first-class hotels have them in each room.

There are two TV channels, with some color, but mainly with black and white transmission. Programming includes news, variety shows, cartoons (often vintage U.S. imports), late-night movies, educational programs, cooking suggestions, and serial melodramas. The 1977–78 smash hit was *Enrique de La Gardere*, which so unfailingly drew large audiences that one could tell the time of evening by the groups of people regularly gathered around the nearest TV set.

Radio. There are numerous stations with as wide a range of programming as television. U.S. radio stations can sometimes be received.

Periodicals. There are several magazines; the most popular are *Cuba, Bohemia*, and *Revolución y Cultura*. The newsstands are well worth a visit, although they do not carry publications from nonsocialist nations. Most publications are in Spanish.

Film. The Instituto Cubano del Arte y Industria Cinematograficos (ICIAC) is a purely post-Revolutionary phenomenon. It produces newsreels, documentaries, and features that are political in content and sophisticated in technique. Directors such as Tomás Gutiérrez Alea and Santiago Álvarez enjoy international acclaim, and indeed Gutiérrez's masterpiece *Memories of Underdevelopment* won a special U.S. film critics' Circle prize, but Gutiérrez was prevented by the U.S. Treasury Department from entering the U.S. to collect it.

Tourists should take any opportunity to see Cuban films, for despite the language barrier they are revealing and informative. Some worthwhile films are *El Brigadista* (about the literacy campaign); *El Octubre de Todos* (about Castro's trip to Africa); *Con las Mujeras Cubana* (about Cuban women); and some longer feature films like *De Cierta Manera, Los Sobrevivientes, Última Cena*, and *El Otro Francisco*.

All major cities have cinema houses, and admission is never more than 1 peso. Small towns have cinemobiles. On Saturday evenings long lines form, so plan accordingly.

THE ECONOMY

Agriculture. You could plant a pencil in most areas of Cuba and it would probably sprout leaves. The island's potential as a garden spot was consistently noted by early travelers. Today its fertility both sustains and limits the economy as Cuba struggles to maximize agricultural output while developing and diversifying industry.''

The Cuban economy relies heavily on the agricultural sector. Following the omnipresent sugar in importance are tobacco, coffee and citrus, rice, potatoes, beans and other root vegetables, and fruits such as the pineapple, mango, and papaya. Since 1959, citrus land area alone has jumped from 25,000 acres to 250,000 acres.

Dairy, cattle, poultry, and hog production have also received serious attention. Through artificial insemination, Cubans have developed a strain of cattle with the milk-producing capacity of the Holstein and the tropical resistance of the Brahma.

A series of Agrarian Reform Laws after the Revolution consolidated land ownership so that now 70% is under the control of the state, which is the only legitimate Cuban merchant. The remaining percentage is in the hands of small farmers, many of whom received title to land they had rented prior to the Revolution. Collective farms operate on the state land, and the workers are salaried.

Small farmers grow crops according to the national plan, but they may keep a portion of the produce for their own use, selling the balance to the state at fixed prices. The maximum size of private farms is 5 *caballerías*, or approximately 165 acres. All large landholdings were confiscated in 1959, but the owners who remained in Cuba were reimbursed by the state for the land value at the time. Today there is constant debate about whether small farmers can be efficient in the modern agribusiness world, but it is clear that for some crops at least, especially tobacco, quality suffers when the personal touch is removed.

Industry. The largest heavy industry is nickel production, which runs second to sugar production. Cuba's nickel deposits are the third largest in the world. There are also fertilizer plants, cement production, construction, and mechanical industries (developed not least of all to make spare parts that were unobtainable after the blockade). Marble, caolin, textiles, clothing, furniture, printing, plastics, soaps, and beverages are also important to Cuba's industrial output. Ingenious new mini-industries, such as the manufacture of baseballs and violins, have been developed to provide jobs and reduce imports. The fishing industry has gone from a basic wooden fleet with an annual yield of 22,000 tons in 1958 to fully mechanized ships now yielding 240,000 tons annually.

SUGAR — THE RAZING OF CANE

The foreman of a sugar shipping terminal strode up close to a mountain of brown grain sugar ten stories in height. Taking a fingertipful and putting it to his tongue, he beamed, "This, this is our gold."

Indeed, sugar might as well be currency in Cuba, for its cultivation and export account for 80% of the nation's foreign earnings. If a school, road, hospital, or apartment house is built, it is because of sugar; if a plan is curtailed, it is because of sugar. The Cuban economy is inextricable from the world sugar market, and when prices drop, the repercussions are felt in Cuba for years.

Cuba owes this unfortunate dependence to many factors. Sugarcane was introduced to the Caribbean by Columbus on his second voyage. Cuban soil is ideally suited to this crop, and the introduction of slavery enabled Cuban landowners to cover the nation with cane fields. As U.S. interest in Cuban sugar grew, more and more land was cleared, and sugar supported Cuba. After the Revolution the sugar mills were nationalized, and diversification of the economy, particularly through industry, was attempted.

Production. Cuba produces almost 7 million tons per year, the world's highest output. In 1970 a national mobilization program intended to reach an unprecedented 10 million tons; virtually every Cuban joined in the cutting. Despite this massive effort the goal was not reached, and Fidel Castro, who had staked the reputation of the Revolution on attaining it, personally accepted the blame. Today, attempts to increase production are going on constantly, but at the same time, careful attention paid to ways of breaking the sugar dependence.

Planting season. Cane is planted beginning in June and until November, but not during rainy periods. Cuttings from the tops of mature cane are used, and fields need not be replanted every year since the same roots can produce crops for up to 15 years. However, rotation of crops and experimentation with new strains characterize Cuba's effort to improve production.

The harvest (zafra). Sugarcane before cutting grows to a height of about 6 feet and a diameter of about 3 inches. Traveling around Cuba during the harvest, December–May, one has the sensation occasionally of being awash in waves of green stalks topped with the plume of the wispy beige "flower of the cane."

Across Cuba, mills operate 24 hours a day, and the air around them is heavy with the pungent, sweet-roasted aroma of milling cane.

The cutting itself is an extraordinary process, a good deal of which has been mechanized. The Cubans have perfected the design of the *combinada*, which cuts, quarters, and delivers the cane to trucks virtually in one motion. These machines are most effective on flat land, since the cane must be cut as close to the roots as possible. Often, the cane is burnt at root level to soften it for the first cut. Occasionally, on the road, one meets convoys of brand new *combinadas,* produced in Cuba, shiny and smelling like Matchbox miniature vehicle toys.

The *combinada* resembles a bulldozer, but in front, instead of the scoop-and-push apparatus, it has two enormous steel noses resembling pencil points and a squared-off chute jutting out like a raised arm. Blades spiral around the noses, which spin rapidly, cutting the cane at ground level, trimming the leaves, then chopping each stalk into pieces about 15 inches in length. The pieces fall into a tray and are vacuumed up into the apparatus, carried through it by conveyer belt, and then sprayed out of the chute into a waiting truck. The truck delivers the cane to a train, and the train takes it on to a mill. A *combinada* can cut a truckload of cane—about 600 arrobas (15,000 pounds) in about 8 minutes.

In contrast, a *millionaria* hand cutter (a *millionaria* brigade racks up 1 million arrobas in a season) produces 180–200 arrobas in an 8-hour day. These master cutters—and even regular cutters—make cane cutting look like a ballet for the hands. With one straight, seemingly effortless stroke of the machete, the cane is cut from the ground; then it is cleaned by skimming the machete along the cane vertically, severing the leaves. The bare stalk is cut into pieces and dropped on the ground to await collection. The cutters advance rhythmically through the field, and sometimes all that is visible are their sombreros; all that is audible, the constant swishing, crunching, and chopping of the machete.

The milling. The cut cane is pressed by giant rollers, releasing a white sugar juice called *guarapo*, which can be drunk ice-cold or mixed hot with rum and a beaten egg for a superb "hot toddy."

Raw sugar remains when the juice has been boiled off.

Sugar by-products include rum and molasses; the tough, squeezed-out stalks, called bagasse, are either used for fuel or recycled into fiberboard and paper.

The shipping. Most sugar is consumed in the white refined variety, shipped from Cuba throughout the world, much of it in sacks. However, an innovation of the Revolution has been the introduction of bulk shipping terminals, the largest of which is the Tricontinental in Cienfuegos. Here, raw sugar arrives by train from the mill. The rail cars tip and pour their cargo through grates onto underground conveyer belts which carry the unrefined sugar into warehouses approximately 80 feet high and 140 feet wide—stadiums of sugar.

Ships from all over dock at Tricontinental, unload their cargo, and take on sugar, which is poured straight into the hold and leveled off by giant spatulas. A boat of 15,000-ton capacity can be loaded in 16 hours—a job which once took a month and about 3,000 workers loading 325-pound sacks of sugar on their backs. The terminal now operates with about 305 workers, including administrators, and during the *zafra* the terminal works 24 hours a day, collecting, sampling, and shipping the seemingly unceasing stream of sugar.

By making arrangements in advance through Cubatur, Tricontinental can be visited by groups.

The taste of cane. At Varadero Beach during the *zafra*, cane-cutting excursions are sometimes organized for interested tourists. These excursions are arranged at individual hotels through the Cubatur representative. You are taken by truck, in the company of experienced cutters, and given the chance to hack away at the cane forests, take photographs, and learn about the entire sugar production process. Just as the tasting is an integral part of visits to wineries throughout the world, so the chomping of cane is the rare treat of the cutter.

At first the sensation is like chewing wood, but when the juice is extracted, the unsugary, but sweet, natural taste justifies the risk to the teeth. Once, on a country excursion by taxi, I had the good luck to fall in behind a convoy of trucks loaded with freshly cut mill-bound cane. Every few feet, a stalk dropped to

the road, and the *taxista* and I, giggling like children, stopped
to harvest the stray stalks until we could chomp no more.

TOBACCO AND THE FAMOUS HAVANA CIGAR

Europe discovered tobacco when Columbus discovered Cuba.
The Indians cultivated *cohiba*, which was smoked during religious or magic rituals through a hollow forked reed inserted
directly into the nostrils from the smoldering leaves. The
tabacs—a word which, via Spanish misunderstanding, became
the name of the plant itself—were leaves rolled in bunches and
smoked through the mouth, the precursors of the famous
Havana cigar. First introduced to Spain, the custom of smoking
and snuffing became European fashion, and by the early 1700s
tobacco was Cuba's main export.

Today, the tobacco industry in Cuba employs 50,000 workers, more than half of them women. About 82% of the tobacco
crop is still grown on small farms owned by experienced *campesinos* who take the personal interest necessary to ensure
superior quality. Cuba exports tobacco for cigarettes, pipes, and
even for chewing, but by far the most famous export is the incomparable Cuban cigar.

Certainly no other industry in Cuba is as dependent on dex-
terity and manual artistry as the cigar-making process. Though
about 30% of the cigars produced are machine-made, only hand
rolling provides the quality demanded by cigar connoisseurs.
On a machine, 4 workers in a 6-foot-square area can produce
9½ Monte Cristos per minute. The average by hand is 110 in 8
hours.

Such painstaking manual labor requires that the cigar maker's
relationship to the product be almost personal. To him or her,
every cigar is a challenge, every one an opportunity to arrive
closer to perfection—in the end, every one a sculpture. Cuba's
largest factory is H. Upmann in Havana, where 23,500,000
cigars are produced annually in 39 different varieties.

Every factory has a strategically positioned platform with a
desk and microphone on it. From here, the "reader" of the day
reads aloud to the workers—newspapers, poems, novels, new

political material. Through the readings, a practice which began in 1864, ideas to which the cigar worker would probably not otherwise have had access become part of the daily routine. This accounts in part for the comparatively high degree of literacy and politicization among cigar workers throughout Cuban history.

Today the platform is also used to introduce visitors, and it is a moving experience indeed to hear your name and nationality announced and to have a hundred cigar workers applaud an enthusiastic welcome.

The cigar-making process. In many tour itineraries, a visit to a cigar factory is included, but often the process is not seen in sequence. Following is a description, plant to cigar.

The leaves arrive at the factory in dry sheets from the field, grouped according to strength, looking very much like thin slices of frozen beef. One tobacco plant produces at least five strengths of tobacco—leaves growing closest to the center, or those left longest in the plant, are the darkest and strongest. Certain leaves, therefore, are picked sooner than others, but the main picking season is October–January. In curing, too, strength is controlled by graduated exposure to sunlight. Cuba's best tobacco grows in the Vuelta Abajo region of Pinar del Río province.

On arrival at the factory, the leaves are tied in bunches and sent to the wetting area. There, in what resembles a religious ritual, the tips are dipped ever so slightly—about two inches—into potable water. To set the water traveling through the leaves, the wetter (*mojador*) waves them gently but rhythmically, in the air and one almost expects him to recite exotic chants. Then, for two hours, the leaves "rest," hanging lengthwise to insure uniform distribution of moisture. (The *mojador* does not spend his day waving his arms. The job is rotated among the workers.)

The perfectly dampened leaves, silky like fine translucent cloth, then go to the stripper (*despalillo*), who removes the center stem in one smooth pulling action. The halves are then bunched, using the stem itself as a tie, and sent to the sorter (*rezagado*), who regroups them according to color and strength. The eyes of the sorter scan leaf after leaf, distinguishing the finest variations in shade, and the sorting room is a rainbow of browns. The sorter puts each new leaf in its appropriate color pile, stretching it out over the ones underneath with care, as though handling a flower petal, opening it fully without ripping it.

Thus sorted, the leaves are ready for the cigar maker (*tabacero*), who receives a few of each color, depending upon the type of cigar he is rolling. Working quickly but very precisely, the roller fingers the leaves and chooses according to texture and color the desired combination; he then rolls them into shape, clips one end neatly, leaving the other loosely unwrapped, and presses the bunch into a mold to hold its shape while he works the next one. When a mold is full of cigars that look as though firecrackers had exploded in the ends of every one, it is put into a press.

Taking the molds from the bottom of the press first, the next *tabacero* begins the final and most important stage of the rolling process. Using a sharp rounded knife, he or she cookie-cuts a circle from a tobacco leaf, removes a cigar from the mold, forms the firecrackered end into a point, and very gently affixes the circular head with a vegetable gum called *tragacanto*. The cigar is thus fingertipped to completion.

The finished cigars are bunched in groups of 50 and then sent on to the *escogido*, who boxes them in as perfect a color harmony as possible. The boxes are usually of pinewood, decorated with embossed lithographs designed for each specific brand—Romeo y Julieta, Monte Cristo, Fonseca, etc. The boxes are elegantly trimmed by hand on the premises of the factory.

Once boxed by color, the cigars move to the bander (*anillado*), who slides a paper trademark ring on each cigar in the box. The banded box then moves to the *revisador*, who painstakingly, almost surgically, inspects each cigar layer, revising, correcting, realigning. Then, after passing inspection, the box is transmitted to the filetiado, where a wafer of cedar wood is inserted to ensure freshness and the box is sealed, guaranteeing the customer a 100% hand-rolled Cuban cigar.

The finest cigars are packed individually in metal cylindrical cases, like the Churchill, or in miniboxes of wood with sliding tops, like the par excellence Diadema. Some cigars are even put in glass jars to guard, as the label says, against the "hazards of varying climates to freshness and fragrance."

Visiting cigar factories. Most group itineraries include a tour of cigar-making facilities arranged by appointment. Cubatur will organize optional excursions for a minimum of six persons. Check with the nearest Cubatur representative to see if any tours are scheduled. The most frequently visited factory is H. Upmann in Havana, but there are many others throughout the island.

SPORTS

Sports fever has swept Cuba in the past ten years, but particularly since 1971 when the National Institute for Sports, Physical Education, and Recreation was created. Today, the country takes sports training very seriously and has incorporated it into every school curriculum, as well as into adult education and recreational programs. One can find almost every sport here: swimming, boxing, tennis, running, squash, bicycling, fencing, weight lifting, wrestling, basketball, volleyball, gymnastics, equitation, diving, handball, soccer, shooting, sailing, rowing, fishing, hunting, and table games. Baseball and dominoes, however, qualify as national pastimes.

Not only do individuals participate, but there is a national matrix of teams which organize for international competitions. Athletes, like artists, are considered workers and part of the society's productive effort, and there are no professional sports in the American sense. In the Olympics, Cuban athletes have excelled in boxing and track-and-field events, and their baseball teams usually sweep the international competitions they enter. Homecoming baseball teams return to street fairs which rival Carnival in splendor. Baseball is played from December to June. Tourists are welcome to watch the games. Admission is free. In Havana, games are held at the Latin-American Stadium near Plaza de la Revolución. Cubatur can provide schedules.

In addition to the hotels, most major cities have sports facilities which are open to tourists, usually free, or for nominal rental charges. Country clubs have been converted to public recreation centers which offer swimming, tennis, and various other sports. For more detailed tennis, golf and other sports listings, see the City-by-City Guide.

CULTURE

There are virtually unlimited possibilities for visitors to participate in cultural activities, and they are heartily encouraged to do so. In every city, there is either a Ministry of Culture office or a *Casa de Cultura*, a "culture house" where schedules of concerts, art expositions, theater performances, poetry readings, and other events can be obtained. Cubatur representatives also have access to this information, and in large cities a *cartelera cultural* ("cultural calendar") is published and posted in hotels. Newspapers also list cultural events under *Culturales*. Every cultural taste, including opera, can be indulged in Cuba.

The Cuban Ministry of Culture tries to expose every Cuban to the full range of cultural possibilities. Consequently, one hears of traveling theater and music groups in the mountains, cinemobiles, opera performed in factories, ballet in military schools.

THE FINE ARTS

The National School of Art. Providing trained artists for the numerous cultural groups is the responsibility of the National School of Art at Cubanacan, Havana, which some special interest tours include. Visits are by appointment through Cubatur for groups only.

Before the Revolution, a golf course wound its way through the woods of the Cubanacan suburb. Today, the National School of Art occupies the grounds—a 110-acre area devoted to the teaching of dramatic and visual arts, music, ballet, and modern dance. The students usually live on or near the premises and are a crucial component of the cultural development of Cuba.

Founded in 1962, the school was yet another brainchild of Fidel Castro. When it was inaugurated, it occupied preexisting buildings, with adjacent residences converted to dormitory and classroom space. The controversial new buildings, added in 1963, combine domes, colonnades, arches, vaulted ceilings, and fan windows so that the school resembles a 21st-century caravansary.

The school provides specialty training in the arts as well as academic preparation. Technically it is categorized as a high school, although where careers demand training at an early age—dance, for instance—young students are accepted. Entrance to Cubanacan is gained through academic and professional examinations. Students who excel technically but lag behind scholastically may be admitted, but graduation is contingent upon academic as well as professional success.

The course of study is four years; during the last two, students are trained in the teaching methods of their profession. Students from Cubanacan are often asked to act as consultants to local cultural groups. All students are provided with lodging, food, and materials free of charge. When the students are working with local groups off Cubanacan premises, they receive a stipend of 35 pesos per month to cover their transportation expenses. After graduation, the students are required to perform two years of social service in their field, usually teaching, after which they are free to join professional groups and pursue their careers or continue their studies.

During the 1977 academic year, Cubanancan had 659 students—506 boys and 153 girls—about half of whom were studying music. These students value their training, and most of them would probably share the sentiment expressed by one of their colleagues at graduation, February, 1978: "In this school, they teach us to see inside, and to take what is good in ourselves and our art and to share it with other people."

The National Ballet of Cuba. One cannot speak of ballet in Cuba without discussing the dynamic presence of Alicia

Alonso. Guided by her extraordinary talent and will, the ballet developed and continued to flourish in Cuba.

Her company premiered in 1948 in Havana, and the first ballet school was established in 1950. However, most dancers went abroad to perform since there were few jobs in Cuba. Alicia, the prima ballerina, toured and gained international recognition. She used the prestige of her company to undermine the Batista regime, and in 1956 government support was withdrawn. The company disintegrated, and Alicia Alonso danced in exile until 1959.

She returned to Cuba after the Revolution, reconstituted the ballet, and has dedicated the company to bringing this art form to as many people as possible. The company has 156 dancers who perform not only in theaters but also in work centers and factories, explaining and demonstrating ballet. The company tours internationally to accolades, has visited some 40 nations including the United States, and combines classic, folk, and Revolutionary choreography. The ballet season in Cuba runs all year, with two performance weeks per month in Havana and throughout Cuba. The ballet schedule can be obtained from Cubatur, through the newspapers, or by phoning the National ballet offices in Havana (tel. 327151).

Alicia Alonso's failing eyesight in no way impairs her talent or inhibits her energy, and her transcendance of the handicap has won her universal respect. An interviewer once asked Alicia what she would have liked to have been if she were not a ballerina. She seemed to look through him and unhesitatingly quipped "A ballerina."

Also, there is a national ballet school, as well as provincial schools and the School of Dance at Cubanacan. The Ballet of Camagüey also operates a ballet school and, although not as prominent as the National Ballet, offers a wide repertoire and very promising young dancers such as Pedro Martes and Mayra Rivero. The first graduation from the school was in 1967, and the group tours Cuba throughout the year.

ARCHITECTURE AND THE CUBAN HOME

Accommodating Cuba's tropical light and climate preoccupied Spanish colonial architects, and their design solutions grace the palatial and not-so-palatial buildings of Cuba still. When walking, note:

The vitrales. These stained-glass arch windows positioned above doors began to appear in the late 18th century, when colored glass imported from Europe was pieced together with wood and later with metal, to diffuse the sun and play color into the rooms. The glass fans out peacocklike, alternating geometric patterns, Moorish swirls, or Romantic floral explosions. The full 180° arches are called *mediopuntos*.

The lucetas. These rectangular windows are placed above doors. They are often stained glass, although marbled glass is more common.

The mampara. This double-swing medi-door, wooden, often with elaborately etched or stained-glass crowns, serves as a room divider or a partial outer door to protect privacy while allowing ventilation.

The rejas. Originally these window screens were wooden, made with rippled rods called *barrotes*. Later they were fashioned from iron and intricately designed both to decorate and protect.

The persianas. These slatted-wood movable panels were placed in windows or *mamparas,* for ventilation.

The portales. These galleried walkways that protect pedestrians from sun and rain were originally built of stone, with grand columns and vaulted ceilings, but later, due to North American influence, squared off and built with wood, à la the porch. In some towns of Cuba, it is possible to walk for blocks without ever leaving the *portales*, particularly around main plazas like Central Park in Havana. The *portales* apparently originated to provide protected waiting and delivery space for the merchants, whose warehouses were often the first floor of their homes.

The entresuelo. On some old Cuban homes, a window occupies what seems like a between-floors position. This is the *entresuelo*. In this area, the house slaves or servants lived, and crates and cargo were stored.

The postigo. This small window or partial opening is set into the massive wooden doors of Spanish homes.

The antepecho. This half-height, ornamented window guard is usually flush with the building facade.

The bohios. These small, often roundish houses with palm frond roofs have been the traditional rural Cuban home since man moved out of the caves. The name itself is Indian, and when Columbus visited Cuba, the Indians told him of *bohío*, which Columbus misunderstood to mean another island. Bartoleme de las Casas, whose abstract of Columbus's diary is the only extant copy, made a marginal reference to the confusion: "The Indians called their houses *bohío*—the Captain did not understand it well."

Since then, the *bohío* has symbolized Cuban rural life, and countless travelers have written of its picturesque, tranquil appearance. Most *bohíos*, however, have no floors, no plumbing, no toilet facilities. There is nothing picturesque about living in them, and today the government has been gradually moving the *campesinos* to modern apartments.

The traveler will notice many spots in Cuba where tiny *bohíos* cling, seemingly by luck, to sheer mountain slopes. They are charmingly remote—for the traveler, an inexorably Cuban landscape signature.

The patio. The classic patio, a Spanish adaptation of the Moorish inner court, is as central to the Cuban culture as the cigar. Stately patios were requisite in palaces and government buildings. But open space is essential in the Cuban climate, and even the humblest *bohío* has its patio—often an open area around the house which serves as an outdoor parlor, a place to sit in the evenings, chat with family and friends, solve problems, sing.

Impassioned discussions take place *al patio*; romances are born. Where there is no patio, there is a balcony at least, even in new housing projects. In Cuba, even some trucks have "patios," platforms built out over the cabs, decorated with what looks like a picket fence!

The rocking chair. In every size and style—carved of precious wood, painted, inlaid, or metal-framed with plastic woven seats—the rocking chair in Cuba is ubiquitous. Called *sillon* in Havana, *balance* elsewhere, the chairs are generally assumed to have been introduced by Spain, although some historians trace them to New England. Especially rare are the *comadritas*, armless rockers intended for sewing, embroidery, or other work with which chair arms might interfere.

The chairs are often casually propped backwards against buildings, rockers out to protect the seats from rain. They are one of Cuba's subtle charms.

FOLK ARTS

Folklore and the Conjunto Folklorico. Cuban folklore is often described as "mulattoized"—a unique mixture of Indian, Spanish, French, and African traditions. Regionally, folklore follows economic-agricultural lines. Where sugar was the major industry, Afro-Haitian culture, transmitted by the cane cutters, prevails; in tobacco and other "white" businesses, the Hispano-European tradition dominates.

A 1957 guide to the Caribbean written for U.S. citizens described Cuban folklore as follows:

> The lack of deep inward appreciation of their own island and folkways keeps the native arts and crafts, literature and music from developing its own genius and makes Cubans curiously one-dimensional. Undeniably, the nearness of the U.S. and its wealth, power, prestige and mass arts doesn't help matters.

This matter was helped in 1962 by the establishment of the Conjunto Folklorico Nacional, which studies and seeks to revive the folk traditions of Cuba. Prior to the formation of this group, work in the area was academic, and the general population remained virtually ignorant of its folkloric past. The Conjunto rediscovers folklore, not as something quaint, but rather as a link between the present society and the popular culture of the past. The major cities each have a performance group supported by the national Conjunto, and these groups tour pro-

vincially. The Conjuntos of Trinidad and Santiago de Cuba are especially notable.
The following terms are bound to come up:

bongo A small African drum.

changani An African ritual song.

comparsa A collective dance culminating in a religious procession.

conga A processional dance frequently seen at Carnival, in which each dancer holds the waist of the dancer ahead.

contradanza A 19th-century Cuban salon dance of French origin introduced via Haïti.

controversias Extemporaneous narratives wherein each participant builds on the improvisation before.

danzon A slow Cuban version of the contradanza.

décima A classic Spanish poetic form. Each stanza has 10 lines, each line 8 syllables.

diablito "Little devil," a popular doll based on the masked men of African religions. Readily available in tourist shops.

filin A kind of urban street blues.

firma-signs used in African religions.

güiro A gourd used as a percussion instrument, also often carved into unusual lampshades.

maracas A percussion instrument made from a gourd with pebbles inside.

punta campesino or *punta guajiro* A country song and dance form most common in the tobacco growing areas. *Décimas* are often recited.

requento A small guitar.

retreta A weekly outdoor concert held in a public plaza.

rumba An Afro-Cuban dance with a number of local variations.

son An Afro-Cuban rhythmic form.

tres A typical Cuban guitar with 6 or 9 strings.

tumba francesa A dance form of the French blacks, half salon, half African; also a kind of drum.

zapateo A *guajiro* country dance, performed with partners separated à la the minuet.

Music. The traditional *trova*, the Cuban version of the medieval ballad form, was sung throughout Cuba during the

Spanish period, through the wars of independence, and in the pre-Revolutionary period. These throaty classics recounted love and loss or told of historical events. Almost every major city has a Casa de la Trova where *trovadores* perform. These are listed in the City-by-City Guide. Performances are usually in the evening. Admission is free.

The *nueva trova* (new song) is a post-Revolutionary *trova* using the poetry and music of young Cubans, who often sing of the Revolution and their hopes for it. The *nueva trova* movement is an entirely new music phenomenon in which both professionals (Silvio Rodríguez and Pablo Milanes are most well-known) and amateurs (El Grupo Moncada) participate.

Those who enjoy rumbas and congas will find them at any nightclub or cabaret, brassy and bold. The Orchestra Arragon, which has toured the United States, is particularly well known for its dance music, and can be heard in major hotels and nightclubs.

TICKETS FOR CULTURAL EVENTS

Tickets are usually sold the day of the performance at the box office. However, contact Cubatur for specific details, as the procedure can vary.

The City-by-City Guide contains further information on regional specialties, theaters, and location of the Casa de Cultura in most cities.

Casa de la Trova, Santiago de Cuba

Hatmaking, Trinidad

Pottery maker, Trinidad

New violin factory, Minas

Mayabe valley, Holguin

Canecutter from millionaria brigade, Las Tunas

A cigar maker, Santa Clara

Triumphant baseball team being greeted in the streets of Pinar del Río

Postigos, the varied doorways of Cuba

Typical street mural

Patio at the Federation of Cuban Women, Havana

Viñales valley, one of Cuba's most famous scenic spots

Moncada barracks and museum, scene of the first attack against Batista, Santiago de Cuba

Las Terrazas, new community built in reforestation area

Poolside at the modern Hotel Camaguey, Camaguey

Velasquez house, Santiago de Cuba

Los Caneyes Hotel, Santa Clara   *Courtesy Cuban National Tourist Board*

Sierra Maestra,
the dramatic mountains of Eastern Cuba *Courtesy Cuban National Tourist Board*

Courtesy Cuban National Tourist Board   Linea Street, Havana

Courtesy Cuban National Tourist Board   Guama Indian village

Famous Tropicana nightclub, Havana
Courtesy Cuban National Tourist Board

Los Jazmines Hotel, Viñales Valley
Courtesy Cuban National Tourist Board

The incomparable Varadero Beach, 10 miles long
Courtesy Cuban National Tourist Board

CITY-BY-CITY GUIDE

INTRODUCTION TO THE GUIDE

HOW TO USE IT

The guide begins with Havana, Cuba's most complex city, and the one most frequently visited by tourists. Thereafter, the organization is alphabetical by city for easy reference, since most visitors will not be familiar with Cuban provincial or topographical divisions.

The alphabetical arrangement is intended to serve not only group tour visitors but individual travelers as well, so that when you arrive in a city, you will have some idea of what there is to see and do.

For each city of size, there is an historical profile; information about what to see, where to walk, museums, cultural events and regional specialties; and hotel and restaurant guides. There are also maps of selected cities. Where excursions or day trips can be made from a given city using it as a travel base, an "Excursions from . . ." section is included. Nearby beaches, if any, are listed separately at the end of the city entry.

Each entry provides basic information in capsule form at the beginning: date of establishment (the year either of official incorporation or of the first reported settlement); population (based on available 1978 statistics); and mileage estimates (based on distance via main roads).

WHAT CITIES ARE USUALLY VISITED

Depending upon length and type of tour, U.S. citizens have visited Havana, Camagüey, Cienfuegos, Varadero, Trinidad, Guama, Santa Clara, Hanabanilla, Santa Maria del Mar, Santiago de Cuba, the Isle of Youth, and Soroa. Some tours have included La Guira National Park and Vinales as well.

As tourism develops, many more Cuban cities will be able to accommodate visitors. Included here are all cities and towns currently on the tourist route, as well as those likely to be in the near future.

TRIPS FOR INDIVIDUAL TOURISTS — THE MUSTS

Getting around without a tour group, even with private transportation, can be a hassle in Cuba, especially for individuals who speak no Spanish. However, those who have plenty of time, some tourist pluck and a little traveler's savvy will find this section handy. The following are some recommended itineraries; the city details are listed alphabetically.

Western Cuba, Pinar del Río and Havana provinces. An extremely worthwhile one-to-two-day excursion is Havana to Pinar del Río, overnighting either in Pinar or at Vinales, traveling at least one way via the north coast road. Those with a car should not miss Las Terrazas, about midway between Havana and Pinar del Río.

Central Cuba. This area is known for plains, prairies, and infinite cane fields. The most interesting cities here are Matanzas, Santa Clara, Trinidad, Camagüey, Cienfuegos, and Sancti Spíritus. All have access to beaches and can be used as convenient travel bases.

Oriente—the wild mountains. This rugged eastern region encompasses the provinces of Holguín, Granma, Santiago de Cuba, and Guantánamo. The city not to be missed is Santiago de Cuba. See Bayamo and Baracoa if time permits.

The best beaches. These are to be found at Varadero and Guardalavaca, outside Camagüey at Playa Santa Lucia, outside Havana at Santa Maria del Mar, and in other areas under development like Cayo Largo, the Isle of Youth, and Cayo Sabinel.

HOTEL LISTINGS

Where available at the time of writing, exact hotel rates are listed. Elsewhere, the visitor is directed to Cubatur. Prices in general are discussed under "Hotels in Cuba" in Section I.

The descriptive information in the listings is intended to convey the atmosphere of a hotel, describe facilities and highlight special features, views, etc. However, group tourists do not have a choice of hotel accommodation since it is arranged for them well in advance but best available hotels are always used.

Individual tourists should book all hotels through Cubatur as early as possible, especially for visits from January to June, during August, and on weekends, when Cubans use the hotels en masse.

RESTAURANT PRICE CODE

Restaurants are described and rated as follows: Deluxe (D), above 7 pesos for an entree; First-Class (FC), 5–7 pesos; Moderate (M), 2–5 pesos. However, the reader should bear in mind that in Cuba all distinctions blur, and no rigid categorization is possible.

DRIVING AROUND CUBA

The Central Highway (Carretera Central) spines the island from east to west. It is a well-paved, straight road presently being expanded to accommodate four lanes. The highway is Cuba's most frequently used road, and there is often truck traffic.

Cuba follows the international system of road signs, and speed limits vary depending upon whether you are in an urban or rural area. On the open road, the driver's judgment prevails. It's safest, however, not to drive faster than 60 mph.

If you have private transportation at your disposal, you might enjoy venturing onto some of Cuba's secondary roads, where the scenery is often magnificent. You should be aware, however, that turn-offs are often unmarked, and road maps generally unavailable. Therefore, you should be able to ask directions in Spanish. If you can't, always travel with a dictionary or phrase book. Hitchhiking is not permitted. Gas stations are regularly located, but repairs and gasoline may not be available at all of them. Some suggested routes follow, arranged by province.

Pinar del Río and Havana province (eastern Cuba).

The north coast road, running east to west between Havana and Vinales via Cabanas and Mariel, passes beaches at Las Esperanza, near Vinales. These are open for swimming, but check locally since many areas are closed for military purposes. Allow 2½ hours for leisurely driving.

Cabanas to Cayahabos is a north-south road used for access to Las Terrazas forestry community, and one of the island's most beautiful. Allow about 45 minutes' driving time.

Soroa to Cayahabos is an east-west road, and another scenic superlative, but accessible only to vehicles with four-wheel drive. *Don't* risk your car—spare parts are scarce, and road service in this area nonexistent. Paving is under way, so check locally before setting out.

Matanzas province. (central Cuba)

Cárdenas to Matanzas, through a short inland spur via the towns of Cantel and Camarioca is a lovely drive, set among small farms. Allow about 30 minutes.

Villa Clara and Sancti Spìritus provinces. (central Cuba)

Sagua la Grande to Cárdenas, on the north coast road,

traversing rolling farmland and interesting rural villages, takes about 1½ hours.

Moron to Santa Clara, along the north coast, goes by beautiful Mayajigua Lake and the lovely towns of Yaguajay and Remedios. Allow 2 hours.

Santa Clara to Trinidad, a north-south road via Manicaragua, passes through tobacco-growing regions patched with mixed shades of green. Allow 1 hour.

Holguin province. (Oriente)

Banes to Guardalavaca is a short north-south route through rolling, green, palm-covered hills. Allow about 30 minutes.

Holguin to Las Tunas, a northerly spur via the charming fishing town of Puerto Padre, takes 2 hours.

Santiago de Cuba and Guantánamo provinces. (Oriente)

Santiago to Chivirico hugs the south coast of Oriente at the foot of the dramatic Sierra Maestra. Paving is underway beyond Chivirico, but again, *don't* take your vehicle unless it's a jeep. Allow 2 hours.

Guantánamo to Baracoa, on La Farola via Sanbanillas, is a spectacular drive, though exceedingly slow-going due to curves. Allow 3 hours and do not drive at night—the road is unlit.

HAVANA (LA HABANA). Est. 1519; pop. 1,900,240; capital of Cuba and Havana prov.

When you arrive in exotic, exciting, beautiful Havana, you will no doubt envy the birds—not only because they get around so easily, but because Havana is a city of moving parts and contrasting images whose collective effect can only be perceived with an unlimited aerial view.

There is the colonial city, walled, colonnaded, balconied, laced with designed wrought iron and carved wood. There are the perfect Spanish plazas, castles and fortresses, churches and public buildings draped with vine—the old stone city that burst its walls, winding itself along the harbor. There is the modern city—squared off neatly into blocks, dominated by tall buildings, commerce, and the affairs of government, alive with traffic and a sense of action.

There are grays and pastels and bright, hot colors, a stone dove of peace blazoned onto a brick wall, a satellite ice-cream parlor, mansions with laundry hanging from the balconies. Children play baseball, volleyball, jacks, and hide-and-seek and run along the seawall with startled tourists in warm-ups.

There are rainbows painted on apartment houses and buildings with plumbing, electricity, and balconies, built on the ash and rags of reclaimed slums. Manicured lawns and trimmed hedges line Fifth Avenue, and a potted yagruma tree leans out over a balcony in old Havana. There are embassies, museums, nightclubs, hotels, and a country club turned into an art school.

There is a concentration of energy common to all capitals— grandeur and simplicity, tranquility and the turmoil of change. In Havana, you must walk and scan, taking in eye level and above. There is music to Havana. All the visitor need do is follow it.

HISTORY

Havana was founded in 1515 by one of Diego de Velázquez's men, Pánfilo de Narváez. It was originally located on the south coast of the island in a province known to the Indians as *Abana*. The site was probably near what is today Batabanó. The southern location was not favorable, as the land was swampy and the agricultural possibilities limited. The port that is now Havana was then known as Puerto Carenas.

After the discovery and conquest of Mexico, the superb harbor of present-day Havana became invaluable to the Spaniards, and the city was moved in a series of steps to its present site. The year of founding is usually given as 1519 but cannot be established with certainty because many records were lost in a pirate raid in 1538.

The newly important Havana experienced rapid growth disproportionate to that of the other Cuban cities, but which also attracted plunderers. The French pirates who were roaming the Caribbean descended almost immediately. After the city was set aflame in 1538, Hernando De Soto, the explorer of Florida,

HAVANA
AND ITS ENVIRONS

Bay of Cojimar

COJIMAR

HABANA
DEL ESTE

ALAMAR

HABANA VIEJA

CENTRO
HABANA

CASA-
BLANCA

TO SANTA MARIA DEL MAR

Gulf of Mexico

VEDADO

Bay of
Havana

MIRAMAR

PLAZA DE LA
REVOLUCIÓN

REGLA

GUANABACOA
(HISTORY
MUSEUM OF
GUANABACOA)

N

CERRO

JAIMANITAS

VIBORA

SIBONEY

MARIANAO

PARADERO DE
LA VÍBORA

SAN FRANCISCO
DE PAULA
(HEMINGWAY MUSEUM)

SANTA MARIA
DEL ROSARIO

PARADERO DE
ARIMAO

PARK
LENIN

Presa Ejército Rebelde

who was then Cuba's captain general, ordered the rebuilding of the city and the construction of a fortress—Castillo de la Real Fuerza.

In 1555, the city was again burned to the ground, and in 1588, the famous Englishman Francis Drake made his appearance at the gates. Fed up with living in constant threat, the Spanish government ordered the construction of El Morro, the imposing lighthouse fortress on the promontory of Havana harbor. La Punta Fortress, opposite El Morro, was built to complement it.

By the end of the 16th century, there were about 4,000 inhabitants in Havana. The 17th century passed in relative peace, although there were minor sea skirmishes. The British capture of nearby Jamaica in 1654 revived the building plans for the Havana city walls, which had fallen behind since the first stone was laid in 1633. (These walls ran along what are now Egido and Monserrate streets, with gates scattered to permit city entry. Fragments are still visible.)

But for the most part, the fortresses provided ample protection, and the city prospered and developed. In 1759, half of Cuba's 140,000 people lived in Havana, which had begun to absorb most of the urban investment in the country.

During the British occupation, 1762–63, Cuban trade mushroomed; but when the Spanish regained Cuba, instead of furthering the trade possibilities England had developed, they reimposed a monopoly. Havana reacted by developing a smuggling business par excellence, especially in rum and molasses. Gambling, prostitution, and harbor crime accompanied the contraband and set Havana on a "sin city" course. After the British departure, Spain again set about fortifying the city, and the Atares and Cabanas fortresses were built.

The flourishing slave trade and growing sugar business inspired tremendous capital infusions, and central Havana became a lavish, beautiful city of sweet shops, theaters, great public buildings, and stately plazas.

By 1863, when the city walls were demolished to permit expansion westward, Havana had a workable system of aqueducts, railroad connections, and gas lighting. The city was rightly considered one of Latin America's most advanced, sophisticated, and elegant capitals.

However, the prosperity was hardly universal. The charms and delights of lush Havana coexisted with filth, squalor, disease, and thievery. The city orphanage had a swinging-door drop chute to facilitate the abandonment of children by those who could not afford them. By the 1950s, the heyday of U.S. tourism in Cuba, even the Americans who ensconced themselves around the National Hotel pool acknowledged that Havana was a city where anything, anyone could be bought—a brothel and sewer dressed up and sold as paradise.

All currents of Cuban political thought manifested themselves in Havana, and important events in the city's history can be found in Section II, "History." Today, Havana is an energetic vital city in transition, the hub of the traveler's Cuban experience.

GETTING ORIENTED

Havana is built on a bay, with the harbor channel on the east and the Alamendares River on the west. It is helpful to visualize the city in four general sections—old Havana (Havana vieja), central Havana (Centro Havana), Vedado, and Revolution Plaza (Plaza de la Revolución). These do not correspond to actual political and administrative units, but they divide a very large city into manageable districts for the traveler.

Old Havana is the easternmost section of the city, bounded on the east by the harbor and on the west by Monserrate and Egido streets, where the old city walls ran.

Central Havana adjoins old Havana to the west and is bounded on the north by the Malecón (Havana's oceanfront drive) and the sea, on the west by Avenue Menocal (or Infanta), and on the east by Monserrate and Egido streets.

Vedado, starting more or less at the University of Havana, is the section where most tourist hotels are located. Vedado runs to the Alamendares River and is laid out in almost perfect squares.

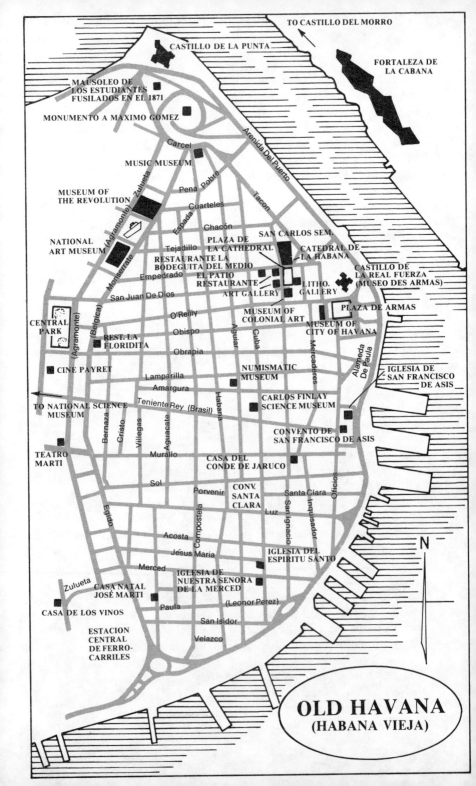

**OLD HAVANA
(HABANA VIEJA)**

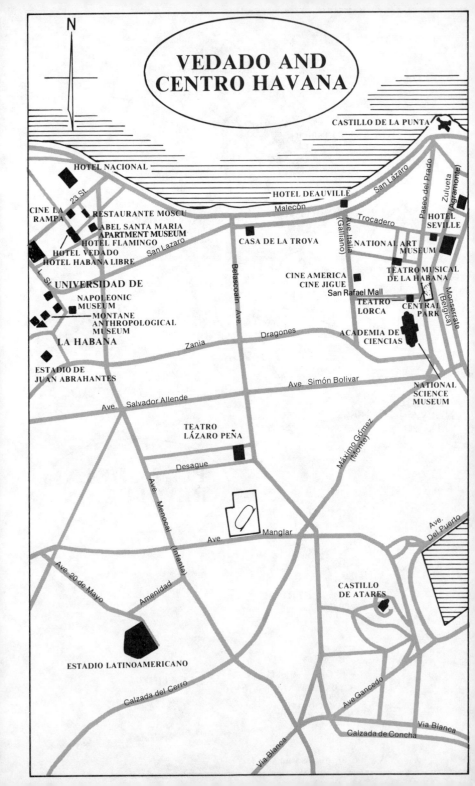

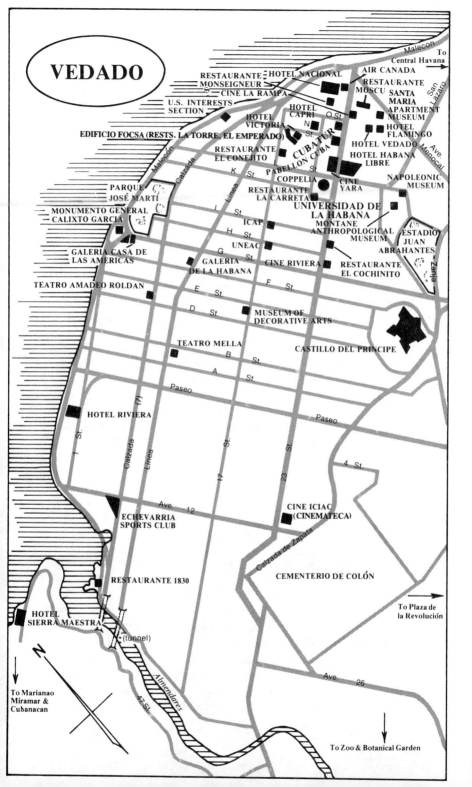

The Plaza de la Revolución area, the political center of the city, is slightly southeast of Vedado and a bit off the regular tourist route.

When asking an address, it is helpful to have at least a vague idea of the section of the city you will be heading toward. Some residential areas located off the tourist routes are Vibora, Cerro, Lujano, Santo Suarez, and Jesus del Monte.

Museums and restaurants have been included in the following descriptions, with a master list of restaurants for cross-referencing following the Havana section. The city is large, and traveling around is often difficult. Therefore, it is best to plan for "serious" sightseeing and cover the city by sections. To visit all Havana's museums and savor its ambience, to wine, dine, and nightclub, would require at least a week, but most tours spend only two or three days there. The city has access to fine beaches, and its comfortable hotels make it an ideal base of operations.

Transportation problems, especially at rush hours, are more acute in Havana than elsewhere in Cuba. Whenever possible, walking is the most efficient method of traveling around. Taxi fare between Vedado and old Havana runs about 1 peso one way, and bus fare is 5¢ within the city, 20¢ to suburbs. Exact fare is required.

OLD HAVANA

An interesting feature of Spanish colonial cities was that, with the exception of the areas immediately rimming the plazas where the very highest officials lived, residential areas were mixed socially and economically. Merchants often lived above their warehouses, town slaves lived in the homes of their owners, workers lived among the aristocracy. Only the Indians lived in completely separate sections, or *barrios*. This mixing was certainly less a function of democratic principle than of economic necessity, but especially in old Havana, there is a constant juxtaposition of the lofty and the humble.

The prevailing architectural influences are pre-baroque, using solid masonry construction and tiled roofs; ornate baroque, heavily sculpted and carved; and neoclassical Greco-Roman. Delicately carved hardwood ceilings with intricate dropped-gable support systems are common. Especially noteworthy are the Spanish doors, high and wide, often decorated with a family coat of arms.

With the development of Havana's suburbs, facilitated by the construction of the Malecón sea boulevard in 1902 and much later by the tunnels on the east and west, old Havana was left to decay. The government never expanded ancient plumbing systems, and beautiful facades were allowed to crumble in the salty sea air. When restoration was undertaken, it was usually by private individuals who had a personal or family interest in the property.

Most of old Havana consists of 18th- and 19th-century constructions, 70% of which have been declared national monuments since the Revolution. The Ministry of Culture, together with the Office of the Historian of Havana and the Department of Public Works, has collaborated on a master plan for the old city. It calls for a sensible restoration, not only to reclaim the beauty of the city, but to provide the inhabitants of these structures with adequate modern housing facilities.

When the city was designed, the Havana gentry traveled around in two-wheeled conveyances pulled by a single horse. The horse was ridden by a *calesero*, usually a black and often a slave, who was dressed in high boots, top hat and a costume trimmed with colorful ribbons. The original carriages were called *volantes* and had a stationary bonnet to protect passengers from the elements. Eventually, the *volante* was replaced by the *quitrin*, with a bonnet that could be moved up and down. (The museums of the City of Havana and Colonial Art each have a *quitrin*. As far as I know, no *volantes* have survived.) Later on, the Victoria, a 4-wheeled traditional carriage, was introduced.

The streets of old Havana, therefore, are just carriage width and, except for a few winding pockets, are squared off at right angles. It is very difficult to get lost.

WALKS IN OLD HAVANA

To hear the music of old Havana, the fruitful walks will undoubtedly be the random ones. However, here are some recommendations. Many of the churches, plazas, and other sights mentioned here are described further under the appropriate heading.

Obispo Street, east to west. This lively, shop-filled street runs from the Plaza de Armas to the city wall boundaries. You will pass the Ambos Mundos Hotel, now used by employees of the Ministry of Education, but once the temporary home of Ernest Hemingway, who no doubt spent many pleasant hours on the roof taking in the glorious view of the harbor. There are high wooden doors with the hotel name etched in the glass. Hemingway's room has been kept exactly as he left it, complete with bedside reading, and there was talk of opening it as a mini-museum. Note also the Drugeria "Johnson" on the corner of Aguiar, with mahogany galleries very typical of drugstores of the Spanish period. At the end of the street near Monserrate is the Moderna Poesia bookstore, one of Havana's best, and the Manzaria de Gomez, an enclosed shopping arcade.

Compostela Street, north to south. This is literally one of the most colorful streets in old Havana, with buildings painted lemon yellow and sea blue. Don't miss the Pharmacy at the corner of Teniente Rey, a national monument with beautiful wood and stained-glass paneling.

Pena Pobre, east to west. This street is the narrowest in Havana, in the La Punta end of the section, near the Santo Angel Church and the Music Museum. It forms a picturesque corner where the streets wind into each other.

San Ignacio, north to south. A must on this street for those interested in architectural restoration is the Conde de Jaruco palace, at the corner of Murallo Street (also called Brasil). The palace, once the home of one of Cuba's oldest Spanish families, is being restored stone by stone and will eventually house a museum.

Cuba Street, north to south. This street is a veritable city in itself. At Merced Street is the church of the same name, and on the next corner, heading toward the cathedral, is the Espiritu Santo church. There are important houses all along Cuba Street, including the O'Farrill house, now occupied by the Motor Vehicle License Bureau. The Finlay Science Museum is also on this block.

Obrapria, east to west. Note the especially striking structures at the corners of Mercaderes (Casa de Calvo de la Puerta) and San Ignacio (Casa Riberos de Vasconcelos).

Empedrado, east to west. Here, along the first paved street in Havana, is the legendary La Bodeguita del Medio restaurant, and a few doors further, the restored house of the Condesa de la Reunion. The park between Havana and Aguiar with a statue of Cervantes is an ideal reading stop.

Mercaderes, north to south. This street is a principal shopping area.

Avenida del Puerto (Alameda de Paula). Skirting old Havana along the port, this street is perfect for lovers of ships and all the activity that attends them. It used to be lined with 24-hour sailors' bars and has a sort of seedy-industrial atmosphere. Nevertheless, at Leonor Perez and the Avenida, there is a marble carved obelisk worth seeing, called Columna de O'Donnell, dating from 1847.

The Walls of old Havana. Bits can be seen in front of the Museum of the Revolution, near the railroad station at Avenida del Puerto and Egido, and at Monserrate and Teniente Rey.

FORTIFICATIONS OF OLD HAVANA

Check with Cubatur for the status of fort visits. Not all are open to the public.

Castillo de la Fuerza, Avenida del Puerta at Plaza de Armas. Havana's oldest fortress, built from 1558 to 1577, is the second oldest fortress in the New World. The tower is crowned with a bronze sculpture which functions as both a weathervane and the insignia for Havana Club Rum. The fortress is open to the public and also houses the Museo de Armas. (See "Museums in Old Havana.")

El Morro (Fortaleza de los Tres Reyes), at the mouth of Havana harbor, on the elevated headland (which is what *morro* means), across the bay from the city. Begun in 1589 and completed in 1630, it was designed by the Italian engineer Antonelli, who modeled it after one which then existed in Lisbon. An irregular polygon fronted by a lighthouse tower that was added in 1844, this is Havana's most famous colonial landmark.

La Punta, opposite El Morro, where Prado meets the Malecón. This fort was begun in 1590 to complement Morro, to catch pirate ships in crossfire. A heavy iron chain was strung from La Punta to El Morro to close the harbor.

La Cabana (Castillo de San Carlos de la Cabana), opposite Cathedral Square on the El Morro side of the harbor. Constructed between 1763 and 1774, after Spain regained Cuba from the British, this imposing fort was used by Spain to execute political prisoners during the war of independence. It is probably the most important of Havana's fortifications, but not open to the public. Traditionally a shot was fired from La Cabana at 9 p.m. to signal the closing of the city, a practice continued today.

Castillo de Atares, in the elbow of Havana harbor. This triple-tiered fortress was finished in 1763.

Castillo del Principe, near the Plaza de la Revolución at Calle G and Avenida Allende. Located on a hill affording one of Havana's best views, this fort is not presently accessible to tourists.

San Lazaro Tower, a lookout at Malecón and Maceo Park.

PLAZAS OF OLD HAVANA

Spanish urban planning borrowed from Rome the principle of retaining open areas for public use. In colonial Cuba, the "public" did not include slaves or servants, but certainly the plazas were rendezvous for other city dwellers, and the weekly *retreta* (evening concert) usually took place in the main square of the town. (Blacks were permitted their own *retreta* once annually.) The Plazas of old Havana are the ventilators through which the city breathes.

Plaza de Armas (Plaza Céspedes), foot of O'Reilly Street opposite La Fuerza castle. This restored, graceful, quadrangle with royal palms, other flowering trees, and marble benches placed along wrought-iron railings, was originally a marketplace. The plaza was the first public square in Havana, laid out in approximately 1519, and was the focus of administrative and cultural life. The Havana *retreta* took place here and still does, usually on Sunday evenings at 8 p.m. Plaza de Armas is elegantly ringed with important buildings.

El Palacio del Segundo Cabo, 1772–1776, is an imposing colonnaded building on the Fuerza side of the square. Formerly the headquarters of the Spanish military governor of Cuba, it now houses the Ministry of Culture. It is not open to the public.

El Palacio de los Capitanes Generales (Museum of the City of Havana), 1776–1791, is adjacent to El Palacio del Segundo Cabo. Perhaps the most beautiful baroque building in Havana, it was built as the residence for the captain general of Havana and later served as the U.S. governor's residence during occupation, as Cuba's presidential palace (1902–20), and as the city hall (1920–67). The patio is draped with ivy and flowers and is probably Havana's most tranquil open space. In addition to its museum function, the building is frequently used for concerts and poetry readings. (See "Museums in Old Havana" for a more complete description.)

El Templete, 1828, is a copy of a Doric Greek temple and was erected on the spot where the first mass was said in Havana in 1519. The paintings inside by Vermay, a French artist who profoundly influenced Cuban art, depict this first mass, the first Havana city council meeting, and the inauguration of the Templete.

The other buildings around the square are in various stages of restoration. Some were hotels and will eventually be once again.

Just off the square on Obispo Street between the Plaza and Mercaderes Street is a typically Spanish house restored since the Revolution, painted pastel blue, with plants gracing the balcony. It serves as a document center for the historian of Havana, presently Mr. Eusebio Leal. Leaving Plaza de Armas, it is most interesting to walk away from the sea to San Ignacio Street, then make a right to the Plaza de la Cathedral, passing imposing Spanish structures with portal doors and delicate *rejas*.

Plaza de la Cathedral. This cobblestoned plaza has become a focal point of tourist interest, mainly because of the art galleries which surround it and the Saturday afternoon art shows which take place here. (See "Cultural Events in Havana.") It is one of the few places in Havana where tourists will be "hustled" by children for Chiclets and other such items. Naturally, the tourist should use his or her discretion in these matters, but the Cuban government discourages this kind of behavior and hopes that tourists won't respond.

The Cathedral of Havana itself is a massive church built in 1704 by the Jesuits. When they were expelled from Cuba, it reverted to the archdiocese of Havana for use as a cathedral. It is a prime example of Cuban baroque architecture, with a many-columned limestone facade, concave and well weathered. The interior of the church has numerous niches and side altars, one of which held the remains of Columbus until their return to Santo Domingo. The main altar of the cathedral is resplendent Carrara marble inlaid with gold, silver, onyx, and carved wood. The sculptures are reportedly by an Italian named Branchini, while the paintings are by Vermay.

Flanking the facade are unmatched towers containing two bells, one from Matanzas and one from Spain, supposedly cast with a dash of gold and silver that accounts for their musical tone. A small museum in the cathedral contains vestments and other valuables.

It is best to visit the cathedral on Sat., 5 p.m.–7 p.m., or during mass on Mon., Wed., Thurs., and Sat. at 6:30 p.m., or Sun. 8 a.m.–10 a.m. Check to see whether the east bell tower is open. The view is superb, but there was talk of closing it to the public.

Directly opposite the cathedral is the *Museum of Colonial Art*, formerly the Bayona Palace, built around 1720. It is the oldest structure on the square. (See "Museums in Old Havana" for a fuller description.) Adjacent is the former Lombillo Palace, which now houses the interesting experimental print and lithography shop, *Galeria del Grabado*. Next to the shop is the former home of the Marques de Arcos.

Directly opposite the print shop is the *Plaza Art Gallery*, which exhibits the work of young Cuban artists. Next door, in the former home of the Count of Agua Claras, is the lovely *El Patio* restaurant.

CHURCHES IN OLD HAVANA

Convento de Santa Clara, 1635, a mini-city bounded by Habana and Cuba Streets in one direction and Sol and Luz in the other. The city's first slaughterhouse, public fountain, and baths were located here. Each building in the convent has a stucco roof, an elaborate carved wood ceiling, and balconies. Was closed for restoration.

Church of Espiritu Santo, Jesus Maria and Cuba Streets. Built in 1636, this is the oldest standing church in Havana, and a lovely building with simple stone interior. Catacombs are under the altar. The dark mahogany furniture case taking up the length of the vestiary was cut from a single piece of wood. The *vitrales* of this church are particularly beautiful.

Santo Cristo del Buen Viaje, Villegos Street between Teniente Rey and Lamparilla. This two-towered structure with tiled roof, located on a small plaza, was built in 1693. The amazing crossbeamed ceiling is the main feature.

La Merced, Cuba and Merced Streets. Built in 1746 and rebuilt in 1792, this is one of the loveliest churches in Havana. The completely frescoed interior was restored in 1963 by the Havana Cultural Council. The garden is a perfect resting spot, with delicate, lacy, wrought-iron gates. The area around the church is well worth a walk.

Convent and Church of San Francisco d'Assisi, Oficios and Teniente Rey Streets. This magnificent complex of religious buildings, built between 1584 and 1738, includes Havana's first convent. The patio and garden are among the city's most elegant. It is now the site of a restoration workshop and antique gallery where furniture, prints, paintings, and other items may be purchased. (See "Shopping in Old Havana.")

El Santo Angel Custodio, opposite the Museum of the Revolution, on Monserrate St. The church is notable for its cream-colored Gothic spires. It was built in 1672 by the Jesuits.

San Carlos Seminary, behind the cathedral facing the harbor, on Avenida del Puerto. This structure, built in 1772, is another superb example of Cuban baroque style, and a seldom visited pocket of tranquility. Open Mon.–Fri. 8:30 a.m.–12:30 p.m. and 3 p.m.–5 p.m.; closed Sat.–Sun.

MUSEUMS IN OLD HAVANA

Museum of the City of Havana (Museo de la Ciúdad de Habana). Tacon #1 between Obispo and O'Reilly (tel. 61-0722). The museum is housed in the former palace of the captain general, and is less a museum of the city than of the history of Cuba itself. It contains important historical documents, furnishings and silverware of the 18th and 19th centuries, portraits and personal possessions of Cuban heroes, a throne room—never used—for the king of Spain, coaches, *rejas,* a *quirin* with *calesero* garb displayed, and cemetery monuments from the colonial period. Don't miss the collection of beautiful copper implements. Open Tues.—Sat. 2:30 p.m.—6 p.m. and 7 p.m.—10 p.m., Sun. 3 p.m.—7 p.m.; closed Mon.

The patio is the site of frequent concerts, poetry readings, and light theater performances. Schedules can be obtained at the museum or from Cubatur.

Museum of Colonial Art (Museo de Arte Coloniale). San Ignacio #61, opposite the Cathedral of Havana on the plaza (tel. 61-1388). This maganificently restored Spanish palace houses a small exhibit devoted to the history of Cuba and has a number of rooms with furniture and implements representative of the colonial period. The room devoted to the design of *vitrales* and *mamparas* is unique in Cuba. Open Tues.—Fri. 1 p.m.—9 p.m., Sat. 3 p.m.—10:30 p.m., Sun. 9 a.m.—1 p.m.; closed Mon. A visit to this museum can easily be combined with the activities of Saturday at the plaza. (See "Shopping in Old Havana.")

Numismatic Museum (Museo Numismatico). Aguiar #456 between Amargura and Lamparilla (tel. 66578). This museum houses a permanent collection of Cuban coins from the colonial epoch to the present, with occasional "theme" exhibits. Open Tues.—Sat. 3 p.m.—10 p.m., Sun. 9 a.m.—1 p.m.; closed Mon.

Arms Museum (Museo de Armas). Castillo de la Fuerza, Plaza de Armas. This recently opened museum depicts the history of Cuba, with exhibits of weaponry used from the Indian period through the Revolution. The installation system using wood and natural stone is elegant. Open Tues.—Sat. 1 p.m.—8:30 p.m., Sun. 8:30 a.m.—12:30 p.m. On Monday, only the fortress is open.

Carlos Finlay Science Museum (Museo de Ciencias Carlos Finlay). Cuba #460 between Amargura and Teniente Rey (tel. 68006). This is an off-the-beaten track museum with particular appeal to physicians and chemists. The building formerly housed the Academy of Science but is now devoted to exhibits of manuscripts and instruments used by Cuba's leading scientific figures. It contains a pharmaceutical collection as well. Open Mon.—Fri. 8 a.m.—5 p.m., Sat. 8 am.—noon; closed Sun.

Music Museum and Archives (Museo del Musica y Archivo). Carcel #1 between Aguiar and Havana (tel. 80-6810). Located on a side street near the Malecón, this museum will be one of Havana's most interesting when it opens in 1979. It contains a history of the musical instrument in Cuba, including rare African drums. There are music boxes from the 19th century, with fine silver moving parts the visitor can watch with the delight of a child. There eventually will be listening rooms for records of Cuban music. (Check with Cubatur for exact hours, or phone the museum.)

Birthplace of José Marti (Casa Natal José Marti). Leonor Perez (also known as Calle Paula) #314, between Picota and Egido, near the railroad station. The small, modest home where Marfii was born and spent the first fosr years of his life contains objects related to the war for independence, including Marfi's work desk and personal possessions. Open Tues.—Sat. 1 p.m.—8:15 p.m., Sun. 9 a.m.—1 p.m.; closed Mon.

SHOPPING IN OLD HAVANA

Saturdays at the plaza, Cathedral Square. Cuban handicrafts, ceramics, books, and records may be purchased here each week from 5 p.m. to 10 p.m. A lively gathering and excellent opportunity to meet and chat with Cubans—it's an experience that should not be missed. Often music or theater groups perform during the outdoor bazaar activities. This is a good time to visit the Colonial Art Museum, the cathedral art galleries, and the cathedral itself.

Galleries. The art galleries around the plaza de la Cathedral sell original artworks and are open normal shop hours during the week, as well as Saturday at the plaza.

Antiques. The Palace of Art, located in the former San Francisco d'Assisi convent, 147 Oficios Street (tel. 61-3331), is worth visiting just to see the convent structure and the wrought-iron open-cage elevator. Cuban furniture, antique prints, table items, porcelains, and china not earmarked for museums are on sale in this restoration workshop and gallery. Shipments of large pieces can be arranged. Open Mon.–Fri. 8 a.m.–noon and 1 p.m.–5 p.m., Sat. 8 a.m.–noon; closed Sun.

Saturdays at La Moderna Poesia, corner Obispo Street and Monserrate. At noon outside this large bookstore, Cuban writers gather to discuss their work and distribute signed copies of their latest releases. Another fine opportunity to meet Cubans and participate in local cultural activities.

Palacio de Artesania, Cuba #64, between Pena Pobre and Chacon. A complex of shops where crafts, tobacco, liquor, clothing etc. can be bought, beautifully arranged around an old Spanish courtyard. 12:30-7:30 p.m. Monday-Saturday Tel. 61-0044.

CENTRAL HAVANA

The line between old and new in Havana is not as pronounced as the division of this guide suggests, and outside the wall line, in this central area, there is a collage of possibilities for the visitor.

WALKS IN CENTRAL HAVANA

Central Havana is basically a shopping center, with numerous cafeterias, cinemas, and stores. The streets, especially during rush hours, are filled with Habaneros going about their daily business. The best way to participate is to walk.

Neptuno Street. Begin at Agramonte, with the Hotel Plaza. This building, painted an eggshell cream color, has an ornate gold-leaf lobby and particularly fine wrought-iron balconies. Walk Neptuno to Galiano, which it crosses.

Galiano (Avenida Italia). This shopping artery is especially active between Neptuno and San Jose. Don't miss the Joyeria

Trianon, a French-style electric blue facade with porcelain inlay and marble columns, at the corner of the San Rafael mall.

San Rafael mall. Closed to auto traffic between Galliano and Central Park, this is probably Havana's liveliest street. On Saturday afternoon particularly, it seems to sway with the rhythm of whatever music may be pouring out of the record shops. The VietNam Bookstore is located here, and the San Rafael Art Gallery, at #105.

Malecón. The word means "embankment," and it's exactly that—a seawall road that binds Havana. Planned in 1857 by Albear, the Cuban engineer who built Havana's aqueduct, it was finally constructed in 1902. The houses which line Malecón were once grand, almost all 20th-century structures gaily painted, with colonnades and arches that recall other eras. One house even used Greek-style caryatids to support its balcony.

The waves crash constantly onto Malecón, sending sea foam up over the wall. The entire skyline of Havana is visible from here, and the walk from its beginning at La Punta to Vedado is about two miles. On a beautiful day, you can enjoy the view of the sea and the fresh air. The walk will take you past the new Havana Hospital, the city's tallest structure, and the bronze and marble equestrian monument to Antonio Maceo. After school hours, an informal baseball game is usually in progress around the monument base, and the plaza comes alive with the shouts of children.

Prado. The boulevard running west of Central Park to the sea is the incomparable Paseo del Prado, or Paseo Martí. Begun in 1771, this is one of Havana's grandest arteries, planted with tall shady laurel trees along its entire length. There is a pedestrian promenade down the middle, fountains scattered along the route, and cross streets punctuated by bronze lion statues. The mosaic tile work on the promenade was added in 1927. Prado was once Havana's most prestigious shopping area.

WHAT TO SEE IN CENTRAL HAVANA

Central Park (Parque Central). Between the Prado and

Zulueta Streest (also called Agramonte Street), this stately rectangular plaza is a focal point, since many public bus routes begin and terminate here. The park itself is lush with palm, almond, and poinciana trees and during the heat of the day is a fine place to catch some shade.

The Capitol building (Capitolio) and Fraternity Park (Parque Fraternidad). Anyone who doubts the extent of U.S. influence in Cuban political affairs need only visit this building, whose white dome can be seen from almost anywhere in the city. Opened in 1929, it is virtually an exact replica of the U.S. Congress building. The interior is almost entirely marble, with vaulted arches, rotundas, and polished brass lamps. The employees who worked there before the Revolution remember how their footsteps echoed throughout because the building was almost always silent—"that's how often the Congress came to work." The construction was mounted at a cost of $16.5 million. Today, the building houses the offices of the Academy of Sciences as well as the Natural Science Museum.

Fraternity Park adjoins the Capitol and draws its name from the fact that a ceiba tree was planted there in soil brought from the home country of each delegate to the Pan American Conference held in Havana in 1928. The park is shady and cool, and you can have a photo taken for a peso by any number of park photographers, whose cameras, developing labs, and offices sit on the same tripod. In the park is the white marble Indian Fountain, dating from 1837.

Around Central Park and the Capitol. Before the Revolution, there was a tremendous concentration of wealth in this area—all the best shops, confectioners, hotels, and theaters were located here, spilling down onto the Prado.

Lorca Theater, opposite the park on the Capitol side, is probably the most ornate theater in Cuba, with four towers each tipped by an outreaching angel. The facade is wedding-cake rich. Constructed as a theater in 1838, the building also used to house the Centro Gallego, an exclusive Spanish philanthropic society whose members were descendants of the original Galician settlers. The Lorca is now a box theater, with velvet seats and crystal chandeliers, where the National Ballet and Opera often perform. *Martí Theater*, Dragones Street between Prado and Zulueta, is also a 19th-century culture center.

Across the street from the capitol is the *Payret Cinema* and numerous cafes with outdoor tables. Also note the colonnaded shopping center, which has one of Havana's best bookstores, at the corner of Prado and Teniente Rey. The *Plaza de San Francisco*, on Monserrate between Teniente Rey and Dragones, has the lovely lion fountain, sculpted in the 19th century by the Italian Gaggini.

MUSEUMS IN CENTRAL HAVANA

National Museum of Art (Palacio de Bellas Artes), Trocadero and Zulueta Streets, opposite Granma monument (tel. 61-3915 or 68198). Cuba's national gallery of art should not be missed. Floors are joined by ramps leading from the atrium garden. Be sure to see the rooms devoted to Cuban painting, especially the works of Portocarrero, Peláez, Raul Martínez, Carlos Enriquez; the permanent exhibition of young artists; and the rotating exhibitions at the back entrance of the museum. There are also outstanding collections of Egyptian, Greek, and Roman antiquities considered the best in Latin America. Open Tues.–Sat. 1:15 p.m.–8:30 p.m., Sun. 9:15 a.m.–12:30 p.m., closed Mon.

Museum of the Revolution, Refugio #1, former presidential palace, facing the harbor and Máximo Gómez monument (tel. 61-5308 or 61-5307). This museum contains a detailed history of Cuba from discovery through each stage of war and revolution—a must. It is the definitive collection of newspaper clippings, personal possessions of the guerrillas, photographs, and other exhibits related to the Revolution. Open Tues.–Fri. 12:30 p.m.–7:30 p.m., Sat.–Sun. 11:30 a.m.–4:30 p.m.; closed Mon.

Granma monument, between Museum of the Revolution and the Museum of Art. The yacht that carried Fidel Castro and his followers to Cuba from Mexico is preserved here under glass. It may be visited during the same hours as the Museum of the Revolution.

Museum of Natural Sciences Felipe Poey, Academy of Sciences (Capitol) Building, entrance to the left of the grand staircase on Prado (tel. 80-0707 or 68536). This museum houses excellent collections of marine life, butterflies, mammals, and birds. The planetarium offers hourly shows in the evening, and the Punta del Este cave, complete with copies of the famous Indian pictographs, is replicated in exact detail. Open Tues.–Sat. 2 p.m.–9:35 p.m., Sun. 9 a.m.–12:30 p.m.; closed Mon. Special guided tours may be arranged through the tourist's sponsoring agency, usually Cubatur. These tours can be made Tues.–Fri. 8:30 a.m.–5:30 p.m., Sat. 8:30 a.m.–12:30 p.m.

VEDADO

Vedado is where the visitor to Havana will no doubt first arrive—most hotels are located here, as are most restaurants. Vedado, once an exclusive section, remains predominantly residential, although the largest mansions have been converted to public use, like the attractive Writers and Artists Union Building (UNEAC) and the Institute for Friendship among Peoples (ICAP) on 17th Street and I.

GETTING AROUND VEDADO

Vedado is divided into square blocks, with odd-numbered blocks crossing lettered blocks and then, even numbered blocks. The letters P to A are used, then Paseo Street, then the numbers 2 to 32. An address written "Calle 23 between E and F" will pinpoint the address within a block. The main streets are Calle 23 (La Rampa), Calle 9 (Linea), and Calle 7 (Calzada). The corners usually have a white concrete ground level marker identifying the cross streets.

After the letter A, at the west end, Vedado becomes a bit more confusing. Paseo, which runs parallel to the lettered streets, divides letters from even numbers. After Paseo, one can have an address written "Calle 23 between 10 and 12." For example Calle 23, #*1155* is located between 10 and 12 on Calle 23. The corners usually have a white concrete ground level marker identifying the cross streets.

WHAT TO SEE IN VEDADO

La Rampa (Calle 23). Vedado's main street, which rises from Malecón up a hill, is lined with airline offices, ministries and other enterprises. Almost all buses travel this route or pass close to it.

Coppelia, Calle 23 between L and K. In a large, shady park, there is a circular tentlike cement structure—the ice cream capital of Havana, a restaurant, snack bar, and outdoor dining area where the menu is delicious Coppelia ice cream. Choose your item from the posted menu—flavor and style (sundae, cone, dish, or "salad,")—buy tickets for the item from the cashier, present them to the counter staff, and enjoy. There are scores of flavors—all the usuals, plus exotic tropical fruits and unusual tastes like wheat (*trigo*), a Havana specialty and a must for ice-cream lovers.

The University of Havana, Calle 27 and L. This shaded, cool campus on Arostegui hill in Vedado has neoclassical buildings arranged around small, scattered parks. The university was founded in 1728, after a few years of controversy between the Catholic bishops and the Dominican friars, under the name Royal and Pontifical University of Havana. Students were admitted on the basis of their purity of blood. Jews, Moors, Negroes, mulattoes, and persons of less than impeccable Christian credentials were barred.

The university was secularized in 1842 but remained "royal" until 1898. Admission, however, was always restricted to children of wealthy families. It was the scene of constant unrest from the first days of the Republic through the Batista regime. The monument at the foot of the steps leading to the campus contains the ashes of Julio Antonio Mella, a Communist student leader assassinated in Mexico by the Machado regime in 1929.

Today, the University has schools of economics, law, philology, journalism, philosophy, history, psychology, science, and geography. Visitors are welcome to stroll around the campus, but unprogrammed classroom visits are not permitted. These must be arranged in advance by your tour operator and Cubatur.

Colon Cemetery, Calle 12 and Zapata (an inset street that would be 27½ if there were such a street). The wealthiest church members used to be buried right in the catacombs of Cuba's churches. However, this practice fostered epidemics, so cemeteries like Colon developed. It is entered through a triple-arched monumental gate, ornately carved, dating from 1870. There are white marble mausoleums larger than some homes, as well as monuments to martyrs of the Revolution, and row after row of simple vaults.

MUSEUMS IN VEDADO

Museum of Decorative Arts, Calle 17 #502 between D and E (tel. 32-1300 or 32-0924). Formerly a private residence, the museum was inaugurated in 1963. A first-floor room is devoted to temporary exhibitions of Cuban popular art, but the collection consists mainly of beautiful furniture, porcelain, crystal, and ceramics from the 18th and 19th centuries. Most of the objects are European, although there are some Cuban pieces. Open Tues.—Sat. 1 p.m.—9 p.m., Sun. 9 a.m.—1 p.m.; closed Mon.

Napoleonic Museum, San Miguel #1159 near Havana University (tel 79-1460 or 79-1412). This collection of artifacts, furnishings, and other objects from the Napoleonic period in Cuba has been closed for restoration. Check hours locally.

Apartment of Abel Santamaria, Calle 25 #164 between Infanta and O, Apt. 601. This simple two-room apartment was used by the rebels during the Revolution. Abel Santamaria, an important leader, lived here. The furnishings, including a desk

Fidel Castro used, have been left in place. Tues.—Sat. 9 a.m.—5 p.m., Sun. 9 a.m.—1 p.m., closed Mon.

Montane Anthropological Museum, Felipe Poey Science Building, University of Havana, 2nd floor, on main university square (tel. 32-9000). This museum contains pre-Columbian Indian artifacts—some very beautiful pieces indeed. Open Mon.—Fri. 9 a.m.—noon and 1 p.m.—5 p.m., Sat. 9 a.m.—noon; closed Sun.

PLAZA DE LA REVOLUCIÓN AREA

WHAT TO SEE AROUND PLAZA DE LA REVOLUCIÓN

The plaza is Havana's political and civic heart, the enormous open space where Fidel Castro gives major national speeches usually to a crowd of no less than a million Cubans. The square is dominated by a tower monument to José Martí (426 feet high) by the Cuban sculptor Sicre, commissioned before the Revolution. Around the plaza are various ministry buildings, the Central Committee of the Communist Party, the National Theater, and the National Library.

The Philatelic Museum, Ministry of Communications Building, Avenida Independencia, is a must for stamp lovers and history buffs. The stamps of 80 nations—including the United States—are assembled in sophisticated pull-out glass panels, with a national profile included in each. The Cuba panel is especially fascinating. The first stamp printed in Cuba was in 1960; prior to that, all stamp printing was done abroad. The post-Revolutionary stamps are particularly beautiful. All the political heroes are represented, along with flora, fauna, and other national symbols. Note the giant stamp commemorating the 400th anniversary of Peter Paul Rubens' birth, as well as the Declaration of Havana stamps, which actually have the entire speeches printed on them microscopically in various languages. There are frequent special exhibitions and a shop where stamps, postcards (the best selection in Havana), and posters can be purchased. Open Mon.–Fri. 10 a.m.–6 p.m., Sat. 10 a.m.—2 p.m.; closed Sun. (tel. 70-5581).

RELIGIOUS SERVICES IN HAVANA

Members of denominations other than those listed here should check with their home church before leaving to see if there is a practicing group in Cuba at this time.

Roman Catholic churches. (See "Churches in Old Havana.") All churches have mass Sunday mornings, as well as on selected evenings during the week and religious holidays.

Presbyterian church, 218 Salud Street, central Havana. Check locally for service schedule.

Baptist church, 502 Zulueta Street, central Havana. Check locally for service schedule.

Synagogues. *Temple Shevet Achim*, Calle Inquistador #407 at Santa Clara, old Havana. Daily and Friday night services. *Patronato Synagogue* on Linea in Vedado, housing the Hebrew Community House also has Friday evening services.

CULTURAL EVENTS IN HAVANA

Cartelera Cultural. This cultural calendar is published weekly by the Ministry of Culture and usually posted in the main hotels. (If not, ask the Cubatur representative.) It lists concerts, theater performances, art shows, cinema, poetry readings, conferences, and other events.

In Havana, there is a national symphony and opera company as well as the renowned National Ballet. Consult Cubatur or the Cartelera, for details, or look in the daily newspapers under *Culturales*. Something takes place every night.

Casa de la Trova, San Lazaro #661, central Havana, between Belascoain and Gerrasio. This beautiful old house with *vitrales, mamparas*, and a carved balcony is used not only for *trova* activities but for poetry readings and other music events.

Dance. In addition to the National Ballet, the Conjunto Folklorico often performs in Havana, as do other national dance companies. Consult the *Cartelera Cultural*.

Cinemas. There are countless cinemas in Havana; admission is never higher than 1 peso. Consult the newspapers, Cubatur, or the film listings posted in the major hotels for schedules. Films run as long as there is demand. Following are the most well-known cinema houses.

Riviera, Calle 23 between G and H, Vedado
Yara, Calle 23 at L, Vedado
La Rampa, Calle 23 at O, Vedado
America, Galliano and Concordia, central Havana
Payret, Paseo Marti, opposite the Academy of Sciences, central Havana
Cinemateca, Calle 23 and 10, an "art" house, Vedado

Theater. At any time of year, there are dramatic performances scheduled in Havana, in Spanish. The performances include Cuban and foreign plays. Consult Cubatur, the *Cartelera Cul-*

tural, and the newspapers for schedules. The main theaters are:

Lorca, Central Park, central Havana
Martí, Prado and Zulueta, central Havana
Carlos Marx, Calle Primera, Miramar
Hubert de Blanck, Calzada between A and B, Vedado
Roldan, Calzada and C, Vedado
Mella, Linea between A and B, Vedado

Art galleries in Havana. In Cuba, galleries are not necessarily places where art may be purchased. They are mainly exhibition spaces, although in old Havana, the Grabado and Plaza galleries do sell their works.

Galería de la Plaza, Cathedral Square, old Havana. Exhibits and sells works of young Cuban artists.
Galería Grabado, Cathedral Square, old Havana. Havana's experimental print gallery.
Galería del Arte, Galiano and Concordia, central Havana.
Galería de la Casa da Cultura, Calzada and 8, Vedado (tel. 30-3419). An important gallery, formerly the lyceum.
Galería Centro de Arte, San Rafael #105, central Havana (tel. 80-0569).
Galería de la Habana, Linea #462 at F, Vedado.
Galería Amelia Pelaez, Lenin Park (tel. 44-3060).
Galería Villena, UNEAC building, Calle 17, Vedado.
Galería Latino Americano, Casa de las Americas, Calle G and 3, 2nd floor (tel. 32-3587), Vedado.
Galería la Rampa, Hotel Habana Libre, Vedado.
Pabellón Cuba, Calle 23 between M and N, Vedado. Photographic and other exhibits relating to the history of Cuba.
Galería Ho Chi Minh, Call O between 23 and 25, Vedado.

Hours: Most galleries, notably Casa de Cultura and de la Habana, are closed Mondays. Others close Sundays. Usually they do not open before 2 p.m. It is best to check hours before going.

Outdoor concerts. In Almendares park, Vedado, concerts are held on Sunday evenings at approximately 8 p.m. Check Cubatur for exact time and location.

SPORTS FACILITIES IN HAVANA

Tennis. If you bring your own racket and balls, you can play at the *Nacional Hotel,* with one court, hotel guests given preference, book through reception; *José Antonio Echevarría Sports Club,* corner Calzada and 12, Vedado, with five clay courts, free court time, open 8 a.m.—6 p.m., but not always available to the public because of tennis instruction; *Julio Antonio Mella Sports Club*, Marianao, with two clay courts, same operation as Echevarría.

Golf. There is no golf in the Havana area. The nearest and only course is at Varadero, about two hours away.

Volleyball. Facilities for this sport are available at Echevarría and Mella sports clubs.

Swimming. Most Vedado hotels have pools, as do the above sports clubs. Fine beaches start at the Marianao suburb and head west to Santa Fe, with a wide assortment of facilities. The best "resort" beaches on the east side of the city are listed in "Beaches Outside Havana."

Running. The Malecón sidewalk is best, though regulation tracks are available at the sports clubs mentioned above. Avoid running in the streets, as Cuban drivers are not used to the omnipresence of runners.

Spectator sports. The above sports clubs sponsor frequent intramural competitions in a variety of sports. Check with the clubs directly for details. The *baseball* season runs from December to June at the Latin American Stadium (Estadio LatinoAmericano) near Plaza de la Revolución, on Avenida 20 de Mayo and Pedrosa Street. Admission is free. Check with Cubatur for schedules.

HOTELS IN HAVANA

All hotels listed have boutiques and tourist shops, as well as money exchange facilities. Rates are quoted in pesos per room as of 1978, exclusive of all meals, for foreign individual tourism. Many U.S. citizens will arrive in Cuba on package tours and therefore will not have choice of hotel.

DELUXE

Hotel Habana Riviera, Malecón and Paseo, Vedado (tel. 30-5051). Considered the finest hotel in Cuba, the Havana Riviera flashes its modern amenities the moment you step inside. A classic of hotel high-rise construction, it was clearly designed with U.S. tourists in mind. The nightclub opened in 1957, starring Ginger Rogers. 2 bars, a cabaret, 2 restaurants, poolside buffet lunch, cafeteria, swimming pool, steam baths, gymnasium, and conference facilities. A favorite with top-brass foreign delegations, but situated outside the Vedado mainstream.

360 rooms, including 26 suites, all with sea view and poolside cabanas; all accommodation with private bath, radio, telephone, air conditioning. Some TV sets. Rates, depending upon floor assigned: 2-bedroom suites, 103 pesos; 1-bedroom suites, 62; triple, 39–51; twin or double, 31–41; single, 23–31.

Hotel Habana Libre, Calle 23 and L, Vedado (tel. 305011). Formerly operated by the Hilton Hotel chain, the Havana Libre retains its busy atmosphere, although the lobby now bustles with as many Cubans as foreigners. A full-service hotel with rooftop dining and dancing; 3 restaurants, 3 bars, cafeteria, shops, swimming pool. Bubble-top lobby dome with spiral staircase. Excellent central location.

630 rooms, all with balcony, phone, private bath, air conditioning, radio. Rates: slightly less than the Riviera.

Hotel Capri, Calle 21 and N, Vedado (tel. 320511). This modern hotel is located on a quiet but central Vedado side street. It has a low-key pace, much less busy than either the Libre or the Riviera. Restaurant, cafeteria, 2 bars, cabaret, rooftop pool, conference facilities, shops, gracious staff and management.

216 rooms, and 23 suites, each with private bath, air conditioning, telephone, and radio. Rates, depending on floor and view: suites, 56–65 pesos; triple, 37–43; twin or double, 31–36; single, 25–29.

FIRST-CLASS

Hotel Nacional de Cuba, Calle 21 and Malecón, Vedado (tel. 7-8981). Built in 1927, this hotel is one of the world's classics, tall, spired building facing the sea, surrounded by lush gardens, entered via a sweeping driveway. Though the building needs restoration and services are a bit uneven, no other hotel in Cuba can match the Nacional for elegance. Excellent restaurant, Old World game room, conference facilities, cafeteria, shops, 2 swimming pools, a tennis court.

504 rooms, all with private bath. Some air conditioning. Rates (approximate): triple, 27 pesos; twin, 25; single, 20.

Hotel Sevilla. Trocadero #55, between Prado and Zulueta, central Havana (tel. 69961). The gracious setting for Graham Greene's *Our Man in Havana*, this hotel was built in 1924; restoration is ongoing. Lobby has *vitrales*, potted palms, velvet settees, and mahogany writing desks. The dining room is operated by the National School of Gastronomy, and the food is extremely tasty. Restaurant, dining room, bar, café, no pool.

189 rooms, some with air conditioning, all with private bath. Rates: triple, 18 pesos; twin, 14; single, 11.

Hotel Deauville, Avenida Italia #1 (Galiano) and Malecón, central Havana (tel. 616901). This hotel has an excellent dining room. Also bar, shops, nightclub, but no cafeteria or pool. 140 rooms, all with private bath, air conditioning, telephone, radio. Rates: triple, 24 pesos; double, 18; single, 14.

TOURIST-CLASS

None of the following offers the range of services of the deluxe or first-class hotels, but most are well located. Hot water is not guaranteed.

Hotel Vedado, Calle O #244 between 23 and 25, Vedado (tel. 326501). A commercial-style establishment with restaurant and bar, this hotel shares a pool with the adjacent Hotel Flamingo. 120 rooms, all with private bath and air conditioning. Rates: triple, 22 pesos; twin, 18; single, 14.

Hotel Flamingo, Calle 25, corner of O, Vedado (tel. 326596-98). This very pleasant, quiet hotel has wicker furniture in the lobby and stained-glass panels in the door. Restaurant with Spanish-style decor, pool, bar, cabaret. 70 rooms, and some suites, all with private bath; some air conditioning. Rates: same as Hotel Vedado; suites, 27 pesos.

Hotel Victoria, Calle 19 and M, Vedado (tel. 326501 or 32-6022). This charming neoclassical mansion began as a small guesthouse some 50 years ago. It has been added to in stages. The garden bar is one of Havana's most pleasant spots. The popular "Varsovia" dining room serves both Cuban and Polish specialties. 32 rooms, including 3 suites, each with a private bath. Rates: suite, 28 pesos; triple, 24; twin, 19; single, 14.

There are, of course, innumerable hotels in Havana besides those listed above, some for as little as 3 pesos per night. However, most of these do not accept foreign tourists. If you need something less expensive than any of the above, contact your Cuban sponsor, who will advise you. In general, hotels in Havana for less money suffer from inadequate water supply, occasional blackouts, and other inconveniences.

Beach hotels are listed under "Beaches Outside Havana."

RESTAURANTS IN HAVANA

Members of tour groups usually have all meals included in the cost of their tour. However, venturing off the meal plan in Havana is well worth the effort, as restaurants are generally very good.

Following is a selected alphabetical list, by category, of a variety of Havana establishments. Reservations are essential on Saturday evenings and recommended at other times. Reserve through Cubatur or by phoning directly, if your Spanish is up to it. All hotels have dining rooms as well, but these have not been listed. If you wish to dine in a hotel other than your own, reservations will be necessary and should be made through the hotel receptionist or the captain of the dining room.

Further restaurant listings can be found under "Beaches Outside Havana."

DELUXE

El Emperador, Focsa apartment building, Calle 17 and M, Vedado (tel. 324948). This restaurant serves about as classy a meal as can be had in Havana—a deluxe establishment catering to Continental tastes, favored by diplomatic delegations. Full-course dinner with wine not less than $25 per person. Reservations essential; jackets required for men.

Las Ruinas, outside Havana. This is one of Cuba's loveliest restaurants, and well worth the trip. See "Excursions Outside Havana, Lenin Park."

La Torre, rooftop of the Focsa apartment building corner M and 17 (tel. 322451). Here spectacular views of Havana accompany the fine Continental cuisine. Bar usually available only to those having dinner. Same price range and style as El Emperador.

FIRST-CLASS

Bodeguita del Medio, Empedrado 207, near Cathedral Square, old Havana (tel. 6-6121). Literally the "little grocery in the middle of the block," this is another of Havana's restaurant legends. Nobody fails to stop in at least for a *mojito*, the rum drink that drew Hemingway to it. It has a joyful bohemian atmosphere where people sign the flaking walls to commemorate their visits. Excellent Cuban specialties, particularly roast pork and black beans. Reservations essential. One of those places that publicity has made impossible, although Martinez, the manager, does his charming best to seat everyone. Avoid the weekends.

Cochinito, Calle 23 #457 between I and H, Vedado (tel. 40-4501 or –4502). This restaurant specializes in pork dishes.

Conejito, Calle M #206, corner of 17, Vedado (tel. 705501 or –5502). Amid brick and wood Tudor-style decor, Conejito specializes in rabbit served 100 ways, including rabbit hors d'oeurves.

El Jardin, Calzada 162, Vedado (tel. 3-7127). This is a pleasant Cuban-style family restaurant with outdoor patio, though a bit far from central Vedado, almost near the Almendares tunnel.

El Patio, Cathedral Square, old Havana (tel. 61-4550). This beautifully converted Spanish house dating from the 18th century was built on the location of the Paris restaurant, dating from the 17th. Typically Cuban food served is on the patio, with soft drinks available on the outdoor terrace.

Floridita, Avenida Monserrate (Belgica) #353, corner Obispo, central Havana (tel 61-2932). Floridita is another Havana legend, immortalized by Hemingway and *Esquire* magazine as one of the world's greatest bars. It is the home of the daiquiri and of lobster mariposa—a succulent dish of lobster grilled with almonds, pineapple, and butter, well worth the 10-peso price.

The restaurant has been operating in the same location since 1819, when it was called Pina de Plata. Subsequently changed to La Florida, the name was finally fixed with the affectionate diminutive form. The house special "Papa" daiquiri is a double, served with no sugar, for 4 pesos before discount. The French romantic decor in the dining room is the antithesis of La Bodeguita, the other Hemingway haunt. Jackets are recommended for men in the evenings.

Havana 1830, Calzada #1252, near Almendares Tunnel, Vedado (tel. 3-6954). This enormous mansion on the sea has served in the past as a public library, hotel, and private residence. There are four dining rooms—the Violet, Gold, Tropical, and Red—with varying degrees of plushness. An outdoor patio bar and gazebo bar jut out into the sea, and the indoor bar has lovely *vitrales*. Continental and Cuban menus.

La Roca, Calle 21 between L and M, Vedado (tel. 22-2551). This standard restaurant offers Cuban as well as Continental food. Intimate atmosphere and piano music.

La Carreta, Calle K #402 at 21, Vedado (tel. 32-4485). La Carreta has a very pleasant atmosphere and a good menu.

Las Bulerias, Calle L #414, opposite Habana Libre Hotel, Vedado (tel. 32-0706). Popular with Cubans, this restaurant serves Spanish and Cuban dishes.

Los Andes, Calle 21 and N, Vedado. Cuban and South American style food is served here in a pleasant atmosphere.

Mandarin, Calle 23 and M, Vedado. As the name implies, Chinese-style food and decor are featured here.

Monseigneur, Calle 21 and O, Vedado, opposite Nacional Hotel (tel. 329884). Classic French elegance accompanies Continental dishes served with soft violin and piano music in the background.

Moscu, Calle P between 23 and 25, Vedado (tel. 796571). This Havana favorite serves Russian specialties.

Polynesia, Calle 23, in the Habana Libre Hotel (reserve through the hotel operator). As the name suggests, this restaurant is Polynesian in menu and decor.

Potin, Linea 715, corner of Paseo (tel. 3-9403). This simple restaurant serves mainly Cuban food.

MODERATE

Casa de los Vinos, Esperanza #1, corner of Factoria, near railroad station, old Havana (tel. 82481 or 610073). This restaurant started in 1911 as a workers' canteen with one communal table. Then a wine exchange developed where wine was sold by the barrel. Now a bar adjoins a restaurant where Spanish-style food—bean soup and various sausages—can be had. Meat is hung over the bar. A uniquely colorful spot whose walls are inlaid with tiles written with proverbs on love and life.

Latino-Americano Club, Prado, between Virtudes and Animas, central Havana. This first-floor cafeteria with second-floor restaurant also has a pleasant tropical wood-panelled bar. Formerly an ambassadors' club, it is now a favorite with Cubans.

Lafayette Restaurant, corner of Aguiar and Teniente Rey, old Havana. This simple, clean restaurant is favored by workers in the old Havana section. It serves Cuban-style food at reasonable prices.

PIZZERIAS IN HAVANA

Cuban pizza makes a fine snack, especially when time is a consideration and you aren't inclined to wait for a restaurant table. There are simply too many in Havana to mention, but all the following can be recommended:

Buena Sera, Calle 23 #451, opposite Coppelia, Vedado.

Vista Nova, Corner of Calles 21 and L, with garden terrace, Vedado.

Montecatini, Calle 15 #252, Vedado.

Malecón, at the foot of Calle O on Malecón, near the Nacional Hotel. The stand also serves meat pies and ice cream.

RESTAURANTS OUTSIDE HAVANA

Barlovento, about 9 miles west of Havana on the Mariel road, is an excellent seafood restaurant at a boating center of the same name. (FC)

La Coronela, a fine restaurant in the suburbs of the city, serves only foreign technician residents. Maybe you'll befriend one who will take you! (FC)

Escalera de Jaruco, near the town of Jaruco, about 25 miles from Havana, is a Middle-Eastern restaurant in the mountains with striking views. It caters to protocol parties. (M) I am also told that an enterprising man in the town of Jaruco proper has set up some tables in his backyard where he serves fresh fish, so look for him. Jaruco is impossible without a car, as there is no public transportation available. A taxi would have to wait there for your return trip.

Rio Cristal, on the Rancho Boyeros road, 8 miles from Havana en route to the airport, is a beautiful garden recreation area on the grounds of a former slave barracks. Lush river vegetation surrounds a large swimming pool and two restaurants serving Cuban-style food. (M)

NIGHTLIFE IN HAVANA

Havana is hardly the Barbary town it once was, but there remains plenty of legitimate nightlife in which the tourist is heartily encouraged to participate. Cabarets and clubs are extremely popular with Cubans, and reservations are essential on weekends. The cabarets have dance floors and stage shows featuring entertainment with a Las Vegas touch, although there are often folkloric and Revolutionary entertainment numbers thrown in. Dancing, drinks, and glitter may be found at:

Cabaret El Caribe, Hotel Havana Libre
Cabaret Capri, Hotel Capri
Cabaret Parisien, Hotel Nacional
El Pico Blanco, St. John's Hotel, between 25 and 23, Calle O #210
Copa Room, Havana Riviera
Turquino Bar, rooftop of the Havana Libre

All hotels have bars available to hotel guests only, although the cabarets are open to the public.

The One and Only Tropicana, 72nd and 31st streets, Marianao (tel. 2-4544) is one of the world's most famous nightclubs, set in the midst of a veritable forest of palm trees and tropical foliage. The dancers and singers wind their way through the trees on platforms and present an indescribable show of great color, energy, and variety. Dinner is served, or just drinks. Reservations are essential, and a package tour can be booked with Cubatur so that transportation is provided. Getting to the club is a snap, but getting a taxi home is something else again. Maintaining the club costs about $1 million per year, and the performers are often students training for other professional positions. This is a must, even for nightclub haters!

El Colmao, Aramburu #366 between San Rafael and San Jose, Central Havana.

A hang-out favored by Cubans, hardly known by tourists. Features traditional Spanish music and floor show, including flamenco, and starring the inimitable La Paulobita and La Curra, well-known Cuban singers. Drinks and light snacks served. Open daily 8 p.m.-2 a.m. Tel. 701113.

El Morro Bar, (Taberna del Morro) recently opened in the famous castle of the same name, overlooking Havana harbor. Eventually, a full restaurant will be incorporated but for now, spend an evening over a pirata, a Cuba libre, a daiquiri or any one of a number of Cuban cocktails, all served beautifully in the restored castle.

SIGHTSEEING EXCURSIONS

Sightseeing trips are often included in the prepaid tour price. Additional optional tours may be purchased locally from Cubatur, either at the main office or at your hotel. Tours include guide services and transportation by luxury air-conditioned motorcoach. *Optional tours* include: Modern Havana, Colonial Havana, An Evening at Tropicana, The Hemingway Museum, Guama Resort, and The New Community of Jibacoa. New optional excursions are being developed, so ask for up-to-date information.

The Harbor Tour is an excursion by speedboat through Havana harbor. It departs daily at 9:30 a.m., 11 a.m., 3 p.m., and 4:30 p.m. from Havana 1830 Restaurant for a minimum of 4 persons. Tours through the channel afford a fine view of the city and the fortifications for 5 pesos per person. (Check with Cubatur representative to verify schedule before setting out.)

EXCURSIONS FROM HAVANA

Hemingway Museum, San Francisco de Paula, at the Finca Vigia, located 20 minutes from central Havana, about 3 pesos away by taxi (tel. 082-2315). Ernest Hemingway lived in Cuba for many years, and his personal effects, including unopened mail, are left in place here. The house is set in a 22-acre garden, located on a palm-studded hill which affords a superb view of the city. The home became the property of the Cuban government after Hemingway's death with the consent of Mrs. Hemingway. Visitors are not permitted to enter the house, but they may circle it and look through the windows. Hemingway aficionados may therefore appreciate having a pair of binoculars in order to perceive fine details. No photography is allowed of the interior of the house. No visits are permitted on rainy days. If in doubt, phone ahead. Open Tues.–Sat. 8 a.m.–12 p.m. and 2 p.m.–4:45 p.m., Sun. 9 a.m.–1 p.m.; closed Mon.

Casablanca and/or Regla. These two small towns are located opposite Havana on the other side of the harbor channel and accessible for 5 centavos round trip (pay on the other side) from Avenida del Puerta. The boat to Casablanca leaves from the foot of Castillo de la Fuerza, to Regla from the San Pedro docks. The boat trips afford excellent views of the city, quite breathtaking at sunset. On the hills above Casablanca stands the enormous Christ of Havana.

Lenin Park (Parque Lenin) 12 miles from Havana, (closed Mon.—Tues.). This 1,675-acre recreation area of green grass, tall palm trees, and fishing lakes was inaugurated in 1970, and much of the landscaping was done by volunteer labor from Havana. Today, it is used frequently by Cubans for picnics, walks, sports, and other recreational activities, especially on Sunday afternoons. The numerous facilities include $1 million amusement park, a horseback riding school, and a lakeside amphitheater that looks like it was lifted straight from Greece—stone seats covered with moss for comfort, with a floating stage used for theatrical performances. A train circles the park, carrying visitors from one area to another. There are several interesting installations here, and two restaurants worth noting.

Galería Amelia Peláez, overlooking the hills of the park, houses temporary exhibitions of popular Cuban artists. The *mamparas* in the gallery are themselves artworks, their steel-blue glass crowns spraying the room with tinted light.

Peña Literaria, a small reading area stocked with Cuban and some foreign periodicals and books, is a quiet nook for study or reading. *The aquarium* contains specimens from local waters, including the rare flat-nosed manjuari. The *Taller Ceramica*, a workshop for ceramicists, attracts amateurs as well as professionals. Supplies and instruction are provided and children often work outdoors on the cool, green grass. Exhibitions of work are on view.

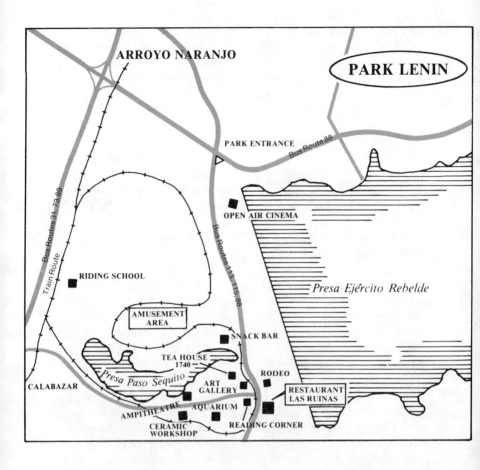

Las Ruinas restaurant (tel. 443336) is one of Havana's most deluxe operations, ingeniously designed around the ruins of a sugar mill and built shortly after the Revolution. The modern stained-glass panels are by the Cuban artist Portocarrero, and the rest of the decor is traditional Spanish—lots of mahogany, crystal, and crisp linen. It's expensive, but the bar serves a wide assortment of unusual tropical drinks and is a fine way to see the restaurant if you prefer not to part with the minimum of 20 dollars per person it will take with wine. (Chicken with rice for two, however, is 10 pesos.) Reservations recommended on weekends. Open noon–11 p.m.; closed Mon.–Tues.

Casa 1748 Teahouse is a charming corner of the park where hot and iced tea is served with sweets, either outdoors or indoors in a converted colonial-style house. A fine spot for a late afternoon "merienda." There are also many other snack bars throughout the park.

To reach Lenin Park, you can take a taxi from Vedado for about 7 pesos one way. Buses that serve the park include #88 from the Vibora station and #113 from the Lisa station. To reach Vibora from Vedado, take #68 or #37; to reach Lisa, #28, or #22. Plan about 1 hour for the bus connections, 15 minutes for the taxi ride.

Santa Fe and Jaimanitas, about 7 miles west of Havana. These suburbs are accessible by public bus (about 3 pesos by taxi). They are small-craft fishing enclaves of interest to those who wish to see more of the Cuban lifestyle.

Miramar and Marianao, Cubanacan and Siboney. Formerly Havana's most exclusive suburbs, they are still residential, but the largest houses have been converted into schools and other public facilities. The #32 bus from La Rampa runs along Fifth Avenue through this area. Get off anywhere and just walk around. It's the best way to understand the wealth that was concentrated in Havana before the Revolution.

Barlovento, about 9 miles west of downtown Havana. This former yacht center is now a public sport-fishing and naval-training center. It is interesting for boat lovers and has an excellent restaurant serving seafood.

Zoological Park, Avenida 26, Nuevo Vedado district. This is a children's recreation park as well as zoo containing a variety of tropical species. Open Tues.–Sun. 9 a.m.–7 p.m.; closed Mon.

Botanical Garden, in La Ceiba south of central Havana, between Calzada de Puentes Grandes and Avenida Rancho Boyeros. This garden is luxuriant with indigenous and exotic plant life, flowers, and trees. Closed Mon.

National Aquarium, 60th Street and 1st, Miramar, about 20 minutes from Vedado by taxi. Closed Mon.

Other excursions. The towns of *Arroyo Naranja, Cojimar, Guanabacoa,* and *Santa Maria del Rosario* are all within a few miles of Havana. See alphabetical listing for details.

BEACHES OUTSIDE HAVANA

Starting about 9 miles east of Havana, there is a 54-mile resort area with 12,000 inhabitants, about 80% of whom work in tourism. The eastern beach area is excellent for family vacations, offering hotel, motel, villa, cabana, and camping facilities along fine sandy beaches, lined with palm and pine trees, plus a full selection of sports and recreational facilities. All beaches are public, and can be visited for the day from Havana.

There are also beaches in the western area, and they are served by the El Salado Hotel and Monte Verde restaurant nearby, on the Mariel road, just outside Mariel itself, about 25 miles west of Havana. Both provide fine food at moderate prices. The beaches, however, do not compare with those of the eastern area, to which the remainder of this section is devoted.

RATES AND RESERVATIONS

Villa bookings for this area must be made through Cubatur and prepaid in full. Rates range from 10 pesos daily for a single room to 30 pesos daily for an entire house, depending on the facilities selected. Hotel bookings should also be made through Cubatur. Rates are listed with each hotel.

RESORT CENTERS

There are three centers in this region: Bacuranao, Santa Maria-Guanabo, and Jibacoa-El Tropico.

Bacuranao, 9 miles from Havana. A cabana complex with a capacity of 150 people, on the beach where the British landed in 1762. Arranged in attractive units, some of which have kitchenette facilities. Each cabana with air conditioning, bath, and hot water. Small sandy bay a favorite with Habaneros on weekends. Served by buses #162 and #62 from Central Park; taxi fare about 5 pesos. Cabanas booked only through Cubatur.

Santa Maria-Guanabo, beginning 12 miles from Havana. A 6-mile stretch of white sand ringed with pine forests, served by the #162, #62, and #262 buses. There are two main tourist centers in this area. One, the Santa Maria del Mar complex, has the larger number of facilities. The other, Guanabo, is a resort town just east of Santa Maria del Mar. There are a few excellent Cuban plantation-style wooden houses on the main road, as well as a small factory for the production of agricultural tools. The town borders the beach, with a camping center used for youth tourism.

El Megano, Santa Maria del Mar, is a cabana complex off the beach with large swimming pool attached. 50 units, all with patio, air conditioning, and hot water.

Villa Los Pinos, Santa Maria del Mar, is a colony of villas that can be rented for exclusive use or on a shared basis. Most houses have 3 or 4 bedrooms, plus sitting room, balcony, and full kitchen. The villas are scattered through the pines, and none are more than a 2-minute walk from the beach. The restaurant serves simple but plentiful Cuban-style food, and cooking can be done in the villas. Rates: on request only from Cubatur.

Hotel Marazul, Santa Maria del Mar (tel. 2531-35), was opened in 1975, the first resort hotel to be built since the Revolution. It is frequently used by U.S. tour groups. 188 rooms, 8 suites, and 29 junior suites. All rooms with balcony, private bath, air conditioning. Showers have hot water, but it is slightly salty. The hotel, just across the road from the beach, with a full-size swimming pool on the premises, is one of

Havana's best. Rates: suite, 30 pesos; triple, 23; double, 20; single, 17. Excellent restaurant, especially the weekly seafood buffet. (Taxi fare to Havana about 7 pesos; bus, 20 centavos.)

Hotel Atlantico, Santa Maria del Mar (tel. 2551-3), was formerly a private club. It is now used mainly for international conferences and meetings. 20 rooms, full restaurants, refrigerators in rooms, air conditioning, radio. Rates: twin, 12 pesos; no singles.

Playa Hermosa, in the town of Guanabo, is a group of cabin units around a large swimming pool and bar area. Accommodation is extremely simple and lends itself mainly to student-youth tourism.

Jibacoa-El Tropico Area, 40 miles east of Havana. A resort center with a range of tourist accommodation.

Jibacoa consists of cabins and tent areas scattered among the forest, ringing a small bay and wider sandy beach. There are 70 bungalows with communal toilet and bath facilities, a restaurant, a bar, and a dance floor.

Villa Loma was opened in 1978. It has 23 cabins and some larger houses similar to Villa Los Pinos. There are also beach facilities and a restaurant.

El Tropico Resort is a full-service resort with a fine Cuban-style restaurant and a sandy beach. It has a very picturesque location, and scuba diving here is reported to be excellent.

SPORTS IN THE EASTERN BEACH AREA

Through the Cubatur desk at each resort, sports equipment and instruction can be arranged. The area offers horseback riding, deep-sea fishing, scuba instruction and diving, snorkeling, bicycling, water skiing. Outdoor squash (using handball courts) and tennis (with cement surface) are also available. Rental charges are nominal, but enthusiasts should bring their own equipment, especially during high season. (Scuba devotees will find French equipment available and therefore may prefer to rent in Cuba.)

Each hotel has a restaurant, and visitors may choose to eat in hotels other than their own, although at present no exchange meal privileges are granted to those on prepaid full-board arrangements. Reservations should be made in advance through Cubatur. In addition to the hotel restaurants, there are numerous snack bars, cafeterias, and ice cream stands. The following restaurants are both good bets on Saturday night when everything in Havana is booked up. Reservations made through the Santa Maria telephone operator, who will connect you to either:

Guanabo Club Restaurant, 13th Avenue and 470 A Street, Guanabo. A brand-new facility overlooking the town, with excellent Cuban-style food, dancing, and outdoor bar. (FC)

Restaurant El Caribe, Santa Maria del Mar, near the Hotel Atlantico, 13th Street off Avenida de las Terrazas, specializing in seafood. An excellent restaurant with gracious service and atmosphere. (FC)

CUBA A TO Z

ARROYO NARANJA. Est. 1845; pop. 154,126; 6 km (3.6 mi) S of Havana; Havana prov.

This suburb of Havana is about 3 pesos by taxi from Vedado. For those whose group trips do not include excursions to the countryside, walking around this town conveys a sense of Cuban rural life. Interesting to note along the road between Arroyo Naranja and Boyeros are the plantation-style wooden mansions which have been converted to schools and clinics. This trip can be combined with an excursion to Lenin Park. (See "Havana" section)

ARTEMISA. Est. 1818; pop. 56,189; 60 km (37 mi) W of

Havana, 115 km (73 mi) east of Pinar del Río on the south road, Havana prov.

One of the first towns of note on the Havana–Pinar del Río road, Artemisa is extremely vibrant. It is surrounded by new construction, and enlivened by the constant comings and goings of *campesinos* on horseback. The highway is Main Street, lined with neoclassical-style pastel-painted houses supported by elaborate Doric and Ionic Greek columns.

Artemisa was an early Castro stronghold, and 24 of the original 150 Moncada attackers were from either Artemisa or nearby Guanajay. These followers held their meetings in the freemasons' hall. A striking bronze cube monument has been erected to commemorate the martyrs of Artemisa. The Casa de Cultura of the town is one of the most active in the province.

BACURANAO. Beach resort outside Havana (see ''Beaches Outside Havana'').

BANES. Est. 1887; pop. 82,622; 80 km (48 mi) NW of Holguín, 30 km (18 mi) S of Guardalavaca resort; Holguín prov.

Banes is about a 1½-hour drive from Mayari Abajo, on a road weaving through coffee and cane fields and passing the Central Urban Norris, the largest sugar complex in Holguîn province.

The town was founded on the site of a pre-Columbian Indian settlement named Bani, and extensive archaeological investigations have been carried out in the region. *The Banes Museum of Indian Civilization* (tel. 2487) displays pottery, tools, stone implements, ivory carvings, and gold animal effigies. There are excellent drawings by José Martinez of the Academy of Sciences, depicting the Indian migrations to Cuba as well as scenes from daily life. There is also a fine collection of local shells. An easy and worthwhile excursion for those staying at Guardalavaca resort. Open Tues.–Sat. 12:30 p.m.–10 p.m., Sun. noon–6 p.m.; closed Mon.

For dining, try *Las Oasis* and the *Hotel Bani dining room*, both on the main street of town. (M)

BARACOA. Est. 1512; pop. 58,416; 201 km (120 mi) NW of Santiago de Cuba, 120 km (72 mi) NW of Guantánamo; Guantánamo prov.

Baracoa is well worth visiting, if only for the drive along La Farola ("The Lighthouse"), a scenic roadway constructed after the Revolution through some of the most majestic mountains in Cuba. La Farola extends 19 miles from Guantánamo and at the entrance, signs proclaim, "Protect your life and the life of others. Check your vehicle." With these warnings, the visitor embarks on the roller coaster, driving through scenery unrivaled in Cuba. Green wild hills rise and fall as though breathing. Small coconut palms with yellowish fronds cover the slopes, looking from a distance very much like beach umbrellas raised by the grass for shade.

HISTORY

Early in December, 1492, during his exploration of Cuba's north coast, Columbus stopped at Baracoa, which he called Puerto Santo. He planted a large cross on the beach and sailed into the Macaguanigua river.

When Diego de Velázquez colonized Cuba, he landed at Baracoa, establishing Cuba's first city there in 1512.

Velázquez soon began his march south and eventually moved the capital from Baracoa to Santiago de Cuba, which was favored for its superior harbor and other geographical advantages. He made his home in Santiago, and his departure from Baracoa consigned the city to decline—it was burned by rebelling Indians, and again by French pirates, and developed a smuggling business which only made the pirate raids worse. The legal economy consisted of some fishing and agricultural enterprises—mainly fruit, corn and yucca. Eventually, cocoa and coffee were introduced, but these crops in themselves could not offset the negative spiral triggered by Velázquez's departure. Baracoa's remote location and mountainous terrain precluded extensive sugarcane planting, so the city's economy never boomed.

During the wars of independence, a number of important battles were fought in the Baracoa region. In 1877, Antonio

Maceo besieged the city for 15 days, and in 1895, 23 expeditionaries landed near Baracoa and engaged Spanish forces. A famous woman fighter Luz Palomares was a Baracoan and joined the Mambisa army there, machete in hand.

After independence and throughout the republican era, Baracoa remained a neglected pocket, and Baracoans today remember bitterly the years they were left to their own devices as Cuba's last outpost.

Specifically feeding their discontent was a road project, La Muleta, which was supposed to connect Baracoa with the Moa area along the north coast. This road was continually promised but never built. The economic situation remained precarious, and when disease destroyed the local banana industry shortly after World War II, Baracoans proclaimed a seven-day general strike to protest the Cuban government's failure to help. Still nothing happened.

In 1958, a large column of Baracoan youth joined the army of Raúl Castro, marking the entry of the region into the Revolution. When the Batista forces finally fled, they set fire to the city's archives, abandoning Baracoa once again to oblivion. This time, however, there was a renaissance.

Though there is still development needed here, the progress of the city is unmistakable. La Farola was an engineering triumph that connected Baracoa for the first time with the rest of Cuba. Where one secondary school existed before 1959, there are now four or five scattered throughout the city and countryside. Minibrigade housing projects sprout daily, and mountain polyclinics bring health care to areas where no doctor ever set foot. Until the Revolution, three doctors served the entire region, and a Red Cross station constructed in 1912 was the major health facility.

WHAT TO SEE

The Cathedral, Independence Plaza, was the first church to be established in Cuba. It was founded in 1512 at another location, but no ruins remain. The present pastel construction is about 150 years old and contains the Cross of Parra, an important relic.

Fortress of Matachine. Built in 1802, the walls and the towers now stand near the city's entrance. The fort was used by the Spanish during the independence wars as a reconnaisance center and as a registry point for persons entering and leaving the city. It is presently being converted to a historical museum of the region.

La Punta Fortress. Built in 1803, this semi-circular structure guards the port. It is presently being converted into a restaurant.

MUSEUMS

Historical Museum of Baracoa, Matachine fortress, at the city's south entrance, is scheduled to open late in 1979. It will house artifacts and exhibits describing the history of the region from Indian settlements to the present. Check hours locally with Cubatur.

HOTELS

Be sure to have Cubatur in your preceding city confirm your hotel accommodation in Baracoa before you arrive, since selection is limited. The unlit La Farola should not be driven after dark, so visitors to the city should plan on at least one overnight. The drive from Santiago is about 3½ hours, allowing no stops. A leisurely tour of Baracoa itself requires about one full day.

Motel Sanguily, Sanguily hill, overlooking the city. This brand new hotel commands a superb view of the city and harbor. It was converted from an ancient fortress which was also the last stronghold of the Batista forces. All modern conveniences have been installed in the antique shell, with traditional Cuban furniture and decoration throughout. A unique hotel experience. Be sure to ask for city-view rooms.

Private bath in all rooms; swimming pool under construction; bar and restaurant available. For rates and reservations, contact Cubatur, in Santiago de Cuba.

Hotel Plaza, Plaza Martí, overlooking the Cathedral, is a simple, clean rooming house. The central location is its prime advantage. Extremely basic accommodation; small rooms, all with private bath and w.c.; no hot water. Rates: 6 pesos per person.

RESTAURANTS

El Tropical, 1 mile from the city center, overlooking the harbor and a small beach, affords fine city views. An open-air dining terrace where excellent Cuban food is served. In the evenings, the dance floor and music make it Baracoa's social center. (M)

El Caracol (also known as Baturro) on Baracoa's seaside Malecón is a small but very pleasant rustic restaurant with picnic-style tables and a "private" dining terrace separated from the main restaurant by a Casbah-like bead curtain. (M)

La Punta, in the fortress of the same name on the harbor, is an unusual restaurant specializing in food of Indo-Cuban origin not easily found elsewhere. House specialties are *ajiaco*, a heavy stew made from root vegetables, and casaba bread. (M)

Watch for these other local food specialties when dining in Baracoa: *cucurrucho*, a dessert served in cone shape, made from coconut, cocoa, and tropical fruits, wrapped in palm leaves shaped into a pyramid; and *bacan*, a ground pork dish cooked with bananas, wrapped in banana leaves, and boiled.

BATABANÓ. Est. 1515; pop. 18,192; 55 km (33 mi) S of Havana; Havana prov.

The original site of Havana, and one of Cuba's first seven cities, Batabanó is now used by sponge divers and as a secondary port for the domestic fishing fleet. Hydrofoils and ferries depart several times a day for the Isle of Youth (Isle of Pines), but it's best to check the exact schedule and fares with Cubatur in Havana before starting out. Hydrofoil trip about 3 hours; ferry about 5.

BAYAMO. Est. 1513; pop. 122,599; 127 km (76 mi) NW of Santiago de Cuba, 841 km (504 mi) SE of Havana; capital of Granma prov.

Those driving between Santiago de Cuba and points west might wish to go through Bayamo, which in itself requires half a day to see properly.

HISTORY

Bayamo, a delightful city, figures importantly in the history of Cuba. It was the second city to be founded by Diego de Velázquez, the site of Céspedes's proclamation of independence from Spain, and the scene of one of the Revolution's first battles.

Bayamo is in the center of fine pastureland, and historians report that in the early days of the settlement, herds of cattle roamed wild and were hunted for sport by the Spaniards. The city had a thriving smuggling business and was more than once sacked by pirates looking for valuables.

The Indians here were constantly fighting the Spanish, with a major uprising reported in 1528. The Bayamo area was used for an "experiment" in which Indians who had not been assigned to Spaniards were offered the opportunity to live "freely" like Spanish farmers if they would renounce their gods, customs, dress, and culture—and pay the crown a fee for the privilege. The experiment died, however, when the officials reported to Spain that the Indians in the experimental village preferred to stay on in service to a Spanish master rather than cope with "freedom." The reliability of the report, naturally, has been questioned.

In 1533, at the gold mines of Jobabo near Bayamo, probably the first rebellion of black slaves in Cuba took place. Four Africans were decapitated, their heads brought to Spanish officials in Bayamo by the mine overseers as trophies of the squelching of the revolt.

The slave trade flourished thereafter as sugar became the principal product. The landowners in Bayamo were fiercely nationalistic, and as early as 1528, Bayamo had spoken out for more local control of politics. The city gradually developed

149

Masonic lodges that were themselves constantly fomenting rebellion. The strongest of these, the Estrella Tropical, was established in 1867. During this period, the national anthem of Cuba was composed by two Bayamo citizens, Cedeno and Figueredo, and was played in open defiance of Spain for the first time in the Bayamo Cathedral.

All the threads of revolt culminated in Carlos Manuel de Céspedes, Bayamo's leading citizen, and owner of La Demajagua, a sugar mill near the city. On October 10, 1868, he freed his slaves at the mill, armed them, and declared Cuba in revolt against Spain. The independence army grew quickly, and by November Céspedes commanded some 1,200 troops and had taken the cities of Holguín and Bayamo.

However, Spanish retribution was swift, and rather than surrender their city, the Cuban Bayamese burned it to the ground.

In 1953, anti-Batista guerrillas attacked the city barracks. The Bayamo attack failed, however, and half the force was captured and killed by Batista's army.

Today, Bayamo is a startling combination of history and progress. Carriages are still used, and horse-drawn pleasure vehicles can be seen coming out of side streets followed by gleaming, brand-new tractors.

WHAT TO SEE

Céspedes Park *(Parque Céspedes)*, one of the most elegant plazas in Cuba, is the city center and hub of the historic area.

Home of Carlos Manuel de Céspedes, Céspedes Park, is a museum devoted to his life and to the independence struggle. Open Tues.–Sat. 8 a.m.–noon and 2 p.m.–5 p.m., Sun. 9 a.m.–1 p.m. Closed Mon.

Church of San Salvador, a block from the Céspedes Museum, one of Cuba's oldest churches and has been declared a national monument for its magnificent stone and wood interior. The national anthem was sung here for the first time.

City Hall Building, Céspedes Park, was the site of Céspedes's proclamation of the abolition of slavery in Cuba.

The Archives Building, Céspedes Park, features lovely Spanish architecture, with delicate black *rejas* against blue window shutters.

HOTELS IN BAYAMO

Inasmuch as hotel facilities in the city are all tourist class, overnight stays are recommended only for those whose demands are minimal.

Hotel Royalton, on Céspedes Park, about three doors from the Céspedes Museum, has an old-fashioned, dark, wood-paneled lobby and a traditional atmosphere. All rooms with private bath but no hot water. Rates (approximate): twin, 7 pesos per person per night.

RESTAURANTS

There are snack bars and cafeterias around the park, but the moderately priced dining room of the Hotel Royalton is your best bet.

CABANAS. Est. 1812; 60 km (36 mi) W of Havana on the north road, Havana prov.

This coastal town is situated at the foot of the Sierra del Rosario and will be traversed by anyone returning to Havana via the scenic northern highway from Pinar del Río or Vinales. The town itself is dispersed on hills, and the *portales* columns, painted deep blue, have the art nouveau lacy white trim at the base that can be seen at Pinar del Río and almost nowhere else.

From Cabanas, a new road leads south into the sierra through an absolutely unspoiled land of small farms, *vacqueros* on horseback, and extensive cane fields. During the cane harvest, the area is alive with activity, and the cut fields resemble patches of wicker laid out on brushed brown earth.

The drive along this road from Cabanas to Cayahabos is

perhaps one of the most interesting and beautiful on the island. An extension road between Cayahabos and the Soroa resort is under construction. This 14-mile stretch is also magnificent, but negotiable at present by jeep only. The trip to Soroa from Havana via Cabanas and Cayahabos, though less direct than the southerly route, is one of the most memorable drives in Cuba.

CAMAGÜEY. Est. 1514; pop. 242,239; central Cuba, 571 km (342 mi) E of Havana, 398 km (238 mi) NW of Santiago de Cuba; capital of Camagüey prov.

Camagüey is situated in the center of what can best be described as tropical range—a Montana with palm trees. In every direction, the land is flat, interrupted only by the granitelike trunks of the royal palms or the figure of a *vacquero* doing roundup chores. There are also expansive cane fields in the region, which the eye can follow but never quite contain. The roads around Camagüey, as in many other areas of Cuba, are lined with piñon trees used as fence posts, some sawed-off but others left to bloom so that the tiny pink flower fans out in the air.

In such an area you might expect to find a rather frontierish town, but Camagüey is among Cuba's most sophisticated cities, combining an elegant, tranquil Spanish style with 20 years of remarkably rapid social progress.

The official sites of the city can be covered in one full day, but leisurely museum visitors and casual strollers will appreciate another day here. The nearby beaches (see "Beaches Outside Camagüey") and the modern hotel facilities make Camagüey a fine base of operations, although most group tours stay for only one night.

HISTORY

The city of Camagüey was founded on February 2, 1514, near what is presently Nuevitas on the north coast. The agricultural conditions in this region were not promising, so the city was moved nearer to a fresh water supply at the Caonao River. Here, there was already an Indian settlement, and a few years

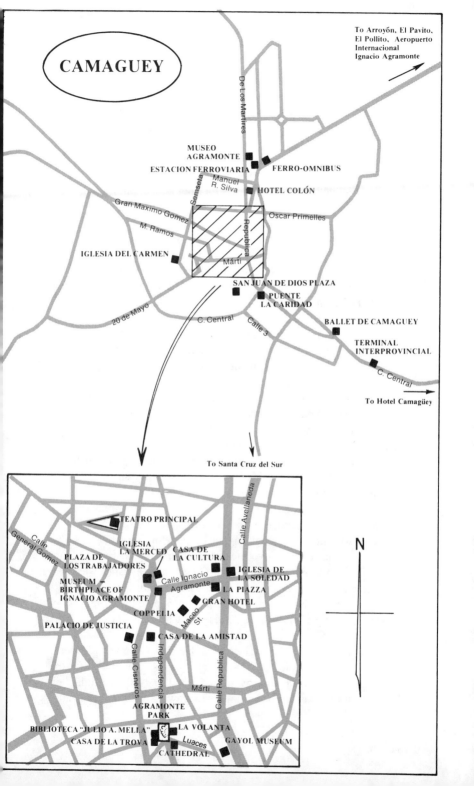

earlier a horrible, unprovoked massacre of some 2,000 Indians had taken place under the direction of Narváez, one of Velázquez's more infamous lieutenants. A new town was established in 1516, but in 1528, the Indians rebelled against the Spanish occupation and the city was moved inland to the present location. Camagüey was originally called Puerto del Principe, but in 1903 the Indian name was restored.

was originally called Puerto del Principe, but in 1903 the Indian name was restored.

There have been many claims that Nuevitas was the port Columbus visited last on his 1492 voyage—as a Cuban archaeologist once joked, "Every city on the north coast wants Columbus." Indeed, he did name one of his stops Puerto Principe, but it is generally agreed that this was what is now called Tanamo, in Cuba's eastern extreme. It is unlikely that Columbus sailed as far west as Nuevitas on his first trip.

After the move inland, Camagüey prospered from cattle raising, but the flat terrain also lent itself to sugar planting. By the mid-18th century, 27% of the population were black plantation slaves. The first slave uprising in the region took place in 1616, and Camagüey landowners strongly favored independence from Spain in hopes of preserving slavery. As Samuel Hazard said, writing about the city in 1871, "This town has always been looked upon with suspicion by the authorities on account of the strong proclivities its people had for insurrection, and its sons have had a greater or smaller share in almost every revolution that has taken place on the island."

One famous son of Camagüey was Ignacio Agramonte, a hero of the independence war. Equally famous was Ana Betancourt, who not only fought against Spain for Cuba but was also an early and fervent advocate for women's rights. Enrique José Varona, an early proponent of Cuban nationalism, was also Camagüeyan. Years later there were numerous outbreaks against the Batista regime here, and in September, 1958, rebel armies led by Camilo Cienfuegos and Che Guevara entered the region.

Progress in the Camagüey area has been remarkable since 1959. Mechanization of the cane harvest has reduced the number of cutters necessary from 70,000 to 14,000. Production of electricity has jumped from 43 megawatts to 269 megawatts.

An entirely new fishing industry based in Nuevitas now produces a revenue of $10 million annually. In the past 5 years, 8,537 housing units have been constructed, and there are 235,000 students, 3 times as many as in 1959.

WALKS

The city demands walking, for it is truly one of the most beautiful in Cuba, especially around 5 p.m. when it comes alive with the purposeful motion of people heading home from work or out for the evening.

The physical center is the triangular Plaza de los Trabajadores ("Workers' Plaza"), which is dominated by the Teatro Guerrero, in the corner, and La Merced church, built in the 1880's, diagonally opposite.

The main street feeding Trabajadores Plaza is Ignacio Agramonte, running east to west. Cisneros Street runs north to south, connecting the plaza with Agramonte Park, the city's other major focal point. In the center of the park is an equestrian statue of Agramonte, and the park is ringed with Spanish buildings almost all converted to official use.

Walks along Cisneros Street, and also Republica, which runs parallel to Cisneros three streets to the east, should not be missed. Between Martí and Luaces on Republica, devotees of the Cuban *rejas* will find a visual feast.

When walking through the city, be sure to watch for the *tinajones*, the folk emblem of Camagüey. These giant clay pots, often 6–7 feet high and 3–4 feet wide, were introduced to Cuba by the Spaniards in the 18th century. They were used to ship liquids and collect rainwater and are still used sometimes to collect rain or plant mariposas—or for children and young-at-heart adults to play in.

WHAT TO SEE

Biblioteca Julio A. Mella, Agramonte Park on Cisneros Street, is the city's public library, which occasionally sponsors art shows as well.

Casa de la Trova, next door to the library, is a 19th-century Spanish building with an unusually large patio. Note the antique bassoon on the wall in the garden where recitals and musical events take place.

Palacio de Justicia, Cisneros Street, is a stately building constructed in the mid-18th century as a religious school. Converted in 1800 into the Royal Court, it now functions as a civic court.

Teatro Principal, 3 blocks northwest of Workers' Plaza, a spectacular theatre with original (1850) exterior and lobby intact, complete with *vitrales*, crystal chandeliers reflected in long mirrors, and potted palms placed along a sweeping marble staircase.

CHURCHES

La Soledad, corner of Agramonte and Republica, is one of the most beautiful churches in Cuba, with entirely frescoed interior. It dates from 1775.

La Merced, Plaza de los Trabajadores, built in the 1880s, is also worthwhile for the interior.

Iglesia del Carmen, outside the city center, was built in 1825 and features outstanding 19th-century architecture.

The Cathedral, Agramonte Park, was established in 1530 but has been reconstructed since. It is dramatic and spacious.

MUSEUMS

Museo Ignacio Agramonte, Avenida de los Martires, #1. Once a garrison for Spanish troops, this building dating from 1848 has been ingeniously converted to a large museum with exhibits of Cuban painting, archaeology, natural science, and modern history. Open Tues.–Sat. 3 p.m.–11 p.m., Sun. 8 a.m.–noon; closed Mon.

Casa Natal de Ignacio Agramonte, Calle Agramonte, #459, opposite La Merced church, is the birthplace of the well-known hero. It has been converted into a museum recounting his life and the independence war. It is by far one of Cuba's most outstanding examples of Spanish architecture. Same hours as Museo Agramonte.

Casa Jesus Suarez Gayol, Republica #69, was the home of a Revolutionary hero who was killed in Bolivia with Che Guevara. The house recounts the role played in the Revolution by various Camagüeyans, especially students. Open Tues.–Sat. noon–10 p.m., Sun. 8 a.m.–noon; closed Mon.

CULTURAL EVENTS

For all information about schedules and tickets, contact the Casa de Cultura at the corner of Republica and Agramonte, or check with the Cubatur representative at your hotel. The city offers a variety of cultural events.

The Ballet of Camagüey is a new company founded shortly after the Revolution. Its repertoire includes the classics as well as contemporary Cuban choreography. The group performs throughout the year, though it is frequently out of the city on national tour.

The Orchestra of Camagüey is a full symphony which performs throughout the year, both in Camagüey and on national tour.

El Grupo de Caidije, based in nearby Nuevitas (see "Excursions from Camagüey"), is one of the most unsual folkloric groups in Cuba. Their dances show a strong Haitian influence. Their annual fiesta performance in April involves elaborate headpieces with lit candles perched on them and features amazing machete dances brought to Cuba by the black Haitian cane cutters.

Casa de la Trova, Agramonte Park, is a beautiful restored mansion open to the public, with nightly *trova* activities.

Casa de la Amistad, Cisneros Street, just off the corner of Máximo Gómez, is an international exchange center that sponsors weekly film showings (Friday evenings usually) and other cultural events. A library and music listening rooms are available.

HOTELS

Hotel Camagüey, Central Highway, 2 miles east of the city (tel. 6218 or 6805), is one of the finest on the island, a modern, airy, bright hotel built in the mid-1970s. After a day of city sightseeing, it is extremely pleasant to return to the large swimming pool and bask in the cool garden surroundings. 160 rooms, all with hot water, air conditioning, balcony, and private bath. Fine restaurant. Rates: twin, 16 pesos; single, 14.

Gran Hotel, Maceo Street #67, near Plaza de los Trabajadores (tel. 2093 or –94), is a gracious classic for those who prefer traditional style and city-center location, though amenities are limited. 72 rooms, each with private bath; no hot water, no pool. The rooftop restaurant is a major plus. Rates: triple, 18 pesos; twin, 14; single, 11.

Colon Hotel, Calle Republica, about 8 blocks from the city center, is another traditional hotel like the Gran, with similar limitations and appeals. Renovation is scheduled for 1979.

RESTAURANTS IN CAMAGÜEY

As everywhere in Cuba, eating at your own hotel is simplest. However, the Gran Hotel rooftop restaurant affords excellent city views, serving fine food at moderate prices. The Camagüey Hotel dining room is also recommended. Others are:

La Volanta, Agramonte Park, on Independence Street. A beautifully restored colonial house with magnificent carved ceiling and Spanish-style furniture and decor throughout. One of Camagüey's most unique and best spots. (FC)

Monte Carlo, near the Hotel Camagüey. An elegant restaurant affording spectacular city views. Located in an apartment complex and usually reserved for protocol or diplomatic delegations. However, Cubatur can assist with securing reservations for foreign tourists. (D)

El Pavito, approximately 4 miles north of the city heading toward Nuevitas. A simple restaurant where turkey is the house specialty. (M)

El Pollito, approximately 3 miles north of the city heading toward Nuevitas. Here, chicken dishes are the thing to order. (M)

Arroyon, just opposite El Pollito. Serves general Cuban menu in pleasant but simple surroundings. (M)

EXCURSIONS

Nuevitas, 46 miles northeast of Camagüey. A veritable boom town, Nuevitas was thrust into industrialization after the Revolution. There are large cement plants, fertilizer factories, and one of Cuba's largest thermoelectric generating stations. There's no reason to overnight here, but just in case, try *Hotel Kaonawa* near the port, offering basic accommodation and simple, pleasant meals. Rates: 7 pesos per person.

There is a history museum now in the planning stages. When operative in 1979–80, it will house a collection describing the development of the region. Check locally with Cubatur regarding hours and location.

Violin Factory at Minas, Minas, 23 miles northeast of Camagüey. The road to Nuevitas from Camagüey runs through perfectly flat territory strung with typical rural towns, the most distinguished of which is Minas, home of the only violin factory in Cuba. Operated by the Ministry of Culture, it constitutes a matchless experience of the new Cuba. The factory may be visited by groups only, with advance permission. Contact Cubatur for details.

The factory was inaugurated on December 23, 1976, the brainchild of Alvaro Suarez Ravinal, who describes its history with a father's pride in his eyes. A guitar maker for 50 years, Ravinal was inspired shortly after the Revolution to develop a new industry for Cuba. He says he literally woke up one morning and decided to try his hand at violin manufacture, since the proliferation of music groups had begun to create a demand for instruments—most of which had to be imported, depleting Cuba's currency reserves. Cuba had always produced guitars, but never violins.

Ravinal tested several models before settling on a beautiful and workable prototype of the first violin ever produced in Cuba. The grain of natural Cuban woods—mahogany, cedar, pine, and many others—was shown to great advantage in his work, and Ravinal was invited to stage a major exhibit in Santiago de Cuba. At that time, he presented two violins to Juan Almeida, a member of the Communist party, who was extremely impressed and asked Ravinal about his plans. Ravinal expressed his hopes that a small violin factory could be built so he could pass the skill on to younger workers. Almeida liked the idea, and a factory—even larger than the one Ravinal envisioned—was built.

Today, 29 young men and women carefully, lovingly work over the wood cut from Cuban trees. None of them have ever worked on violins before. Ravinal teaches the workers everything—how to choose the wood, how to use the tools (most of the delicate process is manual). The shop is alive with the sound of tapping and tooling, and pervaded by the aroma of new wood.

Ravinal is now busy on viola and cello prototypes. Several musical groups use Minas violins, and the Orchestra of Santiago de Cuba owns ten; Ravinal hopes Cuba can eventually export violins. When asked what he does about strings for the instruments, Ravinal replies confidently, "Well, those we still import, but if this keeps going well—in our first 6 months we have produced 80 violins—maybe we'll start a factory to produce our own strings too."

BEACHES OUTSIDE CAMAGÜEY

Travelers may appreciate a break from landlocked Camagüey, and since only the Hotel Camagüey has a pool, the north-coast beaches are the nearest access to swimming and sun. They are among the best in Cuba.

Playa Santa Lucia, 60 miles north of Camagüey by car. This superb white expanse offers excellent swimming and is a favorite with Cuban families. There are hotels and restaurants nearby.

Hotel Tararaco is a beautiful, brand-new hotel, opened in 1978, employing the long, low, white construction with stucco tile roof common all over the island. Swimming pool, restaurant, and full modern amenities. All rooms with private bath, telephone, and radio. Rates: on request from Cubatur in Camagüey; twin, about 20 pesos; single, about 15.

Santa Lucia Cottages are a favorite with Cuban nationals. These wooden cottages have full amenities, including running water, electricity, and television. Some have kitchenettes, which make them desirable for families. Rates and reservations are available from Cubatur in Camagüey.

Bahamas Restaurant, just off Santa Lucia Beach, has an outdoor terrace facing the sea. This excellent restaurant offers typically Cuban food at moderate prices. Black bean soup and beefsteak are the house specialties, and well worth sampling.

Cayo Sabinal, a 10-minute drive from Nuevitas, 1½ hours from Camagüey. This 10-mile expanse of sugary white sand rivals the legendary Varadero Beach in quality. Here, at the rim of virgin marshland, flamingos gather in streams, and reflections in the still, mirrorlike inland pools are broken only by the graceful movements of egrets and cranes.

A tourist village is under construction at Sabinal. According to its developers—a Canadian-Cuban combination—it is expected to be the "finest resort in the Caribbean." Plans call for low-rise cottages to be phased in gradually, to minimize disruption of the ecology, which will be, after all, one of the resort's prime attractions.

Eventually the village will offer golf, indoor and outdoor tennis, horseback riding, nature tours, boating, and other sports. The resort should have its first units in operation by winter 1980.

CAMARIOCA. 25 km (15 mi) W of Cardenas, 25 km E of Matanzas, 20 km (12 mi) SW of Varadero; Matanzas prov.

This small fishing port has notable wooden frame houses. *Boca de Camarioca*, a seafood restaurant on the central highway, provides a welcome dining stop for the road-weary. (M)

CARDENAS. Est. 1828; pop. 69,171; 18 km (10 mi) SE of Varadero, 52 km (31 mi) E of Matanzas; Matanzas prov.

This lively city is well worth a half-day visit, especially for those based at nearby Varadero Beach. Buses run hourly from Varadero to Cardenas, and taxi fare is about 3 pesos.

HISTORY

The city was founded on March 8, 1828 in a swampy area surrounded by large sugar estates. Some of the original fortifications may be seen along the harbor today, and they are scheduled for restoration.

Cardenas developed rapidly as a commercial center, mainly because of the thriving sugar business and well-situated port. However, it is best known as "the Flag City," since the Cuban flag was first flown here, in 1850, by the annexationist Narciso López, who attempted to invade Cuba via Cardenas.

A curious blend of past and present, the city has a small museum and is filled with horse-drawn carriages, bicycle riders, and unusual architecture. The carriages have been in Cardenas as long as anyone can remember, and so have the bicycles. No other Cuban city has as many of either.

WHAT TO SEE

Colon Park. The park is the focal point of the city, as everywhere in Cuba, and carriages may be rented here. Colon Park had been named for various Spanish monarchs, but in 1858 the mayor decided to erect a statue to Columbus and commissioned a Spanish sculptor named Piquier. Cardenians claim this was the first statue erected to him in Latin America. It was built with some government funds but mainly with "donations" from the people of the city.

La Dominica, Colon Park. When Cardenas was founded, it was a swampy area with canals running through the city to the sea. One canal originated from what is now La Dominica, and this point became a loading area for the sugar estates. Eventually overnight accommodations were provided, and a hotel opened. La Dominica was the site of the first flag raising. The building was extended and reconstructed in 1919 and is now a national monument, though still used as a hotel.

The Cathedral, Colon Park. The stained glass windows are considered the main feature of this church, which was built in 1846 at an estimated cost of 90,000 pesos.

The Market-Plaza Molokoff. In the early years after foundation, there was no public market in Cardenas. A leading citizen, Parodi, proposed one and was given permission to build it, provided the facility would pass into public ownership within 25 years. The structure takes up most of a block and is built in a cross shape with full flowing dome and colonnade. It is one of the few, if not the only, iron constructions in Cuba. The dome is about 50 feet high and was constructed in the United States. When the Cardenians saw it, they named it Molokoff, probably after a dome-like crinoline skirt fashionable at the time.

MUSEUMS

Casa Natal de José Antonio Echevarría, 240 Genes Street. Built in 1873, the house is a fine example of neoclassical architecture. The two floors of the museum are joined by a carved wooden spiral staircase of very rare style.

Echevarría, an anti-Batista student leader, was born here in 1932. He was killed in 1957, and the second floor of the museum surveys his life and those of other Cardenians who died in service of the Revolution. The first floor surveys the role played by Cardenas in the overall history of Cuba. Open Tues.–Sat. noon–8:30 p.m., Sun. 8 a.m.–noon; closed Mon.

CULTURAL EVENTS

Cardenas's annual culture week, March 1–8, features various concerts and public events timed to coincide with celebrations of the founding of the city. Contact the Echevarría Museum staff or local Ministry of Culture office for details.

CASILDA. Est. 1808; 7 km (4 mi) SE of Trinidad; Sancti Spíritus prov.

This small fishing town on the south coast serves as the port for Trinidad and Sancti Spíritus. The coast and beaches in the vicinity have some of the finest coral formations and diving walls in Cuba. (See "Beaches near Trinidad.")

CAYO CARENA. See "Cienfuegos."

CAYO GRANMA. See "Santiago de Cuba."

CAYO LARGO. 80 km (48 mi) due S of the Zapata peninsula, 186 km (111 mi) SE of Havana, 119 km (71 mi) due E of the Isle of Pines; in the Caribbean Sea.

This narrow island, about 25 kilometers (15 miles) long and three kilometers (1.8 miles) wide, has an expansive white beach, graduated sea bottom, and clear, crystalline sea.

The cay is being developed as a tourist center, and eventually divers will be able to travel by boat between the Isle of Pines and Cayo Largo, stopping en route to dive and using the boat as a hotel. There are extensive coral reefs around the island, and off the north coast a number of shipwrecks have been discovered and are being investigated to determine their accessibility to tourists. The main diving center will be at Ballenatos Beach; a hotel is under construction and should be operating by 1979–80.

CAYO NARANJO. See "Excursions from Guardalavaca."

CAYO SABINAL. See "Beaches Outside Camagüey."

CIEGO DE ÁVILA. Est. 1849; pop. 72,930; 108 km (66 mi) W of Camagüey, 460 km (276 mi) E of Havana; capital of Ciego de Ávila prov.

Almost every tour bus passes through this lively town. Situated in the central Cuban plains, it is a hub of dairy, cattle, and citrus production. It was founded in the mid-19th century, although the first land grants in the area were made in the mid-16th century. Tradition claims that the king of Spain chartered the land to a Spaniard named Ávila, who operated a large hacienda. The area then was heavily forested, except for a clear central area, or *ciego*. Often travelers used Ávila's hacienda as an overnight stop en route to Puerto Principe or Trinidad. In the 17th century, as a city gradually developed, there was an attempt to name it San Jeronimo de la Palma. By then, however, the conversational "Ciego de Ávila" had become almost an official name and was retained.

There is little here of obvious tourist interest, and an overnight stay is hardly necessary. Still, those with a car, some free time, and a special interest in the lifestyle of Cuban cities will find a stop worthwhile. If you visit, you will want to see *Martí Park*, surrounded by buildings erected mainly in the early 20th century, when the city came into commercial prominence. The most stately of these is the city hall, which was built in 1911 and now houses Poder Popular.

Also worth noting is the *Teatro Principal*, two blocks from the park, built in 1927. The enormous doors are made of hand-carved wood, and the theater itself is decorated with elaborate allegorical statuary, an oval grand marble staircase, and bronze chandeliers. The theater has a 500-seat capacity and is being restored.

The Hotel Santiago Havana, corner of Castillo and Central Highway (tel. 3324 or 3346) is a very basic hotel not recommended to demanding vacationers. However, the dining room serves fine food and is a convenient lunch stop for those driving between Camagüey and Santa Clara. Built in 1957. 75 rooms, basic amenities, no hot water. Restaurant, bar. Rates: twin, 17 pesos; single, 13. *The Hotel Ciego de Ávila*, 4 miles north of the city, is a new hotel under construction. Check with Cubatur, Havana, before planning to use this one.

CIENFUEGOS. Est. 1819; pop. 95,000; 69 km (41 mi) SW of Santa Clara, 337 km (202 mi) SE of Havana; capital of Cienfuegos prov.

HISTORY

Cienfuegos has always been a trade city, mainly because of its wide, deep harbor, in which "all the navies of the world could rendez-vous and not crowd each other," according to a 19th-century traveler. Indeed, the bay has made the city a vital commercial capital, but the residential districts remain insulated from the bustle and go about life in a rather tranquil fashion.

The harbor is dominated by Jagua Castle, begun in 1738 and finished in 1745. At the time, there was no town to speak of, but the Spanish built the fort to protect the coastal villages and inland areas from pirates. The first sugar mill was constructed in 1751, the original town plan dates from 1796. By 1804, harbor construction was under way.

In 1817, a French emigré from Louisiana, Don Juan Luis Lorenzo d'Clouet, presented a settlement plan to the governor, Don José Cienfuegos. D'Clouet's plan called for recruiting colonists—whites specifically—whose passage and initial basic expenses would be paid by the government. Each white over 18 years old and able to work would receive a *caballería* (33 acres) of land. The Spanish Cortes approved the plan, and by April, 1819, the first 137 caballerías had been turned over to the d'Clouet settlers, most of whom came from France. The original village was destroyed by a storm in 1825 and rebuilt in 1831; by 1874, the city had its church, Plaza and aqueduct established.

Cienfuegos prospered, developing a thriving trade based on sugar, tobacco, and fruits. The downtown part of the city reflects this prosperity—the buildings are rather ornate, grand structures. The entire city shows the French neoclassical influence in design—straight, wide boulevards linked one to the other.

WHAT TO SEE

Cienfuegos lacks official "sites," but it is rich for those who love idle strolling and city exploration. In addition, it has two of the best hotels in Cuba, which makes it a very comfortable base of operations. With three nights here and the necessary transportation, one can easily take day trips to nearby Trinidad, Santa Clara, Soledad, and Hanabanilla (see "Excursions from Cienfuegos"). One full day is necessary to see the city itself.

The streets run at exact right angles to each other, with odd-numbered streets crossing even ones. Calle 37, also called Prado, is a tree-lined, double-width boulevard that connects central Cienfuegos with the Punta Gorda suburb. Calle 56 is the principal shopping thoroughfare. For those with cars, a system of preferential and nonpreferential roads determines whether the driver must stop at a given corner, and the visitor will soon notice that there are virtually no traffic lights in Cienfuegos.

Parque Martí and surrounding buildings, corner of 54th and 29th streets, form a gracious square that should not be missed. Dominating the park is the arch and statue commemorating the establishment of the Cuban Republic, built by volunteer labor in 1902. In the square's center is a gazebo bandstand where the city orchestra and other groups often perform.

The handsome stone cathedral dates from 1870 and occupies almost a full block adjacent to the Primer Palacio, now the seat of Poder Popular. The palace, almost as much as the Havana Capitol Building, exemplifies the extent to which Cuban architecture was influenced by North America.

One of the most pleasant buildings on the park is the Jesus Menendez Social Club, formerly the exclusive Lyceo, now open for public recreation. Early in the evening, workers drift into the domino room, and the sound of ebony cube against ebony cube clicks out into the square.

By far the most spectacular building is the Terry Theater, which was inaugurated in 1895 with a performance of *Aida*. The theater underwent restoration in 1965 and has since become the main hall of the province for social, cultural and political events. It seats 920 persons, and the entire interior consists of dark Cuban woods. The frescoed ceiling is a sky of romantic images of women in clouds, trumpets, and gold. The three-tier balconies are of pine, painted with delicate floral patterns. Allegorical figures cling to the arch over the stage. As in most theaters built in Cuba during the 1800s, the theater floor can be mechanically raised to stage level, as was often done during grand balls. The Terry can be visited most easily when an event or performance is scheduled (see "Cultural Events").

Punta Gorda, foot of Calle 37, was once the exclusive residential section, and it remains an area of large homes and manicured lawns. However, most of the buildings have been converted to public use—like the gleaming white bayside yacht club, which has become a recreation camp and sport training school. Some buildings, however, remain in private hands, and with cars parked in the driveway, they evoke Suburbia, USA, except the vehicles are often mint-condition models circa 1949.

Industrial Cienfuegos is an area that the average traveler will probably not have the opportunity or inclination to visit. For those who do, or for special interest tours, permission must be obtained in advance.

The industrial growth of Cienfuegos has been spectacular. The city, in addition to its modern harbor, which is presently being expanded, supports oil refineries, fertilizer plants, electricity generators (the first nuclear facility will also be built here), and wheat mills. Some visitors tour the Tricontinental Bulk Sugar Shipping Terminal, which is a fascinating excursion (see Section II, "The Economy of Cuba—Sugar") but must be booked well in advance by your Cuban sponsor.

MUSEUMS

Museum of Decorative Arts, Valle Palace, Punta Gorda, is located in the spectacular Moorish-style creamy pink colored building diagonally opposite the Jagua Hotel. It contains furnishings, porcelains, and other decorative pieces. Check hours locally.

Jagua Castle, opposite Pasacaballos Hotel at the harbor entrance is accessible by ferry from the hotel, along with the adjacent Jagua fishing village. Open Tues.–Sun. 9 a.m.–5 p.m.; closed Mon.

CULTURAL EVENTS

Casa de Cultura and Music Conservatory, Calle 37, #5615, at 56th Street (shares the building with the Valdez library), publishes a monthly calendar of events and coordinates local culture groups, including the drama club, city chorus, and other music groups.

Casa de la Nueva Trova, Calle 35 at 16th Street, Punta Gorda (tel. 7120), is a modern private home converted to public use, where music students come to study the old *trovas* as well as sing and perform the modern versions. There are evening performances at least once a week.

Roberto Garcia Valdez Public Library, Calle 37, #5615, at 56th Street, has a general circulation library and an art department that often sponsors exhibitions of local artists.

HOTELS

Hotel Pasacaballos, at the mouth of Cienfuegos Bay, 23 km (13 mi) from the town center (tel. Dial 00 and ask the operator for the hotel). Built in 1976, this hotel is considered the most beautiful built since the Revolution. Indeed, the harbor location is lovely, in full view of Jagua Castle and the fishing village opposite. A modern atrium-style retreat from city bustle. Request harbor-view room. 188 rooms, all with air conditioning, private bath, hot water, radio, and balcony. Olympic size swimming pool; excellent dining room; cafeteria, shops. Rates: triple, 26 pesos; twin, 21; single, 13.

A local bus leaves from in front of the lobby regularly; fare to the city is 20¢. Taxi fare is about 6 pesos. By far the most pleasant way is by ferry from the hotel pier, 20¢ to downtown, but leaving at irregular intervals. Speedboats can be rented for transportation to town or for visits to the castle and village opposite the hotel. The cost is approximately 3 pesos per person per hour.

Hotel Jagua, in the Punta Gorda suburb, at the end of Calle 37 (tel. 8195 or 8545). Jagua was operated before the Revolution as a deluxe gambling resort. The gambling is gone, but the two-tier dining room is still the scene of social events like weddings and birthdays. The hotel has a modern atmosphere but is set off on the quiet Punta Gorda peninsula, among palms. Ask for a harbor view on a high floor where you can also see the superb sunsets over beautiful Valle palace, now the Decorative Arts Museum. 142 rooms, all with private bath, hot water, phone, and radio. Shops, 2 bars, cabaret, pool, and excellent restaurant. Rates (approximate): triple, 25 pesos; twin, 20; single, 12.

RESTAURANTS

In addition to the hotel dining rooms, the following are Cienfuegos's major offerings:

La Verja, Calle 56 between 33rd and 35th streets. A beautiful colonial-style restaurant, a former residence built in 1831 and converted into a garden bar and restaurant. Open for breakfast 8 a.m.–10 a.m.; lunch noon–2 p.m.; *merienda* 3:30 p.m.–5:45 p.m.; dinner 7 p.m.–10 p.m. The city's best, serving excellent Cuban food. (FC)

Pio Lindo, 37th and 56th streets, a simple establishment with basic Cuban menu. (M)

Mandarin, 37th and 56th streets, Chinese-style Food. (M)

El Pollito, 37th Street between 56th and 58th, simple but pleasant, specializing in chicken. (M)

Laguna de Cuba, Punta Gorda, a recreation center with adjacent restaurant. (M)

Cochinito, Punta Gorda, 37th Street, specializing in pork. (M)

Govadonga, directly opposite Jagua Hotel. Traditional Spanish food is the fare, with paella the highlight. Very popular with city residents. (M)

Cabaret Mambisa, Punta Gorda, on a barge in Cienfuegos harbor en route to Punta Gorda along 37th Street. Drinks only. An unusual and pleasant seaside atmosphere. (M)

EXCURSIONS

Soledad Botanical Gardens, about 30 minutes from town. Cuba's most extensive botanic collection, not to be missed by plant lovers. (See "Soledad" in the alphabetic listing.)

Trinidad, Sancti Spíritus, and Santa Clara are all interesting, lovely cities within a day's trip from Cienfuegos, for those based here.

BEACHES OUTSIDE CIENFUEGOS

The Pasacaballos and the Jagua hotels both have large swimming pools, for guest use only. For public sea swimming, try:

Rancho Luna Beach, 20 km (12 mi) E of Cienfuegos. This soft white sand expanse has a new hotel under construction scheduled for early 1979 opening. Families might prefer the beach location, but the setting cannot compare to Pasacaballos.

The *Rancho Luna Hotel,* set back from the beach, is a modern low-rise white stone building with stucco roof and will have 285 rooms, all with private bath, radio, balcony. Rates: on request from Cubatur.

COJIMAR. Est. 1646; 8 km (4.8 mi) E of Havana; Havana prov.

This small fishing village on the Cojimar river was immortalized by Hemingway in *The Old Man and the Sea.* Hemingway himself fished out of Cojimar and is remembered by a number of townspeople. Cojimar is adjacent to the Havana del Este housing project and offers an interesting combination of rural, city, and sea life. Definitely worthwhile is a lunch or dinner at Hemingway's old haunt, La Terraza.

Restaurant La Terraza on Main Street, Cojimar (tel. 90-8471), is built out over the river and is one of Cuba's most celebrated seafood restaurants, simple in decor but exceptionally pleasant in atmosphere. It was originally a fishing club but was opened in 1972 as a full-service restaurant. Bar service or meals are available. Shellfish and lobster are excellent house specialties. Hours: lunch, noon–2 p.m.; dinner after 6 p.m. (reservations essential on Saturday evening). About 3 pesos taxi fare from Vedado; #58 bus from Monte Street, near the Capitol Building in old Havana.

EL CORNITO RESORT. 13 km (8 mi) W of Victoria de las Tunas, on the central highway, Las Tunas prov. El Cornito is a rustic cabana resort, with restaurant serving Cuban food, surrounded by palm and banyan trees, near the Hormigo river. Water sports—boating and fishing—are available. 48 cabanas, some air-conditioned, all with running water and bath. Rates (approximate): 14 pesos for twin cabana.

Nearby are the ruins of the home of the famous Cuban poet J. V. Napoles Fajardo ("El Cuculambe"), who wrote during the mid-19th century. An outdoor refreshment terrace has been set up amid the walls and gardens. The enormous sign on the highway directing the visitor to the home is larger than the home itself, but a museum is planned eventually for the site.

EL TROPICO. See "Beaches East of Havana."

GIBARA. Est. 1817; pop. 57,244; 31 km (18 mi) N of Holguín, 52 km (31 mi) W of Guardalavaca; Holguín prov.

Gibara is a bay city, a fishing town that has always attracted
local people during the summers for its seaside promenade and
atmosphere. There is speculation that the name of the town derives from *jiba*, the Indian word for the short shrub that grows
on the shores of lakes and streams in the area.

The town is at its liveliest on Saturday afternoons, particularly around the central square, where Gibarans walk arm in
arm or have a long smoke in a rocker at the Workers' Social
Club. A visit here is an excellent sidetrip for those based at
nearby Guardalavaca. One would not ordinarily expect to find a
museum in a town the size of Gibara, but in fact there are two.

The Gibara Museum of Colonial Art, Independencia #27
(tel. 48), was once the luxurious home of a tobacco-dealing
family and has served various functions during the last century.
In 1972 the museum was inaugurated. Highlights are the enormous *vitrales*, the Austrian furniture made of bent wood
steamed into shape, and a late 19th-century Catalan ceramic.
The furniture collection is modest compared to those of other
museums, but there are craft circles for youngsters, and the
museum's director, Antonio Nicolau, believes that the children's activities are ultimately the museum's most important
function. Open Tues.–Fri. 2 p.m.–6 p.m. and 7 p.m.–10 p.m.,
Sat. 8 a.m.–noon and 2 p.m.–6 p.m., Sun. 8 a.m.–noon;
closed Mon. Phone ahead to verify schedule or to arrange a
special visit, if possible.

The Gibara Museum of Natural History provides precisely
the sort of experience that restores one's faith in life's ability to
surprise.

Joaquin Fernandez de la Vara, a slender, twinkling Gibara
elder statesman who speaks excellent English, is founder-
director of the museum. Although modest in size and scope,
the collection is presented with a skill that rivals the efforts of
larger museums. For 40 years de la Vara went about the business of collecting specimens and in 1966 turned his collection
into a museum with government support. Asked when the idea

for such a museum occurred to him, de la Vara remarks very definitely, "I was born with this idea."

The museum contains a fine shell collection, as well as numerous cases of mounted ducks and other migratory birds. In addition there are a number of Cuban mammal species, and marine life including a formidable 7½-pound crab, a 322-pound sea turtle with exquisite shell markings, and the razorlike jawbone of a Sierra fish. De la Vara devotes much energy these days to informing visitors about endangered species, lecturing, and showing films and slides to the townspeople. The museum, and de la Vara himself, make Gibara a delightful discovery. Open Tues.–Fri. 8 a.m.–noon and 2 p.m.–6 p.m., weekends by appointment only. Call the Gibara Ministry of Culture office (tel. 4) for an appointment.

GRAN PIEDRA NATIONAL PARK. See "Excursions from Santiago de Cuba."

GUAIMARO. 79 km W of Camagüey on the central highway; Camagüey prov.

This historic city was the site in April, 1869, of the Guaimaro Assembly, where the first Cuban constitution was drafted, the national flag adopted, and Carlos Manuel de Céspedes elected president of the Free Republic of Cuba.

Hotel Guaimaro, on the central highway just outside town (tel. 8140 or 8040), is of interest only as a convenient roadside stop-off point. It is a modern, comfortable hotel, though, built in 1977. 40 rooms, each with bath and w.c., no hot water. Pool under construction. Some rooms with TV and refrigerator. Restaurant, bar. Rates (approximate): twin, 14 pesos; single, 13.

GUAMA. 186 km (111 mi) SE of Havana, in the middle of Treasure Lake; Matanzas prov.

This Indian village resort was named for a rebel Indian chief whom the Spanish tried constantly to subdue (he was eventually murdered in his sleep by his own brother). Guama was the Revolution's first tourism project. It consists of artificial islands—seven in all—resting on piles in the lake that are joined by bridges and built up with wooden, thatched-roof cottages. The architecture replicates the Indian style found in the area before Columbus. (The remains of the original Indian settlement, also built on stilts and artificial islands, could still be seen at the turn of the century.) Treasure Lake itself is in the middle of Zapata National Park, and legend claims that the Indians sank their valuables to its bottom in order to save them from the Spanish—hence the lake's name. There has been no archaeological proof of this theory to date.

Guama is an enchanting place, absolutely insulated from the sounds and pressures of the modern world. Before the Revolution, the residents of the area made a meager living on charcoal production, but the resort has given them entirely new economic possibilities.

One arrives at the lakeshore and then embarks in a motor launch through the canals for five miles to the hotel. On the mainland side, there is a ceramic workshop where artisans produce the well-known Guama earthenware used at the hotel, and a crocodile breeding farm, aimed at preserving the species. *Mosquito repellent is a must for a visit to Guama.*

The accommodations at Guama consists of 44 rustic cabins, in Indian style, beautifully dispersed on small islands, each with hot and cold water and bath. Rates (approximate): twin, 14 pesos; no singles. The Boca de la Laguna restaurant serves superb Cuban-style food. There is also a cafeteria. The unique bar is a favorite with honeymooners and lovers of peace and quiet.

Guama has drawn foreigners mainly for its spectacular sport fishing. There have already been a number of professional tournaments here, mainly for bass. Special fishing tours can be arranged (see "Tours to Cuba"). Paddle boats and speedboats to travel around the lake may be rented at the reception desk.

Guama also has 25 outdoor bronze sculptures by Cuban artist Rita Longa that depict scenes of Indian life, as well as an indoor museum housing artifacts and implements found in the area.

All bookings for Guama must be made through Cubatur. Excursions to Guama usually include nearby Playa Giron, a lovely sandy beach where the abortive Bay of Pigs invasion took place.

GUANABACOA. Est. 1743; about 6 km (3 mi) SE of Havana; Havana prov.

One of the most worthwhile side excursions possible from Havana, Guanabacoa is a lively, active town with a rather unique history, well-preserved architecture, and appealing *ambiente*. Taxi fare from Havana is about 3 pesos; to go by bus, take #195 from Vedado, #5 from Plaza de la Revolución, #13 or #95 from Central Park.

HISTORY

The city was formally established in 1743, but the entire history of Cuba can be traced in its development. Around 1555, the Spanish governor Angulo ordered the natives who were roaming the territory to establish themselves in settlements nearby Spanish cities. Guanabacoa, therefore, became a kind of reservation, and in 1574 some 300 Indians were reported living there. At the same time, during pirate raids, the settlers of Havana would retreat to the hills around the town, which led to a mixing of the groups and the eventual disappearance of the Indian community. The town prospered from the fertility of its land and gained a reputation as a resort area because of its sea breeze and medicinal baths.

When the English army attacked Havana in 1762, the mayor of Guanabacoa, "Pepe" Antonio, organized a resistance force, although the British eventually took the city. During this period slavery was developing, and there was a tremendous concentration of slaves around Guanabacoa because of the especially fertile land and the proximity of Havana. Some of the very earliest sugar mills were located in the area. Consequently, Guanabacoa became a center of African culture, as the slaves continued to practice their arts, religion, and dances. (A folkloric museum on the subject—the only one of its kind in Cuba—is located in Guanabacoa.)

During the war against Spain, there were numerous skirmishes in the Guanabacoa area, but the city really came to prominence when José Martíı began speaking at the Lyceum Literary Society. This group had become the intellectual vanguard, and Martí spoke there frequently on themes which were regarded by the Spanish as seditious.

WHAT TO SEE

Museo Historico de Guanabacoa, Martí #108, between San Antonio and Versalles streets (tel. 909117), houses a unique collection of artifacts related to folkloric African customs—dance, music, costumes—including implements used in the Santeria and Abakua religious rites practiced by various Cuban slave cults. The museum is scheduled to reopen after restoration in summer, 1978. Open Tues.–Sat. 3 p.m.–10 p.m., Sun. 9 a.m.–1 p.m.; closed Mon.

Iglesia Parroquial Mayor, Calle Pepe Antonio, was inaugurated in 1721. It has a superb wooden altar inlaid with gold and a statue of the Virgin de la Asuncion.

Casa de Cultura, Máximo Gómez, at the corner of Nazarenes Street (tel. 909-244), is the former Lyceum building, which today serves as a focal point for art, literary, dance, and theater groups. The building itself is a classic with a wide marble staircase.

Conjunto Folklorico Guanabacoa is a group which performs in and around Guanabacoa with emphasis on Afro-Cuban cultural customs. Schedule available from the Casa de Cultura.

GUANABO. Est. 1800; 30 km (18 mi) E of Havana; Havana prov.

In this fishing and resort town, one of the earliest anti-Spanish insurrections took place in 1812. There are numerous hotels and restaurants, as well as some very well preserved turn-of-the-century houses on Fifth Avenue, the main street. (See also "Beaches Outside Havana.")

GUANAHACABIBES PENINSULA. 106 km (66 mi) SW of Pinar del Río, 90 km (56 mi) long and a maximum 30 km (18 mi) wide; Pinar del Río prov.

This rocky, barren, swampy strip of land was named by the Spanish for the Indian tribe that once occupied it. Today, there are few settlements on the peninsula, which has been converted into a national park. The area is known for wild pigs, deer, and *jutias*, as well as for extraordinary bird and plant life. Hunting is forbidden completely.

The Roncali lighthouse marks the southeast tip of Cuba, and there are coastal military installations here. Therefore the motorist (the road is not entirely paved) must check with Pinar del Río tourism authorities before entering the area and know in advance that there are no accommodations, meals, or auto services available inside the park. Limited facilities are presently under consideration but will not be ready before 1980.

GUANTÁNAMO. Est. 1797; pop. 165,613; 81 km (48 mi) E of Santiago de Cuba; capital of Guantánamo prov.

Guantánamo is located on the bay of the same name in the middle of fertile plains and low mountain ranges. The sugar business began in earnest here about 1819, and the population was by then 44% black slaves. In 1871, during the war for independence, the city was penetrated by forces under Máximo Gómez, and it was a center of urban guerrilla activity during the Revolution. The U.S. naval base with which the city is most frequently associated was established shortly after Cuban independence.

Driving through Guantánamo, one need not be a Cuban nationalist to realize how little the U.S. presence did for the city. There were, of course, many legitimate jobs generated by the base, but the attendant consequences were appalling. Connections to the flourishing prostitution business passed from generation to generation like titles to land, and it was not unusual to find three generations of women in service to the base. Guantánamo's economic development appears to have been completely arrested by the base. Housing was scandalous, education and health facilities almost nonexistent. Only base-related industry was established, creating a dependency the

Guantánamerans were hard pressed to break.

The Revolution has revitalized the central area of the city (where there remain a few beautiful Spanish-style houses) by building a park and planting trees on the main street. Education appears to have been a priority—new schools abound—and industrial development has begun. Still, Guantánamo remains extremely underdeveloped, even compared to other major Cuban cities, and its improvement will require many more years of concerted effort. The visitor should spend the night in nearby Santiago, as no suitable accommodation exists here.

GUARDALAVACA. A resort area on the north coast, located on a fine white sandy beach, 186 km (111 mi) N of Santiago de Cuba, 53 km (31 mi) NE of Holguín; Holguín prov.

BACKGROUND

When complete in 1980, this will be one of Cuba's most self-contained resort areas. One hotel and several cabanas are now functioning, and the plans call for a few additional hotels and massive recreational facilities. Unfortunately, the landscape around the beach is quite dull, and there is no town for distraction. But for complete rest and relaxation in the sun, Guardalavaca is perfect.

There is folkloric confusion over whether the name of this resort derives from Guardalabarca, which means "watch the boat," or from the use of the beach as a pirate livestock station (Guardalavaca means "watch the cow").

HOTELS

Hotel Guardalavaca. Near, though not exactly on, the beach, this hotel is the hub of the tourist area. A model pre-fab design, using white stone and stucco tile, with plants and local colors throughout, its style has been copied by other Cuban hotels. Ideal for families, the hotel offers an Olympic-size swimming pool, volleyball, and table games; tennis and horse-back riding are being developed. Other activities, which can be booked through the reception desk, include bicycling (the flat terrain is very conducive to this sport), 1 peso per hour, and speedboat rental, 20–24 pesos per hour, depending on the size of the boat. 176 modern rooms, all with private bath (hot water was being installed in 1978), balcony, and radio. Dining room is excellent, with shrimp enchilada a worthwhile specialty. Rates: twin, 20 pesos; single, 15.

Cabanas Guardalavaca. There are 45 cabins near the hotel, with kitchen facilities, sleeping up to 4 people. No hot water. 32 pesos per week. All accommodation here must be booked by Cubatur.

RESTAURANTS AND NIGHTLIFE

Besides the Hotel Guardalavaca dining room, there is the Restaurant Havana, located about a quarter-mile from Hotel Guardalavaca, specializing in seafood. (M)

There is a large public dance floor, also about a quarter-mile from the hotel, with tables and chairs around it. On Saturday night there is usually a cabaret show. The bar is always open.

EXCURSIONS FROM GUARDALAVACA

Cayo Naranjo is a fish hatchery operated by the Cuban government where fish and shellfish are bred. The Cubatur desk can request a visit and arrange the necessary boat rental. There are also numerous small beaches along the coast that are accessible only by boat. One superb beach is located just outside Cayo Naranjo bay.

Banes is a nearby town with an Indo-Cuban museum. The winding road from Guardalavaca to Banes is one of the love-liest in Cuba (about a 30-minute drive, 7 pesos one way). (See "Banes" for additional information.)

Gibara is a nearby town with a museum of colonial art and a museum of natural history, both worth a visit (about a 30-minute drive, 8 pesos by taxi). (See "Gibara" for additional information.)

HANABANILLA. 52 km (31 mi) S of Santa Clara, about the same E of Cienfuegos, 80 km (48 mi) N of Trinidad; Sancti Spiritus prov.

Located in the heart of the Escambray Mountains, with their marvelous landscape, this tiny town edges Lake Hanabanilla, artificially created 17 years ago when the Hanabanilla River was dammed. The reservoir now supplies both Cienfuegos and Santa Clara with water, and a small hydroelectric plant provides power to the Hanabanilla area.

The main industry in town is the construction of plastic recreation boats. The agricultural workers of the area cultivate tobacco and malanga.

The region is one of Cuba's loveliest. The lake sits in the middle of the hills like a small mirror. In the morning, the light comes up over the smoky green slopes and trails across the water, seeming to follow the waves set up by the occasional boat traffic.

The *Hotel Hanabanilla,* built in 1977 on the shores of the lake (tel. LB-86832), is clearly one of Cuba's best hotels, with a unique setting. 128 rooms, all with air conditioning, balcony, private bath, hot water, phone, radio, and television; Olympic-size swimming pool. The restaurant is excellent, and the kindly chefs will gladly prepare the lake bass you catch—provided you don't overindulge! Rates: twin, 18 pesos; single, 14.

From the hotel, you have a commanding view of lake activity, as ferryboats carry workers to and from their homes in hillside hamlets to the town of Hanabanilla and points beyond. The local boats leave at approximately 7 a.m., 11:30 a.m., and 12:30 p.m., then every hour until 6:30 p.m., from the Hanabanilla town dock. Travelers who don't mind an erratic schedule will find a ferry trip into the hills very worthwhile and certainly scenic.

Activity in the town centers around the lake, where fishing, paddle boats, and motorboats are available. There are a few caves around the lake, and some interesting marsh birds, best observed just before sunset. Family vacations are ideal at Hanabanilla.

For diversion, you can visit Manicaragua, an important tobacco town. Buses leave Hanabanilla every half-hour in the morning and thereafter every two hours. Allow one hour for the trip each way. Taxi round trip would be about 20 pesos, not including waiting time.

Hanabanilla has been featured on many tours from the United States and is used as a base from which Trinidad, Cienfuegos, and Santa Clara can be visited.

HOLGUÍN. Est. 1523; pop. 178,958; 772 km (463 mi) E of Havana, 197 km (118 mi) NW of Santiago de Cuba; capital of Holguín prov.

When Columbus discovered Cuba in 1492, he sent an expedition inland to carry greetings to what he thought would be the Japanese emperor's court. Instead, Columbus's emissaries encountered an Indian settlement of about 50 houses called Cubanacan (meaning "center of Cuba"). This village was probably on or near the site of the present city of Holguín, about a 20-minute drive from the Guardalavaca resort. Holguín sits in the middle of fertile farm and sugarcane land, and the Rafael Freyre Sugar Mill just outside the city is the largest in the province.

The city is very much on the move, although it has as yet received little tourism. Among the notable sites in Holguín are: *the Distrito Lenin*, a housing project built on flat, unforested land unused prior to the Revolution; *the Lenin Hospital*, built in 1965; and *the Vocational High School*, with work-study facilities for about 4,000 students. In the older part of the city, along the Maceo, Spanish-style buildings predominate.

Holguín has two museums. *Museo Historico de la Periquere*, Maceo Square, emphasizes the role played by inhabitants of Holguín province in Cuban history. Open Tues.–Sat. noon–7 p.m., Sun. 8 a.m.–noon; closed Mon. *The Museum of Natural Sciences*, Maceo Square, exhibits flora and fauna of the region. Open Tues.–Sat. 8 a.m.–noon, 1 p.m.–5 p.m., 6 p.m.–10 p.m., and Sun. 8 a.m.–noon; closed Mon.

A new resort-type hotel is under construction near the sports stadium, but to date, accommodation is very basic. Until the new hotel is opened, probably in 1981, overnights here are not recommended. However, the *Hotels Praga (formerly Partallo)* and *Turquino,* both in town, provide adequate accommodation and basic meals, as does the *Mirador de Mayabe,* 6 kilometers (3.4 miles) outside the city (tel. 2160), overlooking the lush Mayabe Valley, with a superb view. The Mirador has an outdoor dining terrace and dance floor and is open for lunch and dinner. The staff loves to point out the donkey who drinks beer, but who appears, like most museums, to have Mondays off. A few wild peacocks strut up and down the stone steps. Accommodation is available in 20 cabins, each with bath and air conditioning. Hot water is to be installed. Horseback riding and table games are available, and a swimming pool is under construction. Rates: twin, 8 pesos.

For dining, try *Restaurant El Valle,* 4 kilometers (2.4 miles) from Holguín, an attractive Spanish-style mansion serving full meals. It also has a swimming pool and is near a recreation area with an artificial beach. (M)

ISLE OF YOUTH (formerly Isle of Pines). Disc. 1494; pop. 60,000; 2,199 sq km (859 sq mi) in area, 146 km (87 mi) S of Havana, about 97 km (60 mi) off the south coast of Cuba.

The Isle of Youth is a microcosm of the Cuban Revolution. It offers not only resort potential but also a number of unique cultural and historical attractions. The island, for individual tourists, can be covered easily in two full days, but education or agricultural specialists will find more time invaluable.

Cubana operates regular flights to the Isle of Youth (50 minutes, 25 pesos one way). The sunrise flight is spectacular. You can also take a hydrofoil or ferry connecting with buses from Havana and departing from Batabanó on the south coast (about 3 hours by hydrofoil, 6 by ferry; 10 pesos one way including bus fare). Tickets should be obtained from Cubatur.

H I S T O R Y

The island was discovered by Columbus during his second voyage in 1494 and has changed names 15 times since. The *is-*

lita ("little island"), as Cubans fondly call it, has been variously a pirates' refuge, a Devil's Island prison compound, a last outpost, a mineral springs resort—and always a frontier. After Cuban independence from Spain, the Platt Amendment passed by the United States expressly excluded the Isle of Pines from territorial settlement, and there was constant talk of annexation. Finally, in 1925, the island became part of Cuban national territory, although by then many U.S. citizens lived on the island and owned large tracts of virgin land there. The town of Santa Fe (now called La Fe), developed during this period as a resort, is favored by salubrious climate and mineral springs.

Today, the island is a center of citrus production and a model for the Schools in the Countryside program. The name was changed officially to Isle of Youth in 1978 to acknowledge the contribution young Cubans have made to the island's development.

THE ISLAND TODAY

The name Isle of Pines conjures up images of lush tropical verdure, yet topographically the north part of the island is quite flat and dry, and much more reminiscent of Cuba's central plains than of an island paradise. The main mountain ranges are the Sierra de Canada (1,368 feet above sea level) and the Sierra del Caballo (936 feet above sea level). The south coast, however, is ringed with white sand beaches; the sea is crystal clear, and the resort possibilities of the island have attracted increasing attention.

Before the Revolution, the island had about 60 miles of road and a population of approximately 10,000. Today, one can drive virtually everywhere, and the population has jumped to 60,000, including 15,000 or so students. This student population has made the difference in agriculture—before the Revolution, only 600 square hectares were cultivated; today, 23,000. For miles and miles, grapefruit, tangerine, and orange trees, with pine and mango barriers to protect them from the wind, fill the visual fields. From September to December is the citrus harvest. The scent during blossoming season, January and February, pervades and refreshes as it is carried along on the sea breeze. In addition to agricultural enterprises, Isle of Pines marble is quarried extensively, and caolin, used in the production of porcelain, is also processed here.

WHAT TO SEE

Nueva Gerona, the island's main town, with Calle 41, the main north-south street, leading into Avenida Abraham Lincoln.

Micro '70 is Nueva Gerona's new housing project, entirely microbrigade-built. This fascinating model town is well worth walking through.

With advance permission obtained through Cubatur, you can also visit several interesting workshops. There is a *marble factory,* Calle 23 between 55th and 57th streets, where large marble stones quarried on the island are cut and polished. No photography is permitted. The *woodworking shop,* west side of Calle 43, midway between 18th and 20th streets, is a small craft shop where artisans cut, carve, and stain wood objects, using about 15 different varieties of local wood. The shop is set back from the street and has no sign, so ask for exact directions. Everyone knows it. Premolded wall figures are painted at a *ceramics workshop* called Fria 28 de Enero on Calle 45 at the corner of 24th Street. Those interested in the more sophisticated firing process should inquire in Micro '70 for the Primero Enero area. Isle of Pines ceramic work is particularly attractive.

The harbor is a pleasant area at Rio las Casas and 32nd Street where various craft dock and discharge passengers and cargo. And every tour of the island includes a stop at *Playa Bibijagua,* a black sand beach—hardly a headline attraction, but interesting and different.

If you are spending some time in Nueva Gerona and want further information about what to see and do there, you may find the following addresses useful:

Cubatur, Calle 39 between 22 and 24 (tel. 2200).
ICAP, Calle 39, a recently opened center. Inquire about local cultural events, especially performances of the *sucusucu,* a popular regional dance.
Bookstore Frank Pais, Calles 26 and 39.
Art School and Gallery, Calle 39 between 26 and 24.

The Prison Museum (Museo del Presidio), 2 miles east of Neuva Gerona. The Machado regime constructed this "model" prison in 1926, basing it on U.S. precursors, and Fidel Castro and other Moncada prisoners were incarcerated here during the 1950s. It was finally closed in 1967. The visitor may tour the enormous—168 feet in diameter, 78 feet high—circular prison blocks (one sign sinisterly proclaims "Welcome to Circular #4"). The historical museum attached relates prison and island history. Open Tues.—Sat. 9 a.m.—5 p.m.; closed Mon.

Planetarium and Natural History Museum, Calle 41, south of Nueva Gerona. The museum contains geological and archaeological information on the island, as well as copies of the cave drawings from Punta del Este. (The cave itself is accessible, but only by jeep.) The museum also traces the island's history, and the planetarium presents shows on the Cuban sky. Open Tues.–Sat. 8 a.m.–noon and 2 p.m.–6 p.m., Sun. 8 a.m.–noon; closed Mon.

El Abra, 2½ miles south of Nueva Gerona. This is the house where Martí, at the age of 18, was imprisoned by the Spanish authorities for having written a seditious letter.

Outside Nueva Gerona

La Fe, 16 km (9 mi), south of Nueva Gerona. A former inland colony, with large shaded square and a number of plantation style houses. A worthwhile side trip for those who are interested in how a former U.S.-colony town evolved during the Revolution.

La Victoria, 13 km (7.8 mi) from the Colony Hotel. One of Cuba's first "new towns," it used small one-family units instead of high-rise apartments houses. The town, centered around a dairy plan, has its own schools, polyclinic, day care center, telephone and telegraph office, grocery store, etc.

Punta del Este, 57 km (34 miles) southeast of Nueva Gerona. The road to Punta del Este is not entirely paved, and a jeep is needed for the last stretch. It features a beautiful beach and two caves used by the Indians, painted with celestial plans and other tribal markings—the Cuban equivalent of Lascaux, France. (The caves are reproduced exactly in the Natural Sciences Museum in Havana.)

WHAT TO DO

Scuba diving. The waters around the Isle of Youth are crystalline and rich with shipwrecks, black coral, and underwater caves. The Colony Hotel is the center of scuba activities. French equipment can be rented, and instruction is available. Excursions are organized regularly by Cubatur to Cape Francis and Pedernales, considered the most excellent scuba locations.

Fishing. Local waters are particularly well known for tarpon and bonefish. Regular excursions are organized from the Colony Hotel.

HOTELS

The island, frankly, is hotel-poor. Only the Colony offers the resort amenities the island will require to reach its maximum tourist potential, but there are plans to construct a variety of new facilities in the next few years.

Hotel Colony, 25 miles south of Nueva Gerona (tel. 8181 or 8282). Built in 1958, this hotel is the best on the island, with a long white sand beach, large swimming pool, and lush, landscaped gardens (kept impeccably by Heriberto Ruiz and his team) around a 2-story arc-shaped hotel. 45 rooms, all with air conditioning, bath, hot water, balcony, telephone, radio, 8 suites, 24 beach cabanas. Ask at the reception desk about a weekly sailboat cruise to Cape Francis for diving and snorkeling. Scuba and fishing also available. Rates: suite, 20 pesos; twin, 16; singles available at twin rates.

Las Codornices, just outside Nueva Gerona Airport. Named for a tiny bird common in the Sierra Caballos mountains near the hotel, this simple cottage colony is just right for the budget-minded. 16 rooms, each with private bath, radio, TV, and self-service bar; air conditioning, but no hot water. Restaurant; pool, but no beach. Rates: triple, 12 pesos; twin, 8 pesos, no single rates.

Hotel La Cubana, Calle 39 at 18th Street, in Nueva Gerona. This commercial-style hotel, overlooking Calle Camilo Cienfuegos, offers basic facilities. Rates available from Cubatur. It's the only hotel in the center of town, but quite spartan.

Hotel Treasure Ranch, Brazo Fuerte, outside Nueva Gerona. This cottage complex caters to hunting (in season) and horseback riding. It was closed for renovation in 1978 and latest rates and other information are not available. Cubatur should be consulted for latest data.

RESTAURANTS

Hotel restaurants. All the hotels have restaurants, though the Colony is best, with unfailingly excellent food. Seafood is a house specialty. Also order the grapefruit supreme for breakfast—locally grown sections served in a grapefruit skin hollowed into a basket, topped with mint. What grapefruit was meant to taste like.

Other restaurants. In addition to the hotel restaurants, the following (M) are worth a try: *El Cochinito*, Calles 39 and 24, Nueva Gerona, serves pork specialties; *El Corderito*, Calles 39 and 22, Nueva Gerona, serves lamb specialties; *INIT Seafood House*, Rio las Casas and Calle 32, has fine view of the comings and goings of ships; *El Jaguey and El Ranchon*, in La Fe, specialize in Cuban food, with rustic Indian-style atmosphere; *Viet Nam Dam* is a pleasant refreshment center overlooking an artificial lake. For snacks, try: *Coppelia Ice Cream*, Calle 37 between 30th and 32nd streets; *Pizzeria Isola*, Calle 35 at 30th; and *Merendero Italianito*, Calle 39 at 24th. All three are in Nueva Gerona.

JIBACOA. 72 km (43 mi) E of Havana, Havana prov.

This new community built in the hills around a dairy plan is about an hour from Havana. Weekly optional excursions are organized by Cubatur, departing from the Marazul Hotel in Santa Maria del Mar.

LA FE. See "Isle of Youth."

LA GUIRA NATIONAL PARK. 55 km (33 mi) E of Pinar del Río, 132 km (79 mi) W of Havana; Pinar del Río prov.

La Guira is situated in the Sierra de los Organos Mountains, marked by a castlelike gate into which the name Hacienda Cortina has been set in stone. Cortina was the landowner to whom La Guira belonged before the Revolution. The family wealth had been acquired through dealing in precious woods—mahogany, cedar, and pine—trading, and agricultural activity. Workers who remember that era report that they earned 15–25 pesos per month.

After the Revolution, the property was declared a national conservation area, and it is clear that the Cubans, once kept from the premises by a private guard force, now bask in the opportunity to walk, hike, and ride horseback through the extraordinary grounds of the park.

The forests are still thick with precious woods, now protected from logging, and hunting is prohibited by the Wildlife Service in an attempt to build up the pheasant and deer population. Fishing is permitted in season, and the area is famous for trout, carp, and other native freshwater fish, notably the *viahaco*. Bird watching has also begun to flourish in the park (see Section I, "Tours to Cuba").

La Guira offers horseback riding, fishing, and hunting under the supervision of Cubatur. There is also a small lake with rowboats and peddle boats, as well as two Oriental houses constructed by Cortina for his private art collections—one Japanese, the other Chinese. These are open Tues.–Sat. 9 a.m.–5 p.m. and Sun. 9 a.m.–1 p.m.

Overnight accommodation in La Guira is provided at the *Cabanas de los Pinos,* perfect for those who want to completely escape city life. Set deep in the park, this colony of guest cottages was conceived by Celia Sanchez, a member of the Communist Party Central Committee. It was begun in 1965, and there are now 23 cabins perched on wooden stilts and scattered discreetly through the pine forests. Each has electricity and running water, though hot water must be brought in from the restaurant kitchen nearby. The accommodations are simple but clean, and exactly right for a national park environment. To complete the emphasis on the natural, keys to each cabana are attached to a large wooden seed (a "donkey's eys") rather than a clumsy brass weight. Rates: twin, 8 pesos. Book through Cubatur only.

The Cabanas Restaurant, adjacent to the cottage colony, is constructed completely from pine and cedar, with curling dried vines interwoven for decorative purposes. It serves excellent Cuban-style food and has a bar. (M) You may also want to try *Restaurant La Guira* at the park entrance, a modern restaurant with scenic overlook. (M)

LAS TERRAZAS. Est. 1969; pop. 1,200; 75 km (46 mi) W of Havana, Havana prov.

Situated quietly in the Sierra de los Órganos, its white cottages arranged to flow with the green land, Las Terrazas is one of Cuba's unsung beauties. Happening upon it revives one's faith in the harmony between man and nature. Once, on an incomparably clear day of crisp air and sharp light, I visited the town with a poet who had not seen it since it completion. We arrived coincidentally on the day of the town's tenth anniversary. A rodeo was in progress; all the townspeople had turned out to celebrate. Pablo Armando, my companion, said we had crossed paths with the essence of the Cuban Revolution.

Las Terrazas is a new community attached to a reforestation plan. The plan comprises 12,500 acres (5,000 hectares) of land replanted with precious woods—teak, mahogany, cedar, pine. Before Las Terrazas existed, the area was inhabited by a few *campesinos* who were completely isolated from civilization—no roads, schools, electricity, or housing, except *bohíos*. The mountainous terrain was ill suited to farming, a situation made worse by the constant erosion of topsoil. It had been planted with coffee at one time, but a nomadic population leveled the land, neglecting the coffee, felling other trees and exporting the wood, or burning the trees as charcoal. They traveled from one hill to another until the entire region was a scrubby wasteland.

In 1967, the area was slated for reforestation, and immediately the government began to bulldoze the nude land into terraces—hence the town's name—damming streams and rivers and planting trees. But the population was too low to support the plan, so the government recruited *campesinos,* offering them houses and jobs on the plan. Some were reluctant, because farming and charcoaling were the only skills they had, but they learned building, engineering, landscaping, forestry.

The terraced nature of the plan made it feasible to construct individual housing units, and it was begun with white wooden houses, each with two or three rooms, a stucco tile roof, balconies, and orange shutters. They look almost Alpine, dispersed and arranged irregularly along the terraces. Later, larger apartment blocks were built on raised stilts, but using the same colors and style. The entire town cascades—every house a terrace on the terraces.

Reynaldo González, a Cuban novelist and historian who spent a year working in Las Terrazas during the early days, is compiling a book which will record the impressions of the *campesinos* who built the town and whose lives have changed because of it. His initial interviews are available in Spanish at the Las Terrazas museum.

The most scenic way to approach Las Terrazas is from Havana via the northern coast to Cabañas, then south from there. Between Las Terrazas and Cabañas is some of Cuba's most spectacular scenery (see "Cabañas"). Las Terrazas is 25 pesos from Havana by taxi one way; public bus service is not available except for plan workers. A visit is feasible only for those having a private car or willing to shell out the hefty taxi fare. But, especially on a beautiful day, the trip is exquisite.

LAS TUNAS. See "Victoria de las Tunas."

LA VICTORIA. See "Isle of Youth."

LA YA YA. Est. 1972; pop. 1,235; 20 km (12 mi) from Santa Clara; Villa Clara prov.

This new community was named for a flowering tree found in the vicinity. It is entirely self-contained and overlooks a flat, wide valley dotted with grazing cattle and dairies. Fidel Castro conceived the project in 1970 when touring the area. He recognized that the terrain was far more suited to dairy enterprises than to cane cultivation, the main activity at the time. Farmers made a meager living trying to grow sugarcane on small patches of land. There were no schools within traveling distance, and everyone lived in *bohíos*. Today, the inhabitants live in five four-story apartment buildings, the first of which was occupied in January, 1972. La YaYa has become a showcase.

All apartments have kitchens, baths, and either two or three bedrooms. The inhabitants of La YaYa pay no rent—only electric and gas bills. They work on the cooperative for a salary—about 100 pesos per month—and the family retains the right to live at LaYaYa even if the breadwinner dies and no family member is working on the plan.

The *campesinos* were offered an apartment at LaYaYa if they would trade their land so it could be merged into a state-owned dairy cooperative that would pasteurize and process milk, cheese, and butter. At first, the farmers were reluctant to surrender the land, not least because many of them had just received title to it under the Agrarian Reform. After years of working for someone else, they wanted to enjoy landowner status. However, most farms were miniscule and produced very little. Dora Gutierrez, LaYaYa's administrator, reports that when the government explained the LaYaYa concept to the *campesinos*, many of them scoffed and said, "Those things only happen in movies. They never can happen in Cuba." To dispel the skepticism, the government started building, and the first families moved in. Eventually word spread through the valley that the apartments had real floors, lights, hot water, balconies, schools, bus service—and that the dairy-farm workers earned more in a month than the subsistence farmers ever considered possible.

The Cubans are quite candid about the transitional problems which beset LaYaYa and other similar communities. *Campesinos* who had lived for generations in *bohíos* were unaccustomed to the citified style. They brought their animals—including goats, calves, and chickens—into the apartments and often "grazed" them on the balconies. There was vandalism as well.

When the problems began cropping up, the government realized that the community would have to be more meaningfully drawn into the planning and construction process. All the green areas, for example, were landscaped and maintained by volunteer laborers, many of whom commuted from their *bohíos* every day after work while their apartments were being completed. At the same time, the theater group produced skits that explored the vandalism and other problems inherent in new-community life exposing them to public scrutiny, often with typically Cuban humor. The group also produced plays intended to shatter *machismo,* since many male *campesinos* did not approve of their wives working in the dairy plan, as many women wished to do. Today, La Ya Ya prides itself a model of revolutionary progress.

LaYaYa is most easily accessible from Santa Clara (by taxi about 8 pesos one way). Consult Cubatur for information about public buses. Tourists should note that the dairy project may not be visited; visits to LaYaYa, unless previously arranged to include all facilities, are restricted to public areas.

MANICARAGUA. Est. 1802; pop. 73,527; 30 km (18 mi) S of Santa Clara; Villa Clara prov.

The drive to Manicaragua from Santa Clara affords some wonderful views of tobacco land, sharp green patches against greener rolling hills. The town itself brims with activity and is laid out in typical crossroads fashion. In addition to the tobacco industry, there is now an ice-cream factory, as well as a cheese factory and a number of new schools. The town typifies Cuban rural life.

The day I visited Manicaragua, I intended to look up a friend whose address I did not have but whose phone number I did. Having tried to call ahead with no luck, I drove into town anyway and asked the first person I saw if there was a phone anywhere. The extremely kind Manicaraguan paused for a moment and then proceeded to list for me all the phones in town, including the ones in the polyclinic and the Communist party office. When I explained that I wanted a public phone, he slapped his side and asked good-naturedly why I hadn't made that clear in the first place. He pointed me to the phone booth, which was not coin operated, and I waited for the operator to assist. I provided the number and said it was in Manicaragua. The operator replied incredulously, "But you're *in* Manicaragua!" This particular phone booth was long-distance only. I then asked a few people outside if they knew my friend. The wonders of small towns! Because the man of the family was a well-known sports hero, I was led directly to his door by an adoring fan who said that in the future when I was visiting sports heroes, all I needed to do was say so!

Manicaragua is a one-hour bus trip from Hanabanilla resort, for those who are staying there and wish a little contact with the village life of Cuba. (See "Hanabanilla.")

MARIEL. Est. 1762; pop. 29,968; 48 km (28 mi) W of Havana on northern coastal road; Havana prov.

Hardly the spot for a nature retreat, Mariel's interest lies in its rapid post-Revolutionary industrial growth. The British established a naval station here while they held Havana, and by 1768 fishermen had begun setting up a village. A naval academy dominates Mariel's highest hill, and the intensive industrialization below is a marvel. Mariel has a brand-new thermoelectric plant (inaugurated in February, 1978), Cuba's largest cement factory, shipyards, sisal-processing plants, and lots of new housing and school facilities. Those returning from Pinar del Río via the north road might find a stop worthwhile. The *El Salado resort* and *Monte Verde restaurant* are located just outside town, and both provide fine meals (M). The beach at El Salado is not one of Cuba's best, however.

MATANZAS. Est. 1690; pop. 95,728; 100 km (60 mi) E of Havana, 38 km (22 mi) W of Varadero; capital of Matanzas prov.

Situated between the Yumuri and San Juan rivers, graced by bridges, Matanzas is one of Cuba's most pleasant cities. Its favored location on the bay in the midst of extremely fertile land has made it also one of the most commercially important. At least one full day is needed to satisfactorily explore this city.

HISTORY

In contrast to the city's tranquil atmosphere, the name Matanzas means "slaughter" or "killings." Much has been written about the derivation of the name, and although controversy persists among historians, three theories have emerged. First, there is the report that the local Indians tricked the colonialists by promising to guide them inland and then, at the first opportunity, overturned their canoes, drowning all but a few survivors who lived to tell the tale. The second version reverses the roles, claiming that Indian massacres took place in the region. The third asserts that because of the salt-meat production in the area and the attendant slaughter, the area came to be known as the city of "killings," where travelers could collect food supplies.

In addition to salt-meat production, the area during the 17th and early 18th centuries was a prime exporter of tobacco and coffee. But Matanzas was destined to be a sugar capital, producing more than half the national output during the 1851—61 period. This was due partly to the red soil in the area, particularly well-suited to growing cane, but also to the bayside location, which made Matanzas a favored slave depot. Often, the Africans traded through the port received less humane treatment than the salted pork, and Matanzas was a constant center of slave rebellion.

On this sugar and slave foundation, Matanzas erected a highly sophisticated *salón* culture—a mini-Renaissance occurred during the 19th century. Wealthy Matanzans often went abroad to absorb ideas and trends. As a result, Matanzas became the home of many well-known Cuban poets, scientists, and artists of the 19th century and earned itself the nickname Athens of Cuba. Among its most famous sons and daughters were José Jacinto Milanes, José White Lafitte, José Maria Heredia,

Bonifacio Byrne, and Gertrudis Gómez de Avellaneda, all of whom were either born in or long-time residents of Matanzas.

During the anti-Batista years, an unsuccessful attack was made on the Goycuria barracks. After the Revolution, the barracks was converted to a school.

WHAT TO SEE

The Bridges of Matanzas. In the 18th century, Matanzas consisted of just the main city, but in the first quarter of the 19th, the districts of Versalles and Pueblo Nuevo were added. The residents went by raft from district to district; carriages and carts traveled over wooden bridges that were often displaced by storms and high winds. Today's bridges are, of course, much more solid: *Calixto García*, over the San Juan River, built in 1899; *Concordia*, over the Yumuri River, the most artistic of the bridges, inaugurated in 1878 to commemorate the signing of the Zanjón pact; and *San Luis*, over the San Juan River, built in 1917.

Parque Libertad and environs. This area has considerable architectural interest, and the park itself is lovely. *Sala White*, formerly the Lyceum Club, on Calle Byrne, now houses the Casa de Cultura. *Gener and Del Monte Library*, formerly the Casino Club, on Calle Byrne, was founded 1835 and is one of Cuba's oldest libraries.

Poder Popular, formerly the City Hall, on Calle Ayuntamiento, also houses the Matanzas Gallery of Art. The grand mahogany doors are notable. The private home at #28203, Calle Byrne, off Parque Libertad, possibly has the most elaborately tooled iron doors in Cuba, with bold lion door knockers.

La Viña, corner of Santa TERESA AND Calle Milanes next to the Pharmaceutical Museum, is a typical Cuban grocery store dating from the 19th century. It is being restored and should be open in 1978 as a restaurant.

Sauto Theater, Plaza de la Vigia, at Matanzas bay. Undeniably one of the most important buildings in Cuba from the neo-classical period, the theater was built in 1863. It was once the scene of sumptuous classical evenings but had fallen into disrepair and was used as a cinema until the Revolution. In 1969, an intensive restoration campaign was mounted to revive the delicate frescoes and carved wood. The theater, a sister to the Terry in Cienfuegos and the Milanes in Pinar del Río, is a three-tier affair with circular balconies supported by thin bronze poles. The present seats are exact replicas of the originals, and the capacity is 750 persons. The Sauto is constantly booked with local and traveling classical and folkloric cultural groups, so one can easily combine a visit with a performance.

Cathedral of Matanzas, corner of Milanes and Jovellanos. The present building dates to 1878 (construction was begun in 1693 on a much smaller scale) and has opulent frescoed ceilings and walls. The park around the church, dedicated to the poet Milanes, is cool and shady, and the adjacent side streets are closed to traffic, making the area a very inviting place to pause for a rest.

Castillo de San Severino, Avenida del Muelle, along the harbor, north of town. The oldest construction in Matanzas, the castle dates from 17th-century pirate and smuggler days. In 1628, when Spain was at war with Holland, the Dutch captured an entire flotilla of silver-laden ships here and sailed off to Amsterdam, San Severino notwithstanding.

Monserrat Hill and church. Both overlook the city, affording a superb panoramic view.

Reynol Garcia Housing Project, along the easterly road toward Varadero Beach. This example of the extensive post-Revolutionary housing construction in Cuba combines high-rise and individual units.

The rail station and bus depot, in Pueblo Nuevo between San Diego and Luis Cuni Streets. A confection of spires built in 1883, this building is presently being restored.

Bellamar's Cave, about 2 miles west of the city center. Discovered accidentally in the 1850s by workers in the area, the cave is one of Cuba's biggest attractions. For cave lovers it is a dream—1½ miles of vaulted stone ceiling, stalagmite and stalactite cathedrals, and underground streams—a bit like being held in the mouth of the earth. The air is thin and the temperature high, so asthmatics and claustrophobics should beware. There are guides at the site, and tourists are not allowed into the cave unaccompanied. Open Tues.–Sun. 9:30 a.m.–4:30 p.m.; closed Mon. The adjacent restaurant serves excellent roast pork and beans for 3 pesos.

MUSEUMS

Pharmaceutical Museum, Parque Libertad, Avenida Milanes, corner of Santa Teresa. This magnificent, perfectly restored pharmacy dates from 1882, when it was opened by the French pharmacist Triolet. It is said to be the only pharmaceutical museum in Latin America. A must for physicians and pharmacologists, but of surprising interest to laymen. There are complete collections of original porcelain jars, pharmaceutical instruments, potions, salves, dried plants, pill forms, peelings, and oils. The building functioned as a pharmacy until 1964, when it was converted into a museum.

The excellent condition of the rooms and implements should be credited to the descendants of Triolet and the Spaniard Figueroa, whose daughter married into the French family. Her son retained the pharmacy exactly as it was, including the laboratory in the back decorated with frescoes of medicinal plants. Note especially the bright *vitrales*. Originally, the glass was the color of the French flag, but the Spanish authorities insisted that the colors of Spain predominate—hence the bright red and orange. The museum guides who are exceptionally able and gracious, will be happy to point out these and other details. Open Mon.–Sat. 2 p.m.–6 p.m. and 7 p.m.–9:15 p.m.; closed Sun.

History Museum of Matanzas, Parque Libertad, corner of Ayuntamiento and Contrerais. This interesting museum depicts city and provincial history. It has a complete collection of cigar-box labels, manuscripts of Matanzan poets, and documents pertaining to the rise and conditions of slavery. There is also an unusual collection of newspapers and a moving collection of documents about the young men who died during various insurrections, including the Revolution. Open Tues.–Sun. 3 p.m.–6 p.m. and 7 p.m.–10 p.m.; closed Mon.

Palacio Junco, at the waterfront. Restoration of this building is in progress. It will eventually house the Polivalente Museum, and the history collections will be incorporated. Ask about its status at the Casa de Cultura on Libertad Park.

HOTELS AND RESTAURANTS

To date, Matanzas has not been included as an overnight stop on prepaid bus excursions because it lacks modern hotel facilities. Usually, visits are arranged as one-day excursions from Varadero or Havana. However, for the individual traveler, there are at least three hotels which offer basic accommodation in rather ornate surroundings. Rooms are approximately 10 pesos per twin.

Hotel Velasco, Calle Byrne on Libertad Park, has a fine restaurant with marble columns and gold-leaf ceiling.

Hotel Louvre, Calle Milanes on Libertad Park, next to Pharmaceutical Museum, has fine *vitrales, mamparas,* and mahogany fixtures, and equally fine food.

Hotel Yara, Calle Byrne, around the corner from Liberstad Park, is the simplest of the three.

MAYABE VALLEY. See "Holguín."

MAYAJIGUA. Est. 1820; 106 km (63 mi) W of Santa Clara on north coastal road; Sancti Spíritus prov.

This quiet town lies on the lake of the same name, which is

itself a beautiful blue dot in the midst of palm and other tropical vegetation. There are recreational facilities and a restaurant. Worth a stop for those driving the northerly route between Moron and Remedios.

MAYARI ABAJO. Est. 1814; 124 km (75 mi) N of Santiago de Cuba, 80 km (48 mi) E of Holguín; on the Bay of Nipe, Holguín prov.

Readers of Jose Yglesias's excellent book *In the Fist of the Revolution* will recognize this town, in which the author spent three months documenting the changes wrought by the Revolution. The name "Mayari" is of Indian origin.

Leyte Vidal is the town's main street, overlooking a vast and fertile plain. The small shops on the north side—barbershops, groceries, and the pizzeria so eloquently described by Yglesias—open onto a panoramic view of the plain and the sea beyond. To live in Mayari away from the main street would be somewhat akin to living in a garden. Palms, bananas, and thick floral bushes seem to surround the houses, many of which have scallop-edged patios, uncommon elsewhere. The region recently has received tourist attention because of the Sierra Cristal National Park, north of the town proper—a wild area of pine forests and mountain trails.

There are several hotels and restaurant facilities in the Mayari region, all quite suitable for tourists. In the town itself, *Hotel Bitiri* (tel. 740), hardly operational in 1969 when Yglesias lived here, is clearly the place to be nowadays. There is a lively restaurant and cabaret, as well as a large swimming pool. 21 rooms, each with private bath but no hot water. Rates: twin, 7 pesos with air conditioning, 6 with fan; single, 4. For dining, *El Patio Espanol* serves typically Cuban food at moderate prices. Ask anyone to point you to it, as it is on the back streets.

In the national park you will find *Pinares de Mayari*, 18 miles south of Mayari proper, a complex of buildings offering rooms, suites, and apartments constructed entirely of pinewood to blend with the surrounding landscape. The dining room with cathedral ceiling is an architectural marvel, and the food is excellent. Pinares de Mayari is especially recommended for hikers and lovers of isolation. 18 units, all rooms with electricity and running water, private toilet and shower, some with hot water. Free tennis (1 court) and volleyball; horseback riding (3 pesos per hour); steam baths (20¢ per hour). Swimming pool under construction. Rates: 2 bedrooms with kitchen, 18 pesos; suite, 12; ordinary twin bedroom, 6. Book with Cubatur in Holguín.

MAYARI ARRIBA. 53 km (31 mi) N of Santiago de Cuba; Santiago de Cuba prov.

Until the Revolution, Mayari Arriba was three to four hours from Santiago by jeep and horse through the Sierra del Cristal remote village without a school or hospital of its own. Today, the mineral-rich area is served by a paved road, putting it within 45 minutes of the provincial capital. The drive is spectacular.

The Spanish colonialists never penetrated the area, but Céspedes established his revolutionary government here in the 19th century. During the Revolution, Raúl Castro opened and operated the second front from the town. Of interest is the *Museum of the Second Front*, which documents the battles of this period. Open daily, except Mon., 9 a.m.—6 p.m., by previous arrangement through your sponsor.

MEGANO. See "Beaches East of Havana."

MORÓN. Est. 1750; pop. 36,537; 36 km (21 mi) N of Ciego de Ávila; Ciego de Ávila prov.

This small coastal city is near the recreational area of Laguna de la Leche. The lake is used for fishing and sailboat racing and takes its name ("Milk Lake") from the somewhat whitish color of the water, which is due to its calcium content. Morón has a large park area, and an enormous fan palm tree welcomes you to town. An ornate clock in the form of a rooster was erected by the Spaniards in the middle of the park, but it was removed after the Revolution. A tall monument marks the spot.

The turn-of-the-century railroad station is architecturally interesting and contrasts with the sparkling new housing projects opposite (note the striking graphic designs on their facades). Canals lead into the city from the lake, and a good part of the city's income derives from the transportation of charcoal.

Tourist facilities include the *Moron Tourist Center*, a restaurant and cabaret on the canal leading to the lake; and *Laguna de la Leche*, a restaurant at the boating center, serving typical Cuban cuisine. Sunfish may be rented at the center, and races watched.

MINAS. See "Excursions from Camagüey."

NUEVA GERONA. See "Isle of Youth."

NUEVITAS. See "Excursions Outside Camagüey."

PINAR DEL RÍO. Est. 1699; pop. 118,321; 175 km (105 mi) W of Havana; capital of Pinar del Río prov.

The entrance to Pinar del Río is lined with large shady carob trees, bending away from the road. The city itself conveys a sense of rural isolation, and the neoclassical architecture that predominates is out of step with the times. Yet the bustle of Pinar de Río commands attention. Somehow, the city is beautiful—the blue *portales* columns, some with lacy art-nouveau bases look as though they were designed under the supervision of a patissier. And on the outskirts, the city is a veritable boulevard of new buildings, among which are a stadium and a nurses' academy, the first in Cuba.

HISTORY

Though the first land grants in this region were made by Spain in 1544, actual colonization did not begin until the 17th century. The very earliest Indians, the Guanahacabibes—now grouped among the Pre-Ceramic tribes—settled over the peninsula, and there are some 169 archaeological sites in the region. However, very little evidence of contact between the Spaniards and this particular Indian group has been found.

The city of Pinar del Río is situated in the middle of the highest-quality tobacco land in Cuba (some say in the world), the Vuelta Abajo. Early tobacco cultivation had been centralized in Havana, but because of government monopoly of the trade in the 1700s, growers scattered into the Pinar del Río region, where soil quality was excellent and where smuggling would be easier, away from the watchful eyes of the Spanish governor. The first tobacco factory was established in the area in 1761.

When sugarcane became Cuba's gold crop, Pinar del Río slipped in national esteem. Not as severely neglected as Baracoa and Guantánamo in the extreme east, it nevertheless suffered from administrative indifference. Since 1959, however, extensive rural development in the form of new communities and state dairy farms has taken place here, although the small tobacco farm remains central to the success and quality of the Cuban tobacco industry.

WHAT TO SEE

A solid half-day is necessary to visit the sites of the city of Pinar del Río. Individual travelers might enjoy spending the night at the new Pinar del Río hotel, and then driving on to Viñales for lunch the next day, returning to Havana that night. The drive direct to Pinar del Río from Havana is about two hours without stops, and though Pinar can be seen in one day from Havana, it might be wiser to stay over.

The Milanes Theater, Avenida Martí at Colon, was begun in 1898 and restored in the late 1960s. It is a lavish, entirely wood theater with a 520-seat capacity. The round, tiered interior is similar to that of the Terry in Cienfuegos or the Sauto in Matanzas. Check posters out front for frequent cultural performances.

Casa de Cultura and library, Máximo Gómez #108, is an art gallery and information center where a schedule of performances and other cultural events can be obtained. It is opposite the neoclassical Justice Palace, which now houses *Poder Popular*.

Political monuments are numerous throughout the city. The most notable, at Avenida Pinares near the Museum of Natural History, is dedicated to Pinares, a guerilla fighter.

Marti Street is a thriving thoroughfare that seems to carry you along with it. Note particularly the recreation center, formerly a private club on Martí at the corner of Coro; and the former lyceum, with open patio and three-pronged porcelain-globed light poles outside. This is now Pinar del Río's wedding palace.

The Cathedral, Antonio Maceo and Medina, is a neoclassical structure dating from 1883.

Vinales Valley, about 15 miles north of Pinar del Río, is certainly one of the most beautiful spots in Cuba. See "Vinales" for more information.

Regional specialties are an added attraction for the visitor. Some of the highest quality ceramic and woven work is produced in Pinar del Río, including much of the decoration at Rumayor Restaurant. The *taller* at Maceo, #119 where the craftspeople work may be visited with advance permission. Contact Cubatur, Calle Maceo, opposite the Justice Palace.

The *punta campesina* is a folkloric dance performance involving *controversias*, a Cuban poetry form in which the farmers, or *guajiros*, recite poetry to each other in conversational fashion, each building on the work of the other. Contact the Casa de Cultura for schedules. *Guayabita del Pinar* is a dry and sweet liquor made from tiny guavas, typical of the region.

MUSEUMS

Museo Antonio Guiteras Holmes, Avenida Maceo #52 between San Juan and Ormani Avenado, contains artifacts related to the life of Guiteras and the anti-Machado campaigns. The history of the region is also included. Open Tues.–Sat. 2 p.m.–10 p.m., Sun. 8 a.m.–noon; closed Mon.

Museo Hermanos Saiz, University City, is a small museum commemorating the Saiz brothers, who were active in the clandestine July 26 Movement before the Revolution. (Note also the public housing just opposite the museum—lovely garden apartments.) Open Mon.–Fri. 8 a.m.–noon and 1 p.m.–5 p.m., Sat. 8 a.m.–noon; closed Sun.

Natural Science Museum, Avenida Pinares and Martí, is devoted to the natural and earth sciences. This museum should be visited, if only for the building itself. It is housed in the former Guasch palace, an eclectic building with Egyptian hieroglyphics, Gothic gargoyles, Athenian columns, and art nouveau swirls. It was begun in 1909 as a private home for a wealthy doctor and his family. Guasch had traveled extensively and decided to incorporate a bit from every voyage into the design. Scheduled to open in 1979 or 1980. Check hours locally.

Provincial Museum of History, Avenida Martí, a few doors from the Milanes Theater, will cover the history of the region, expanding the collection already housed in the Guiteras Museum. It is scheduled for a 1979–80 opening.

Tobacco museum, Antigua Carcel, Maxímo Gómez and Ajete streets, will explain the tobacco process from seed to cigar. It is also scheduled for a 1979–80 opening.

HOTELS

Hotel Pinar del Río, University City, was inaugurated 1978. It is a modern hotel with spacious lobby and full amenities. 136 rooms, all with air conditioning, hot water, phone, radio, and balcony. Restaurant, bar, shops, pool. Rates not established at time of writing, but will be comparable to the Hotel Camagüey in Camagüey.

Club Maspoton, 45 miles west of the city, is the only hunting club in Cuba. For those who shoot from duck blinds. Dove season, Oct.—Feb.; Duck season, Oct.—March. Rooms can be booked only from the United States on a group basis. Contact Club de Patos, Suite 123, 5025 Roswell Road, NW, Atlanta, GA 30342.

RESTAURANTS

Rumayor, just outside town at the city's east entrance, has an outdoor cabaret and rustic decor, with wood and woven decorations intended to recreate an Indo-Cuban atmosphere. The specialty is smoked (*ahumado*) meats, and the smoked chicken is excellent. This is one of Cuba's best restaurants, due in large part to the impeccable deportment of Juanito, the maitre d', and his staff. (FC)

La Casona, Calle Colon at Martí, is a quiet Spanish-style restaurant serving traditional Cuban food. (M)

PINARES DE MAYARI. See "Mayari Abajo."

PUERTO BONIATO. See "Outside Santiago de Cuba."

RANCHO MUNDITO. pop. 5,000; 119 km (71 mi) W of Havana, 45 km (27 mi) W of Soroa resort; Pinar del Río prov.

Along the south coast route between Havana and Pinar del Río, there is a turnoff at San Diego de los Banos leading to this lovely town. Set deep in the forest, Rancho is one of the most pleasant rural towns in Cuba—so pleasant, in fact, that there were, before the Revolution, plans to construct a swank hotel with a golf course in the region.

The turnoff from the main road to Rancho Mundito winds deep into the mountains for about 25 minutes of sharp turns, affording fine views of fertile valleys covered with various green palms, bright orange popili, and white-shaded yagruma. For those with private transportation, a side trip from Soroa resort is well worthwhile. The town once supported a large estate surrounded by tenant farms. Today, the Rancho Mundito center is an open plaza, with a workers' social club. There is an outdoor bar, in full view of the old stone steps, now overgrown with grass. Here at Rancho, horseback riders have the right of way; beyond the town, only they and jeeps can venture. The area is a center of guava production, yielding 57,000 quintals per season. Malanga is also grown here.

A small brook cuts through town, near the club, banked with mariposa plants and lush tropical vegetation. The air is fragrant. Though the sensation is of having arrived in a pocket where time has not passed, the people of Rancho Mundito are right in tune with the Revolution and will tell you all you ever wanted to know about how it has affected their lives.

REMEDIOS. Est. 1692; pop. 44,752; 53 km (31 mi) NE of Santa Clara; Villa Clara prov.

BACKGROUND

This exquisite town actually dates from 1514, when a land grant was made to Vasco Porcallo de Figueroa. However, it did not figure in the first seven cities because Porcallo never permitted a city hall or municipality to be established. The town was called Santa Cruz de la Sabana, or de Porcallo, and was moved a short distance inland in 1544. Pirate raids were constant, and in 1578 the town was again moved, and the name changed to San Juan de los Remedios del Cayo. A complete reconstruction took place in 1692, but provincial administrative direction was moved to Santa Clara, considered less vulnerable to sea rovers.

Remedios remains a center of sugar and cattle production, and a number of new schools line the entrance to town. The overwhelming atmosphere, however, is Spanish-colonial. The city fans around the Plaza Martí, with a beige gazebo, tall royal palms, and superb white marble benches, seats divided one from the other by wrought-iron lutes. The park is stately, and very reminiscent of the Plaza Mayor in Trinidad. Remedios is an easy half-day trip from Santa Clara, but there are no major hotels or restaurants in Remedios itself.

WHAT TO SEE

Church of San Juan Bautista de Remedios, Plaza Martí. Construction dates from 1570, but the present building is from 1692, with a series of subsequent extensions. The church is one of Cuba's oldest. In the 1950s it enjoyed the patronage of a wealthy Remedian who financed its restoration, donating valuable European paintings as well as engineering labor. The visitor is most impressed by the altar, carved cedar with 24-carat gold-leaf coating. However, the real masterpiece of the church is the ceiling, which had been covered by plaster until the restoration. The original, now revealed, is carved mahogany in the Moorish style—gabled, fluted, and painted with the flower of Granada. The painting is only partly conserved.

Church of Buen Viaje, opposite San Juan, on the square.

Calle Maceo and Calle Andres del Rio feature exquisite old buildings, among them the Academy of Science building and the archives of Remedios.

The Parrandas of Remedios. These fiestas, typically Remedian, began in 1822 as noisemaking parties to rouse the townspeople on Christmas Eve for midnight mass. The sport of the occasion was enjoyed, and a competition ensued between the two sections of the city—El Carmen, represented by the hawk, and San Salvador, represented by the rooster. Victory went to the district that made the loudest noise. Each section attempted to outdo the other, developing elaborate costumes, cart decorations, and "works of the Plaza," which were gaily painted, imaginative floats. The noisemakers, however, were the *raison d'être* of the *parrandas*. Unique devices were developed, including a piece of well-used plow hit with an iron rod. Like fine wine, the plow improves with age, and to preserve the "vintage," it is buried in the earth every year and dug up only for the *parranda*. Special *parranda responsables* were, and still are, in charge of the secret burial.

The *parrandas* flourished, and in 1921 electricity provided the first illuminated floats in Remedian history. Then fireworks were introduced. Eventually the competitive nature of the *parranda* receded—everyone became a winner. The *parrandas* culminated in a parade of the carts and floats.

After the Revolution, the date of the *parranda* was moved to July 24, two days before the Moncada anniversary and the culmination of Carnival. The *parrandas* are still preceded by 15 days of rehearsal and anticipation. The "works of the Plaza" often have Revolutionary themes, and the nearby town of Camaguani has its own smaller version. Those in the vicinity at Carnival ought not miss the festivities.

A small museum is planned to describe the evolution of the parrandas. Inquire at the Caturla museum for details.

MUSEUMS

Museo de la Musica "Alejandro Garcia Caturla," Plaza Martí. This museum is a rare find that should not be missed, especially by those with even the remotest interest in music. The house itself dates from the late 19th century and was the home of the parents of Alejandro Garcia Caturla, one of Cuba's foremost avant-garde composers and musicians. He was born in 1906 and had begun writing music by age 14. The house, declared a national monument in 1970 and inaugurated as a museum in 1975, is devoted to a collection of Caturla's manuscripts, and to his biography. Caturla, a lawyer by profession, was respected throughout Cuba for his versatility and integrity. His life is a minitableau of Cuban history, and for those who cannot read the Spanish labels in the museum, a brief resumé follows.

Caturla was born into one of the most wealthy families of Remedios, which owned not only the family house but many of the adjacent homes as well. His father had been an officer in the army of Máximo Gómez, and he passed a fervent nationalism on to his son. Caturla's talent as a composer emerged early, but his mature music, based on the rhythms and sounds of Africa, was what placed him in the avant-garde. In addition, he developed modern harmonies, experimenting with new tonal combinations and rhythms clearly influenced by Stravinsky. With his colleagues, he organized the Orchestra de Concierto de Caibarien, a sort of music cooperative, and brought modern music to Cuba. Caturla traveled and was well received, even in the United States, but his music was little played or published at home.

Caturla was radical in every way. Not only was his music avant-garde and his political stand antiestablishment, but his personal life also defied convention. He married a black woman, had eight mulatto children, and then proceeded to marry his sister-in-law when his first wife died.

Caturla was assassinated in 1940 by a policeman who was due to come before him (he was a judge at the time) the next day on charges of having nearly beaten a woman to death. Though no connection between the policeman and the government could be proven at the time, the general feeling was that the murderer was part of a plot by judicial officials to rid Cuba of Caturla. Only the day before, Caturla himself had cabled the Supreme Court of Cuba in an effort to protect himself and his family from the murder plans he sensed were in the wind. In fact he had written a song in 1939 in which he predicted his violent death.

The museum building itself is elegant, featuring *mamparas* tinted with light green glass crowns, *vitrales*, and typical Remedios planters with tiles embedded in the sides. There is a room where visitors can listen to tapes of Caturla's music. The last room in the museum provides temporary space where local exhibitions are mounted. Open Tues.–Sat. 8 a.m.–11 a.m. and 2 p.m.–6 p.m.; Fri. and Sat. eve. 8 p.m.–11 p.m.; Sun. 8 a.m.–11 a.m.; closed Mon.

Historical Museum of Remedios, Antonio Maceo #56, between Carilla and Ariosa sts. This fine 19th-century house contains Spanish furnishings and objects relating to the history of the city. Hours are the same as for the Caturla museum, except no weekend night hours. Check locally.

RIO CRISTAL. See "Restaurants Outside Havana."

SAN DIEGO DE LOS BANOS. Est. 1793; 119 km (71 mi) W of Havana; Pinar del Río prov.

This small town was once known as the Saratoga of the Tropics, since the mineral waters of the nearby Tigre and the Templado springs were found to be healthful. Legend has it that a slave who'd been shut away in isolation because he had contracted leprosy was cured in the waters, and the "miracle" put the town on the map. Many 19th-century travelers were enraptured by the village, and it was widely advertised in the United States.

Today a polyclinic staff supervises use of the baths. The town mixes the Cuban rural and Revolutionary styles—wooden houses stand adjacent to handsome new apartment blocks.

SAN PEDRO DEL MAR. See "Beaches Outside Santiago."

SANCTI SPÍRITUS. Est. 1514; pop. 90,000; 386 km (231 mi) E of Havana; 69 km (41 mi) NE of Trinidad; capital of Sancti Spíritus prov.

This little-visited city has much to offer the tourist. One of Cuba's oldest cities, it is rich architecturally and culturally, though its commercial atmosphere makes it less glamorous than nearby Trinidad. Those in Trinidad, however, ought to attempt a one-day side trip if only for the contrast; comfortable overnight hotel accommodation is available outside the city.

HISTORY

Sancti Spíritus was founded some four miles from the present location, on a site which had been determined by the ample Indian labor supply nearby. However, three years later the city was moved to improve irrigation, as well as to escape a plague of biting ants.

The city's co-founder, Fernandez de Cordoba, led the Spanish expedition to the Yucatán, a voyage which fueled the expansionist dreams of Hernán Cortés and resulted in the conquest of the Aztec empire and the incalculable enrichment of Spain. During the late 16th century and early 17th centuries, Sancti Spíritus suffered from piracy and was burned twice. Valuable documents were lost, as elsewhere in Cuba. The agricultural wealth of the area, which had fostered the growth of Trinidad and Scanti Spíritus, continued to attract pirates until 1750.

Sancti Spíritus contributed a number of major generals to the war of independence, among them Honorato Castillo y Cancio, Serafin Sanchez, and Ramon Bonachea. In return it got very little. The years of independence brought "nothing at all," according to residents. "Imagine a city with a 450-year history, without a library, a museum, a music school, adequate schools or roads?" they explaim, recalling those times. Since the Revolution, some 30 new installations have been developed in the area, among them schools, a folkloric center, a pre-university, and several branches of the University of Las Villas.

During the Revolution, Che Guevara's column came close to Sancti Spíritus, incorporating the local fighters, of whom some 300 died. After 1959, Sancti Spíritus functioned as a command post during the Escambray fighting.

What is most interesting about Sancti Spíritus is how it managed, mainly by virtue of its position on the main road, to escape the eclipse that befell Trinidad.

WHAT TO SEE

Paroquial Mayor Church, Placido and Menendez streets, is one of Cuba's oldest and most well-preserved churches. Virtually every brick and stone is original. In 1536, money was donated by local landowners to reconstruct the church, which had functioned before the city was moved to the present location. A building was completed in 1620 but was destroyed during pirate raids, along with many records. Remaining church records date to 1652. During this period, a solid gold rooster which had been donated to the church by a wealthy parishioner, Don

Pedro Perez de Corcha, was carried off as loot. A stronger and safer church, the present one, was begun in 1671 and completed in 1680. The tower, which is constructed in three pieces, was finished in 1764, and the cupola added in the middle of the 19th century.

The most exquisite part of the church is its carved ceiling, with circular center and dropped gables, each intricately fitted and carved in cross patterns. Note also the paintings and statues in the church, including the porcelainlike (in actuality painted, carved wood) crucifix, and Christ with Humility and Patience.

Other important structures include: *the Academy of Sciences*, on Independence Street, a 19th-century structure; *the public library*, on Independence Street off Sanchez Park, the former lyceum, built in 1927; *the Cubatur office*, on Sanchez Park, built in 1843; *the Yayabo River bridge*, built in 1850, one of the few stone bridges left in Cuba; and *the Teatro Principal*, built in the 1870s, but less valuable architecturally than the Milanes, Sauto, or Terry theaters because of extensive interior renovation.

Coro de Clares are amateur singing groups typical of the city. For further information about them, contact Cubatur.

MUSEUMS

Museum of Colonial Art, Placido and Menendez streets, is a fine 19th-century structure with iron balconies and *rejas*, all constructed locally, housing a collection of furniture and artifacts from the Spanish period. Open Tues.–Sat. 3 p.m.–10 p.m., Sun 3 p.m.–6 p.m.; closed Mon.

Life Museum (Museo de la Vida), Independencia #52, is a small museum dedicated to the natural sciences, in particular the structure of cells and life cycles. It is operated by science students. Usually open Mon.–Sat. 8 p.m.–10 p.m., though it has no official schedule. Contact Cubatur for details.

Parque Honorato (slavery museum), Indepencia Street, is

213

scheduled to open in 1980. The park and surrounding buildings will be restored, and a museum will depict the history of slavery.

Casa Serafin Sanchez, Calle Céspedes, is the house where Sanchez was born. It is being converted into a historical museum of the area that will not only explain Sanchez's life and his role in the independence war, but also include information about the Revolutionary battles which took place in the area.

HOTELS

Zaza del Medio, a few kilometers from the center of town (tel. 2027 or –29), is clearly *the* hotel in Sancti Spíritus. It began operating in 1977. 128 rooms, all with air conditioning, hot water, and bath. Two swimming pools. Overlooks lake with full water sports and fishing. Excellent restaurant, pleasant bar, and cabaret. Rates: twin, 18 pesos; single, 13.

Hotel Colonial, Independence Street, one block off Sanchez Park, is a stately wood construction with *postigo* doors that require you to step up in order to enter. The hotel does not yet accept foreign tourists. However, the restaurant and bar are available, as is the garden terrace.

Hotel Perla, right on Sanchez Park, also does not yet accept foreign tourists, but the Arabic tile writing which appears in the lobby—imported via Spain—is noteworthy.

RESTAURANTS

All the hotel restaurants are available to tourists. In addition, try:

Sancti Spíritus 1514, corner of Lavorri and Céspedes, one block from Sanchez Park. Inaugurated in February, 1978, this restaurant has an elegant Old World atmosphere for lunch or dinner. It's the best in town. (FC)

SANTA CLARA. Est. 1689; pop. 169,157; 299 km (179 mi) E of Havana; capital of Villa Clara prov.

BACKGROUND

Santa Clara was founded by a small group of Remedios families who were fed up with the constant coastal pirate raids and moved inland. Located in the middle of a fertile plain, the new enclave rapidly developed and became the provincial capital in 1878.

Of crucial strategic value, the city has always been a plum of battle. In 1896, Leoncio Vidal attacked the Spanish garrison, and a fiery battle raged in which he was killed. In 1958, Che Guevara's troops swooped in, captured the Batista stronghold, and disrupted a train that was en route to reinforce government troops. A fierce battle ensued in the Santa Clara Libre Hotel, whose facade still bears the scars.

Today, Santa Clara pleasantly combines rural old-fashioned charm with the rustlings of development. The INPUD factory, employing 1,700 workers, was inaugurated in 1964 as the first appliance plant in Cuba. There are over 130 educational institutions in the area, ranging from primary school to university and including the enormous Ernesto "Che" Guevara Vocational School, with a capacity of 4,500. (All these require permission to visit, through Cubatur.) It seems that construction in the city takes place overnight. The city life, however, reflects a somewhat more subdued pace. Activity concentrates around Vidal Square, where the trees are full of birds whose calls and songs actually drown out the honk and blare of the local traffic. The monument in the center marks the spot of Vidal's death.

The city itself can be covered easily in one day, but visitors on sociocultural tours usually spend two. The numerous interesting excursions available outside the city—Remedios, Manicaragua, La YaYa—make Santa Clara well worth two or three nights' stay.

WHAT TO SEE

Municipal Palace, Vidal Square, was built in 1922 on the site of the original (1797) Spanish city hall. It now houses the radio station.

Caridad Theater, Vidal Square, was built in 1885 on the initiative of the philanthropist Marta Abreu. It has a beautifully painted interior by the Spanish artist Camilo Zalaya and is used for most cultural activities in the town.

Museum of Santa Clara, formerly located in the lyceum building, a grand-staircase, chandeliered structure next to the Santa Clara Libre, was built in 1925. It contains historical materials, particularly relating to the Escambray post-Revolutionary struggles. It is scheduled to move to a new location, so inquire locally.

Buen Viaje Church, two blocks east of Vidal Square behind the Exposition Hall, is a beautiful structure built on the site of a church founded in 1765. On the patio, black slaves listened to the services, since they were not allowed in the church.

Iglesia del Carmen, on Park Tudury, was built in 1748. It has been declared a national monument, and restoration is scheduled. A monument in the church consists of several columns, each representing a Santa Claran founding family.

The cathedral, three blocks behind the Hotel Central, off Vidal Park, is an imposing 20th-century structure.

University of Las Villas, cannot be visited without advance permission from Cubatur, although many prepaid tours from the United States include a stop here.

CULTURAL ACTIVITIES

Casa de la Trova, Colon Street opposite Coppelia, one block off the Vidal Square, features Cuban singing. Climb the winding steps over the shoe shop and knock hard. (Cubatur can advise you as to what evenings performances are scheduled.)

Other events besides the Casa de la Trova performances are held frequently at the Caridad Theater or at the youth club, located on Máximo Gómez opposite the theater.

HOTELS

All hotels in Santa Clara should be booked through Cubatur, located next to the Hotel Santa Clara Libre.

Santa Clara Libre, on Vidal Square in the dead center of town (tel. 7540 or –48 or –49), has a commercial atmosphere but an extremely convenient location. 158 rooms, simply furnished, pleasant dining room, air conditioning. Some rooms have hot water, all have private toilet and shower. Lack of a swimming pool is a drawback. Rates: twin, 15 pesos; single, 14.

Motel Los Caneyes, 1½ miles from the town center (tel. 6193 or 3714), is definitely the spot for those who prefer the rustic. The #11 bus connects the hotel with Vidal Square (fare, 5 centavos). Taxi fare is about 2 pesos. It's a unique hotel consisting of thatched-roof huts called *caneyes*, all with private bath. Check before you go to make sure there is hot water as it was in the process of being installed. Large swimming pool surrounded by palms; poolside bar. Excellent restaurant and lively cabaret, Santa Clara's leading night spot. 54 rooms. Rates: twin, 15 pesos; single, 14.

Hotel Central, on Vidal Square, was built in 1929 and recently renovated. Lovely bright yellow and blue tile lines the central staircase, but accommodation is simple. Rooms still offer only basic amenities. Lobby cafeteria is an excellent refreshment stop.

RESTAURANTS

All hotel dining rooms are worthwhile, especially Los Caneyes. Other restaurants include:

1878, on Máximo Gómez, between Independencia and Vidal Square. A lovely colonial style atmosphere and typical Cuban food. (FC)

El Pavito, Vidal Square, diagonally opposite Hotel Libre. Specializes in turkey. (M)

EXCURSIONS

The towns of Manicaragua, Remedios, and La YaYa are within 35 minutes of Santa Clara. Other accessible cities, each requiring one full day, are Trinidad, Cienfuegos, and Sancti Spíritus.

BEACHES NEAR SANTA CLARA

The nearest sea swimming is at Rancho Luna in Cienfuegos. Lake swimming and other water sports are available at the Minerva dam, two miles from town.

SANTA FE BEACH. See "Outside Havana."

SANTA MARIA DEL MAR. See "Beaches East of Havana."

SANTA MARIA DEL ROSARIO. Est. 1732; 16 km (10 mi) E of Havana; Havana prov.

This beautiful town was partially restored before the Revolution by a wealthy patron and resident. Around the park are a number of pastel-colored buildings all dating from 18th and 19th centuries. The highlight of the town is the massive church, called colloquially "the Cathedral of the Countryside." In 1733, a smaller church occupied the same location, and it was expanded in 1760. The baroque-style building's highlight is the wooden altar, entirely covered with gold leaf, and the resplendently carved ceiling. The building has been declared a national monument, and restoration is under way.

Santa Maria del Rosario is easily visited by taxi from Havana, a 3-peso trip one way.

SANTIAGO DE CUBA. Est. 1514; pop. 324,000; 967 km (580 mi) E of Havana; capital of Oriente prov.

Santiago—compact, built on hills, snugly situated in the center of the Oriente region, on a wide and beckoning bay with the wildly beautiful Sierra Maestra as a backdrop—is a lovely city with an irresistible *ambiente* that seems to pulse incessantly through the winding streets. It is an historic city where all of Cuba's revolutions have been born, a clearinghouse where all the cultures of Cuba came together. Santiago, in its streets, its history, even in the lilting accent of the Santiagueros, is one of Cuba's most spirited cities. It is a city to walk in, take time with, to discover at various times of the day, in varying lights.

Santiago easily deserves two nights' stay—three full days—to allow time to visit all the monuments and museums of the city and environs, plus a day for just aimless exploration. For any necessary information, contact the especially efficient Cubatur office, Céspedes Park, on Calle Lacret, under the Casa Grande Hotel (tel. 7278), Alejandro Cumberbatch, director.

HISTORY

Diego de Velázquez founded the city and named it for the patron saint of the king of Spain. It immediately assumed strategic importance because of its fine harbor and was the capital city until 1549. Hernán Cortés was Santiago's first mayor, and he used the position to recruit troops and support for his Mexico expedition. The city quickly became a center of slave trading, since cheap labor was required to run the large copper mine at El Cobre. This mine and the limited extraction of gold in the area were Santiago's main source of income in the early years. Like all Cuban cities, Santiago suffered pirate attacks during this period and was also victimized by earthquakes, necessitating the rebuilding of the city more than once.

Santiago is perhaps more of a melting pot than other Cuban cities—not only were there Spaniards, and blacks, but most of the 27,000 French planters who fled to Cuba after the revolution in Haiti in 1791 settled in the Santiago area. These exiles brought French customs and manners that are still obvious in the architectural flavor of Santiago; they also brought sugar and coffee technology that transformed the economy of the area. Many original French plantations still cover the hills around Santiago.

In 1793, Spain allowed the unlimited importation of slaves to meet to economy's ever-increasing labor needs. Since Santiago was a major slave port, it benefited directly from the change in regulations, but slave resistance, which had begun as early as 1731 at the El Cobre mines, increased.

In 1836, in an attempt to liberalize the government of Cuba, Spain ordered local elections, which Havana's governor Tacon refused to permit. Santiago, in a liberal and rebellious gesture, proclaimed elections anyway. This mini-defiance of Tacon ended in surrender, but Santiago's presence was definitely asserted. During the wars for independence, Santiago contributed numerous personages, among them the brothers Maceo. The greatest leaders, Céspedes and Martí, are buried in the city cemetery. The actual surrender of Spain in 1898 took place in Santiago, and then the city slipped into oblivion as the affairs of the Republic became centered in Havana.

Fidel Castro was born in Oriente and knew the Santiago area well. Capitalizing on its distance from Havana as well as its tradition of nationalism, he launched his first attack against Batista on July 26, 1953, at the Moncada barracks in Santiago. Since the Revolution, development in Santiago—a city that was previously without electricity in most areas and adequate plumbing everywhere—has been extraordinary.

WALKS

A car in Santiago is totally encumbering, and serves only to keep the visitor from contact with the city's pulse. Often the streets in the city have two or three names. Therefore I have used the nomenclature most likely to get you there.

Céspedes Park. Start with the life-center, where all manner of activity is on view. Magazine vendors, musicians, strollers, readers—everyone comes through here. The square itself is dominated by the cathedral, the Velázquez house, and the

Casa Grande Hotel. Also note the grand-staircase wedding palace on Lacret Street next to the hotel and the Galeria de Oriente next door, as well as the white and blue city hall, which houses Poder Popular. The Grande Hotel patio offers a perfect spot from which to watch the life of the square.

The streets of Santiago. Heading away from the center, you should not miss San Basilio, one of Santiago's oldest streets, still lined with gas lamps and paved with cobblestones. The main shopping streets are Heredia, Aguilera, and Saco, full of activities—bookstores, clothing shops, even a musical instrument store at Heredia between Lacret and Felix Pena, for those who want to take home a guitar.

For the quiet life, there is Padre Pico, the famed staircase street climbing high into old Santiago. From the top, the whole city shines, and along the steps, Santiagueros gather to play dominoes or cards and to strum guitars.

Other areas. Early in the morning is the best time to walk Loma Pio Rosado, a tree-shaded, bench-lined hill near Santa Lucia Church, dating from 1701. Follow Castillo Duany behind the cathedral, and ask someone to head you toward Pio Rosado.

The Loma del Intendente area, where the first French settlers lived, is south of the cathedral. Here Santiago's first theater, the El Tivoli, and the first hospital, San Juan de Dios, were erected.

WHAT TO SEE

The cathedral, Céspedes Park. The original cathedral was begun in 1528, and the present pink cream-colored building is the fourth to occupy the site. There is a small museum in the church where the main treasures of the cathedral are stored, along with all historical documents pertaining to its development (open Mon.–Sat. 9 a.m.–11 a.m.). Of particular note in the cathedral itself is the large choral area, the seats for which were hand carved from a variety of precious woods and date from 1810. A museum visit is usually followed by a tour of the

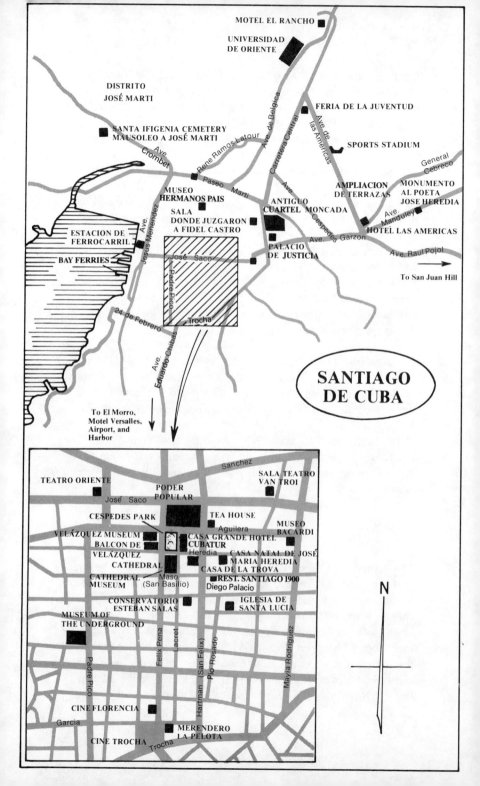

cathedral by the museum director, Luciano Hernandez, but appointments are required.

Casa Heredia, Calle Heredia between Hartman and Pio Rosado. The restored home of the 19th-century poet is now used for poetry readings and other cultural events. Open Mon.–Fri. 8 a.m.–noon and 1 p.m.–5 p.m.

Granjita Siboney, on the Siboney beach road, 8 miles from Santiago. This small farm was rented by the Castro rebels to provide a base from which to prepare the Moncada attack. The road to the farm is lined with monuments, each one dedicated to a soldier who died at Moncada and noting simply the fighter's name and occupation. The farmhouse itself contains a museum which details conditions leading up to and events following the assault. On display are uniforms, weapons and personal possessions, including the rebels' shopping lists. There also are the newspaper stories that appeared after the attack, reporting outrage at the murder and torture of the captured rebels. Only six attackers were actually killed in the battle. The rest—about 68—were captured and killed in cold blood by the Batista army, which left bodies strewn around the farm in simulation of battle. Open Tues.—Sun. 9 a.m.—t p.m.; closed Mon.

Moncada Barracks, Trinidad and Central Highway. Site of the first attack against Batista on July 26, 1953, the barracks has been converted into a primary school. However, the first wing of the building contains a museum which outlines the history of Cuba from the Indian period to the Revolution. Details of the Moncada attack are provided, with a small model outlining the maneuvers. There are also valuable and interesting photos of the guerrillas training in Mexico and camped in the Sierra Maestra. The closing rooms of the museum depict Cuba's advances since the Revolution, under the slogan "This is the banner of Moncada." Open Mon. 8 a.m.–6 p.m., Tues.–Sat. 8 a.m.—10 p.m., Sun 8 a.m.—noon.

Santa Ifigenia Cemetery, Avenida de las Américas, north of the town center. Cemeteries are always sociologically informative, and Santa Ifigenia is particularly so. Before the Revolution, the cemetery was segregated by race and social position, and some private mausoleums are as grand as Martí's. Martí's tomb was placed so that it would always lie in the sun. The sculpted shields around the tomb symbolize the six original Cuban provinces. Carlos Manuel de Céspedes is also buried here.

Jose Martí Housing District, north of Avenue Crombet, about 10 minutes from the city center. A project begun in 1965 to replace the San Pedrido slum adjacent, this was one of the Revolution's earliest large-scale housing efforts, and indeed one of the prettiest—the trees have grown, the gardens have bloomed. There are 40,000 inhabitants, 5 day-care centers, 6 primary schools, and recreation and sports facilities. Visitors are welcome to walk around the district, but schools and day-care centers are off-limits without advance permission.

Morro Castle, on Santiago Bay. Begun in 1640 and completed in 1642, this fortress is perfectly positioned at the mouth of the bay. It was designed by Antonelli, the Italian engineer who also designed Havana's Morro. Having undergone extensive restoration, the castle is in nearly perfect condition but is virtually empty except for a storage room containing some colonial furniture and a wood crucifix dating from the late 17th century. A small bar outside the Morro serves cold drinks and ice cream, with a patio overlooking the sea. The view of the Oriente coast from the castle and bar is incomparable, and sunsets and sunrises here are among Cuba's most memorable. Open Mon.–Sun. 9 a.m.–5 p.m.

Zocapa Point and Cayo Granma, on Santiago Bay. Visible from the Morro, Zocapa Point is the peninsula which juts into the bay, accessible by car and then on foot or by boat. It is a small fishermen's colony with fine wooden houses and an old cemetery.

Cayo Granma (formerly called Cayo Smith for the English slave trader who lived there) is the island in the middle of the bay that seems to have been plucked from the Mediterranean. Today, 1,397 inhabitants commute to and from their homes on the Cayo to offices and factories in Santiago. Some still make their living fishing. There is a tiny, tree-shaded park where the islanders gather for a beer and a game of dominoes. There is also a small grocery store, several schools, a Coppelita ice-cream stand, and a series of large, impressive wooden harbor buildings housing the Pioneer camp and harbor control offices. Boat construction is a major industry of the Cayo as well.

Cubatur has been contemplating a sunset cruise in Santiago harbor to include a stop at Cayo Granma. In the meantime, the Cayo can be reached by ferry from the Alameda harbor in Santiago for 1 peso. Boats leave roughly every hour, but beware of erratic work-on-demand schedules. You can also rent a speedboat and driver for 3 pesos per hour at the Punta Gorda restaurant, opposite the Cayo and about 10 minutes from downtown Santiago. Though more expensive than the ferry, this allows more freedom of movement and permits an interesting tour along the Punta Gorda beachhead, where wealthy Santiagueros once lived.

Sunset is best for the bay, and once serendipitously, my Punta Gorda speedboat broke down just in time for me to watch the sky go orange, and for the bay water to break into the flickering lights of fish swimming close to the surface. After some admirable rowing by the boatmen, we were finally "rescued" by a ferryboat which had been summoned to our side by the SOS signals of a nearby Soviet oil-tanker.

Other sites of interest. *Park Abel Santamaria*, Trinidad between Central Highway and Calle Nueva, commemorates the Revolutionary fighter. Open Mon.—Fri. 8 a.m.—noon and 2 p.m.—6 p.m., Sat. 8 a.m.—noon; closed Sun. The *birthplace of Antonio Maceo*, Calle Los Maceos between Rastro and Corona, is open Tues.–Sat. 8 a.m.–noon and 2 p.m.–6 p.m., Sun. 8 a.m.–noon; closed Mon. *El Viso*, on the road to El Caney, is a small fort of the colonial period.

MUSEUMS

Museum of Colonial Art, Casa Velázquez, on Felix Pena, Céspedes Park. This former residence of Diego de Velázquez, first colonizer of Cuba, has been converted into a magnificent museum containing furniture of the Spanish period. The house was begun in 1516 and completed in 1520. Some outstanding pieces are the *tinajero*, a water-filtering cabinet of mahogany, which passes water through a porous stone and into a waiting vessel; the smoker's chairs; the *ropero* for displaying crystal; and the ceramic bowls in the Spanish-style kitchen. The *vitrales* are particularly beautiful. Much of the furniture in the house was built with wood cut in Cuba, sent to Spain, and returned to Cuba as tables and chairs. Open Tues.–Sat. noon–5:15 p.m., Sun. 8 a.m.—noon and 4 p.m.—8 p.m.; closed Mon.

Museum Hermanos Pais, Avenida General Bandarez #226, between Trinidad and Habana. This simple house was the home of the Pais brothers, underground heroes who were killed during the Revolution. The house contains personal possessions, clothing, and documents pertaining to their role in the Revolution. Open Mon. 2 p.m.–6 p.m., Tues.–Sat. 8 a.m.–noon and 2 p.m.–6 p.m.; closed Sun.

Bacardi Museum, Pio Rosado between Aguilera and Heredia. This collection of archaeological artifacts illustrates local Indian culture as well as more distant ones. There are Peruvian mummies from the Paracas period, one Egyptian mummy, and Cuban and European paintings. Open Mon. 2 p.m.–8 p.m.; Tues.–Sat. 8 a.m.–10 p.m., Sun. 10 a.m.–4 p.m. (tel. 4240)

Museum of the Underground. (Museo de Clandestinidad) Loma del Intendente, corner Padre Pico and Santa Rita. This museum details specific actions of the July 26 Movement before and during the Revolution, in a beautiful reconstructed colonial mansion. Open Tues.—Sat. 8 a.m.—noon and 2 p.m.—6 p.m., Sun. 8 a.m.—noon; closed Mon.

CULTURAL ACTIVITIES

Santiago supports almost innumerable cultural groups, an art school, a music school, Cuba's only magician school, and a musical instrument factory.

The most well-known groups are the Santiago Chorus, the

Conjunto Dramático de Oriente (theater), the Symphony and the Conjunto Folklórico (dance). Following is a list of regular events, but specific schedules can be obtained from the Ministry of Culture, located at Carniceria #461 slightly outside town (tel. 7935), or from Cubatur.

Casa de la Trova, Heredia Street 208 between San Felix and Lacret. In what seems to be the most ancient building in Santiago—it dates from the 18th century—with dark wood-ribbed swinging doors and a nostalgic photo collection on the walls, the heavy tones of the *trova* reverberate. This folk ballad form originated in Santiago de Cuba, and today trained professionals as well as talented amateurs make their way to the Casa each day to sing and be sung to. Admission is free. Manuel Castillo, himself a *trovador* and the Casa administrator, is happy to welcome tourists with a genuine interest in the music. Photography is permitted, but tape recordings are not, unless you have express permission. Activities are usually held Wed. and Sat. around 8 p.m., and Sun. around 9 a.m. Check locally, however.

Teatro Muñecos, at the Teatro Guignol, Maceo Street, one block from the Cathedral. This children's puppet theater usually performs Tues.–Sat. 7 p.m., Sun. 10 a.m. and 5 p.m.

Teatrova, at the teatro Guignol. This drama and trova combination can usually be seen Fri., Sat., and Sun. at 8 p.m.

Poetry readings, Casa Heredia, Calle Heredia between Hartmann and Pio Rosado. The readings are given in Spanish, Fri. 8:30 p.m.

Concerts in Céspedes Park, Thurs. and Sun., 8:30 p.m.

Art Galleries. The following are open Tues.–Sat. 2 p.m.–8 p.m., closed Mon.: *Galería de Arte de Oriente*, Call Lacret #656, between Aguilera and Heredia; and *Galería de UNEAC*, corner of Saco and San Augustin. *The Santiago Exposition Hall*, Saco between Placido and Barnada, usually mounts temporary political exhibitions. Check hours locally. *Casa de la*

Amistad, Maso (San Basilio) between Pio Rosado and Hartmann (tel. 9445) occasionally sponsors art shows.

Carnival in Santiago. The most colorful of all Cuban carnivals is Santiago's. La Trocha—Avenida 24 de Febrero—lights up with dancers, floats, and merrymaking.

HOTELS IN SANTIAGO

Motel Versalles, 3 miles from the city center, just outside the airport (tel. 85152-4). Excellent food. Clearly the best in the city, it is also one of the best in Cuba, and one of the few to make extensive use of wood and native materials. A workshop of weavers on the premises have made the backboard of the reception desk, the chairs in the lobby, the menu covers, etc. 60 rooms, located in low rise bungalow groups, all with bath, hot water, radio, and telephone. Swimming pool is the biggest plus, though the location is somewhat inconvenient. Rates: twin, 18 pesos; single, 15.

Hotel Las Américas, Avenida de las Américas, 10 minutes from center of town (tel. 8046). This pleasant new hotel is modern and clean, though the rooms are small in size. 68 rooms, all with private bath, no hot water, no pool, but located close to the center of town. Excellent restaurant and lively cabaret-bar. Rates: twin, 15 pesos; single, 14.

Motel El Rancho, overlooking the city, about 10 minutes from the center (tel. 8991-3). The view here is spectacular. 30 rooms in bungalow groups, simply furnished, some with hot water, no pool. Excellent Cuban-style restaurant and cabaret. Rates: quadruple, 16 pesos; triple, 10; twin, 8.

Casa Grande, Céspedes Park. This beautiful grande-dame hotel is presently undergoing renovation. The patio is a favorite gathering place for visitors in the city. Excellent location, but very simple accommodation. 60 rooms, all with bath, no hot water. Rates: twin, 7 pesos; single, 6. Book through Cubatur.

San Pedro del Mar, on Santiago Bay, 20 minutes from the

center of town. San Pedro is best for those who have private transportation. 34 cabins on the beach, pool, restaurant, and cabaret. Rates: twin, 10 pesos; single, same. Book through Cubatur.

NIGHTLIFE IN SANTIAGO

San Pedro del Mar has the liveliest cabaret and dance floor, but El Rancho is not far behind. Casa Grande has a rooftop bar which affords the best views of the city.

RESTAURANTS IN SANTIAGO

All the hotels have restaurants; probably the best is in Motel Versalles, with El Rancho second. In addition, however, try:

Santiago 1900, San Basilio between Hartmann and Pio Rosado. Undoubtedly one of Cuba's best and loveliest restaurants, Santiago 1900 is housed in a former Bacardi mansion, with garden patio and unusually colored sea green and white *vitrales*—an absolute must. Cubabellas—cocktails made with a daiquiri base with mint and bitters added—are graciously served *al patio* with hors d'oeurves. Dinner is table d'hôte, served and prepared by students of the National Gastronomy School. All furnishings are turn-of-the-century.

A highlight, however, is the music provided by the unlikely-named Trio Kon-Tiki, an ensemble of female pianist and male drum and base players. They have been together for 20 years, 6½ of them at Santiago 1900. Gracious and professional, the trio earnestly pours forth Cuban favorites as well as nostalgic familiar tunes. It is one of those unique travel moments to be dining in Revolutionary Cuba, in a colonial Spanish restaurant, listening to the dreamy piano strains of "As Time Goes By." (FC)

Punta Gorda restaurant, opposite Cayo Granma. This former yacht club now specializes in seafood dining. The outdoor dining area affords wonderful views of the bay. (FC)

El Baturro, off Céspedes Park, on Aguilera at San Felix. This small restaurant specializes in chicken and pork dishes. A favorite with Santiagueros.

Santiago Tea House, corner Aguilera and Lacret, on Céspedes Park. In this tiny shop iced and hot tea is served. A fine refreshment spot.

The Library Soda Bar, Biblioteca Elvira Cape, Heredia #259, between Pio Rosado and Hartman, Tel. 4669 and 9126. A quiet perfect spot located in the library, serving soft drinks, including superb mango juice for a few centavos. Favored by students and those who want to take a rest from strolling.

El Bodegon, on the old Plaza de Delores, corner of Aguilera. This is Santiago's answer to Havana's Bodeguita del Medio, featuring Cuban specialties. (M)

Puerto Boniato, 15 miles north of the city. This site, almost 3,000 feet above sea level, provides a lovely view of the city and simple but adequate Cuban-style meals at the Mirador Boniato. (M)

EXCURSIONS

El Cobre and Mayari Arriba are within a day's trip. However, the most common excursion is to Gran Piedra National Park.

Gran Piedra National Park, 20 miles northeast of Santiago, over a narrow circuitous road still frequented by more horse-backed *vacqueros* than automobiles. (In fact, large tourist buses cannot make the trip and so minibuses must be used.) The road winds through the Sierra Maestra to the national park area, some 4,100 feet above sea level, climbing through ravines and hills as the eyes strain to distinguish between the fine shades of green which cover the hills. Verdant with vegetation, including many coffee plants which were introduced by the French, the route is 45 minutes of scenic superlatives.

At the park itself, you can hike up to the Gran Piedra (Great Stone) over a series of steps and trails, and finally up a steel ladder onto the rock's surface. The weak of heart should not attempt the climb, but the view of the mountains and coast is incomparable. The main park attraction is hiking, though horseback riding and other sports are planned. Seven ruined coffee-plantation houses are scattered through the grounds, and one of them, the Isabelica, has been restored and is scheduled to open as a museum in 1979.

In 1974, the government built eight stone and wood cabins in the park. They are lovely, and utterly private. Each has a kitchen, electricity, hot water, fireplace, and rustic furnishings, as well as a balcony from which to contemplate the natural surroundings. Rates: 1 bedroom, 16 pesos; 2 bedrooms, 25. Book through Cubatur, Santiago.

The Mirador Gran Piedra serves excellent Cuban-style food. The ceramic plates and cups used are made locally. (M)

BEACHES OUTSIDE SANTIAGO

The climate in Santiago is hotter and more humid than elsewhere on the island, and relief is often necessary. Few hotels have pools, and the beaches of Oriente generally can't compare in quality with those of the north coast. But the nearest are:

Playa Caleton, 15 miles south of the city on the Siboney road. Cabanas and refreshments are available.

San Pedro del Mar, 6 miles from town, at the harbor mouth. Cabanas and refreshments are available.

The Santiago-Chivirico road, heading west of the city. This excursion is feasible only for those with a car. Once one sheds the city and its ring of industry, the terrain goes wild—rough, craggy, undulating mountains in deep South-Pacific green. The coast here is pocketed with small bays and beaches, perfect for privacy and picnics, especially if you enjoy floating on your back looking up at mountain rises.

SIBONEY. See "Granjita Siboney, Santiago de Cuba." Siboney is also a suburb of Havana.

SOLEDAD BOTANICAL GARDENS. Est. 1852; 43 km (25 mi) SW of Hanabanilla, 25 km (15 mi) from Cienfuegos, Cienfuegos prov.

A 90-acre area devoted to the cultivation of some 2,000 species of endemic and exotic plants, the garden has a rare bamboo collection, as well as 45 of the approximately 60 types of palm tree which can be found in Cuba. It began as a private effort of the Atkins family, sugar magnates who used the territory to test sugarcane strains. Eventually supervision was turned over to Harvard University, but after the Revolution, the Cuban Institute of Botany assumed control. Soledad offers an unparalleled opportunity to explore the flora of Cuba. Open daily 9 a.m.–5 p.m. Closed Mon. An easy side trip from Cienfuegos or Hanabanilla.

SOROA RESORT. 81 km (49 mi) W of Havana in the Sierra del Rosario; Pinar del Río prov.

This mountain resort is located in an area formerly owned by the Spaniard Don Ignacio Soroa, who used the land primarily to cultivate coffee. The resort developed in a series of stages after 1928, when private sulphur baths were installed. Activities include horseback riding, bike riding, and swimming in the Olympic-size pool. For botany enthusiasts, there is an Orchid House with 700 varieties of orchids. Flowering trees are arranged to shade these ornamental plants, which require only partial sunlight.

The somewhat overrated highlight of Soroa is the waterfall, which is reached from the main road via a well-paved path. It's a ten-minute walk through a forest of pine and wind-bent coruba trees, fragrant with refreshing tropical air. The resort itself is attractive, especially if one hikes through the back hills.

The accommodations at Soroa consist of cabins arranged around the pool and through the woods, providing peace and quiet in lost mountain surroundings. 49 rustic cabins, each with running water, toilet and electricity, but no hot water. Restaurant, cabaret and bar also available. Book through Cubatur. Rates (approximate): twin, 10 pesos.

TOPES DE COLLANTES RESORT. 21 km (12 mi) N of Trinidad; Sancti Spíritus prov.

Deep in the Escambray forest, at the end of one of Cuba's most tortuous roads, Topes de Collantes eventually will be one of Cuba's largest resort areas, emphasizing mountain recreation—horseback riding, hiking, bird watching, medicinal baths, and controlled hunting. The resort also provides access to Ancon Beach, the finest on Cuba's south coast. The rugged mountains are covered with pine and palm trees, and the hope is to develop the resort with a minimum of ecological disruption. There is a forestry station nearby, as well as the small town of Topes de Collantes.

A series of hotels is presently under construction; they will vary in category and price so as to make the resort accessible to visitors at every budget level. A heated swimming pool is included in the plans so that the resort can function year-round.

Topes is well-known for its fresh, clear air, and the town is dominated by a heavy stone building which served as a sanitarium before the Revolution. Begun in 1936, the building was completed in 1954. After the Revolution and the eradication of tuberculosis in Cuba, the building was completely sanitized and served as a pedagogical institution for primary-school teachers. It is presently being renovated and will be incorporated into the tourism project. Topes's first hotel was opened in spring, 1978, and the complex will develop gradually as need and construction possibilities dictate. Once finished, Topes will be a self-contained resort, ideally suited to families.

At present, the *Hotel Topes de Collantes* provides pleasant accommodations. It is a brand-new hotel with 250 rooms, each with balcony, air conditioning, hot water, bath, and superb mountain view. Garden terrace in the middle of the hotel, large table, game room. Bar and restaurant.

TRINIDAD. Est. 1514; pop. 35,000; 461 km (276 mi) SE of Havana, 78 km (46 mi) SE of Cienfuegos; Sancti Spíritus prov.

Overlooking the bay of Casilda, tucked in the folds of hills, and seemingly out of the current of time lies Trinidad, preserved and restored—Cuba's national museum city. To walk in it is to harvest images that do not belong to this century. If you have a choice in your schedule, plan to spend at least two nights here, longer if you want to use the nearby beaches.

HISTORY

Diego de Velázquez founded the city near rivers that seemed to promise gold. The Indians of the area panned for it, and in the early years of the city did indeed return some gold to Spain. But once the spectacular treasures of Mexico became available to Spain via Cortés—who had in fact recruited expeditionaries in Trinidad—the gold of Cuba was hardly worth working for.

During the 16th and 17th centuries, Trinidad derived its wealth from a thriving slave trade, both legal and illegal. Its south-central position was perfect for dealing with England via Jamaica, which was clandestine until the English invasion of Cuba in 1762. Naturally, the ready availability of black labor stimulated the development of sugar lands, and several large fortunes were made in Trinidad.

The development of the far superior port at Cienfuegos in the 1820's and 1830's soon eclipsed Casilda, Trinidad's port. Add to this the upheavals in the slave trade, the pressures for abolition, and the events of 1868, and Trinidad was out of business. The owners of large estates broke them up to raise cash to ride out the bad times. During the war of independence, Trinidad sent approximately 1,000 troops into battle, but after the establishment of the Republic, the city slipped from prominence. The "central" system of sugar production never flourished here because the land had already been parceled out. Physically, too, Trinidad was cut off from the Cuban mainstream. If a giant were to stand on the central highway north of the Escambray mountains and reach around them, one can picture him trying vainly to touch Trinidad; it would probably fall between the grasp of both his hands. So it was with communication. The city clumbered in the ruins of a glorious past. Poverty and misery accompanied the lack of progress, and Trinidad's public health and education record was lower than elsewhere in the province.

In the 1950s Trinidad was recognized at least for historic value and declared a national monument. This, however, actually worsened the situation because it prevented any new construction which might have altered the quality of the city. No restoration work was begun until the mid-1960s. Presently, a Restoration Commission controls Trinidad's development, and all building or alteration plans must be submitted for approval. Trinidad is divided into three main areas, with varying degrees of alteration permitted in each. Restoration of the central area, around the Plaza Mayor, is complete, and no exterior or interior alterations are permitted. Projects fan out from the Plaza, revitalizing with paint, refacading with adobe and wood, repaving with cobblestone, reroofing with original stucco tiles.

But despite Trinidad's outright embrace of the past, it is a dynamic city. The streets can be silent with history just as they can be lively with Afro-Latin rhythms or TV news. Walking in Trinidad, one can encounter a sombreroed *vacquero* on horseback delivering bread behind a pickup truck delivering brandnew desks and chairs for a school. One can glance into wide and spacious street level 19th century living rooms, sometimes to catch the sight of a just vacated rocker, its lingering motion breaking rhythmically into the rainbow light field of the *vitrales*. Or one can listen to the hum of machinery in small factories dispersed through town.

A piano teacher lives off the Plaza Mayor, and sometimes the not-quite notes of a hopeful student filter into the square, as do the playful shouts of children playing stickball in the church courtyard, as do the certain tones of the tower bells.

Trinidad is a restoration in process—not prissy, not perfect, and not comparable to the fabulous Mexican and South American cities which have remained in nearly pristine condition—but everywhere in use, living its present. In the indelible shadow of history, elegant and eloquent, it is clearly one of Cuba's highlights.

WHAT TO SEE

Plaza Mayor and the streets of Trinidad. The Plaza Mayor

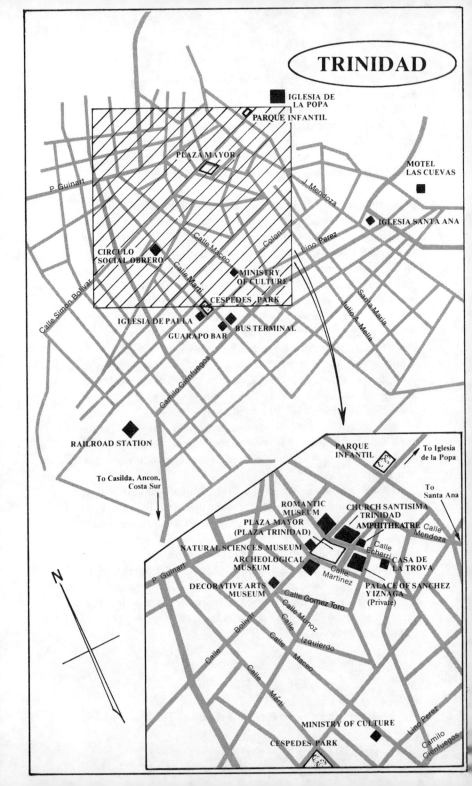

can be described as the centripetal force of Trinidad, and truly the most elegant square in Cuba—landscaped, presided over by royal palms and two bronze hounds vaguely reminiscent of the wolverine Romulus-Remus twins of Rome. A full moon on a clear night over the square is one of those rare travel privileges, and those with flexible schedules should attempt to catch it.

Many of the streets of Trinidad were paved with cobblestone brought from New England as ship ballast. Embedded in many corners are old cannons that formerly served to protect the corners as carriages turned them, but also to denote stature of the house owners.

Bolivar Street, north of the square, has been fully restored, and is one of the city's grandest thoroughfares. Three museums flank the area, as does the Casa de Iznaga, the home of one of Trinidad's oldest families, and still occupied by descendants. Other streets of interest include *Santa Ana and Jose Mendoza streets, Guinart and Villena streets* (note the house at the corner with blue painted facade), and *Calle Nuevo*, ironically one of Trinidad's oldest.

The guarapo bar, corner of Martí and Cienfuegos streets. One of Cuba's few remaining on-the-street stands for the sale of *guarapo* (sugarcane juice) exists in Trinidad. Long stalks of fresh cane are fed through the narrow "mouth" of the press, and milky cane juice is released through a wider opening into a waiting ice-lined bucket. Served cold, *guarapo* is refreshing but very, very sweet.

Iznaga Tower, 8 miles from town. This former sugar estate has the house and slave-watching tower preserved.

Other Trinidad activities. With advance permission, obtained through Cubatur or your sponsor, you can visit: *El Alfarero Ceramica*, a pottery workshop on the city's outskirts where ceramics are exhibited and produced; *the weaving factory*, a small artisan shop where straw-hat weaving and basketwork are done by hand, located on Bolivar Street in a building dating from 1879 that used to house the Sociedad de la Luz, "a social club for negroes;" and *Taller Palacio de Artisano*, an artisan workshop on Guinart Street.

CHURCHES

La Santisima Trinidad, Plaza Mayor, Calle Echerri. The site has been occupied by a number of different constructions, and the current church dates from 1894. There are fine mahogany altars and unusual carved statuary.

Iglesia de Paula, Céspedes Park. This church was built in 1872 and is one of the oldest churches still functioning in Trinidad. It features beautiful use of marble and carved wood throughout.

Iglesia de la Popa, north of Plaza Mayor. Built in 1726 on a hill overlooking the city, this church is used only twice a year now, during Holy Week. It affords a full panorama of the city and the bay.

Iglesia de Santa Ana, Jose Mendoza Street. An empty, ruined hull scheduled for restoration, Santa Ana dates from the 1700s.

MUSEUMS

All museums in Trinidad are subject to the following schedule: Winter (Dec.–May): Open Tues.–Sat. 9 a.m.–1 p.m. and 2 p.m.–5 p.m., Sun. 9 a.m.–1 p.m.; closed Mon. Summer (June–Nov.): Tues.–Sat. 8 a.m.–noon and 2 p.m.–6 p.m., Sun. 2 p.m.–6 p.m.; closed Mon.

The Romantic Museum, Palacio Brunet, Echerri Street, above Plaza Mayor. The house was built before 1740 as the home of Trinidad's Brunet family. It now houses a collection of furniture from the romantic period, although only an armchair in the master bedroom actually belonged to the family. The museum was opened in 1974, after a restoration period of three years followed by a two-year research period during which the collection was assembled. Under the supervision of Carlos Joaquin Zerquera, historian of Trinidad, every detail of the house was painstakingly researched. The main staircase has been decorated with a spiraling vine design that comes as close as possible to the original, based on records of similar houses.

Notable immediately are the wooden window screens with mediopunto arches, carved from cedar, made in Cuba in 1807. Other beautiful work includes the dining room set with Victorian English table and chairs made in Cuba in 1835. The ceiling in the main hall is solid carved cedar, worked from 1770–1780. Off the museum patio is a small exhibition room used for temporary shows, especially for popular artworks done by museum employees. This is clearly one of the finest museums in Cuba—a must.

Archaeological Museum, Plaza Mayor, corner of Bolivar and Martinez. Housed in the former Ortiz family palace, the museum was inaugurated in 1976. Only the first floor is currently operative. It contains Indian artifacts and materials, as well as explanatory data designed for children as well as adults. Numerous hand tools, pots, and other implements are included, along with skeletal remains. There are also reproductions of cave paintings and drawings by José Martinez of the Taino and Siboney Indian rites. The museum is the lovechild of archaeologist Alfredo Renkin and his wife, Manuela Bravo, who are also responsible for the Museum of Natural Sciences.

Museum of Natural Sciences, Plaza Mayor, diagonally opposite from the Archaeological Museum. This museum houses an extensive collection of Cuban fauna and flora, which includes models and specimens. Note the manatee and the guaican, a suction fish the Taino Indians used as a hook to catch other fish.

Museum of Decorative Arts, Calle Bolivar, corner Gomez Toro, a block south of Plaza Mayor. Scheduled for opening in 1980, this museum is housed in the former Cantero palace— where, 19th century travelers reported, the Roman style bath once spouted eau de cologne for the ladies and gin for the men. Currently in restoration, presumably without intention to recreate the bath. The restoration work can be watched through the windows on Calle Bolivar and will be of special interest to artists and architects.

CULTURAL ACTIVITIES

Casa de la Trova, Calle Echerri, one block east of Plaza Mayor. This restored house offers performances by Cuban singers, usually in the evening, but check with the Ministry of Culture or Cubatur. Watch for *madrugadas*, performances of a regional song sung in the streets in the early morning.

Ministry of Culture, Maceo Street between Lino Pérez and Colon. This office coordinates all cultural events, including outdoor park concerts. The Conjunto Folklorico de Trinidad is especially noteworthy and performs African dances originally brought to the region by slaves.

Culture Week, a full week of activities, usually in late summer or early fall. The stone amphitheater next to Santisima Trinidad church is the focal point. (tel. 2337)

Cubatur, Calle Martí, between Cienfuegos and Lino Perez, near Cespedes Park (tel. 2554). Cubatur can be contacted for further information about cultural events in Trinidad.

HOTELS

Hotel Ancon, next to Costa Sur, on lovely beach. Brand new, 192 rooms with all amenities. Scheduled to open in 1979.

Motel las Cuevas, on a hill overlooking the city, about half a mile from Plaza Mayor (tel. 2178 or 2680 or 2633). This is by far one of Cuba's most charming hotels, although amenities are simple—stone cottages, all with balconies and a view of the bay and valley. At night, one can sip *mojitos* on the terrace and listen to the sound of clopping hoofs on old stone as the grazing horses of a nearby ranch drift onto hotel property. 54 rooms, each with shower and toilet, no hot water yet. Pool, restaurant, bar, no air conditioning. Rates: twin, 12 pesos; single, same.

Hotel Costa Sur, 5.4 miles from Trinidad at Ancon Beach (tel. 2107 or 2773 or 2074). Inaugurated in 1975, this modern hotel has a large swimming pool and access to a fine beach. 72 rooms, all with hot water, bath, air conditioning and radio. Rates: twin, 15 pesos; single, 13.

The reef formations and sea life off Casilda port and Ancon Beach are reported to be among the best in Cuba. Cubatur is currently developing these resources and will use the Costa Sur and other area hotels as a center of snorkeling and diving activities. Check with hotel receptionists for equipment rental information.

RESTAURANTS

Trinidad lacks sufficient restaurant facilities, though the *El Pavito* on Calle Bolivar (turkey specialties) and *El Canada* in Céspedes Park serve simple meals at moderate prices. An elegant colonial restaurant is being planned for the pink building behind Santisima Trinidad amphitheater, but it will be some time in coming.

For the time being, the Trinidad hotels offer the best dining facilities. Las Cuevas Motel serves meals in one of the caves that lends the hotel its name, as well as in the main dining room. Food is exceptionally good. A house dessert is the *cascos de naranja*, whole orange peels, boiled and then syruped. Not as sweet as it sounds, and very delicious. The Costa Sur Hotel also serves excellent food. Those with private transportation could try the restaurant at the new Topes de Collantes Hotel. (See "Topes de Collantes Resort.")

TURIGUANO. 28 km (17 mi) from Moron, 64 km (38 mi) N of Ciego de Ávila; Ciego de Ávila prov.

With advance permission, this genetic cattle-breeding plan can be visited and has been included in certain special interest tours.

Before the Revolution, Turiguano was a private estate used for cattle raising and banana export. It was separated from the mainland by swampy marshes, with only boat access. About 25 or 30 families lived on the land, all of whom worked for the American owner. After the Revolution, an intensive development project began. The swamps were drained, and a two-lane paved highway built. Of the 40,000 available acres, 20,000 are now functioning as part of a cattle-breeding project aimed at producing high-yield Santa Gertrudis beef cattle.

The first houses in the development were built in 1960–61 in Dutch style—and the flat, reclaimed landscape and architecture do indeed give you the feeling of having just driven into Holland. Since 1960, new apartments have been added for the more than 1,000 inhabitants. The complex has its own day-care center, social club, and primary school, with a secondary school planned. New pastures have opened, and hog production to meet Turiquano's needs was introduced. The plan is virtually self-sufficient, even to the point of having extended the banana groves to supply the inhabitants.

At the guest house, pet deer roam the garden and rocking chairs line the back porch. The La Tinaja beach is 6 miles from the town itself and offers swimming as well as a restaurant and cabaret.

VARADERO. Est. 1880; Pop. 9,000; 34 km (20 mi) NE of Havana, 140 km (84 mi) E of Havana; Matanzas prov.

There is no doubt about where you are the moment you enter Varadero. Lush landscaping, Spanish-style and modern villas, tall sea pine discreetly placed to provide privacy—it is clear that the gentry of the world once played at Varadero. The peninsula juts slightly north into the Caribbean—ten miles of fine white sand, so fine it slides like silk across the feet, and transparent, equally silky sea, with a graduated stoneless bottom. A paragon beach.

HISTORY

The peninsula supported Indians before Columbus and was called Punta Hicacos for the trees that were prevalent. The Spanish exploited the sea and forest resources, developing small charcoal and salt-pork businesses. However, little attention was paid to the potential of the beach until the turn of the century, when private summer houses began cropping up. By 1910, the Hotel Varadero was operating, providing accommodation to the wealthy residents of Cardenas.

In 1930, the U.S. industrialist Irene Du Pont made extensive property purchases and built a large estate. Thereafter, resort development quickened, mainly on large tracts of land held for private recreational use. The prime beach real estate supported individual homes, inadvertently saving Varadero from the high-rise blight which was creeping in on places like Miami and Honolulu. In the late 1950s, however, hotel speculation was spurred by the construction of the Varadero International, a child of Miami's Fountainbleau if ever there was one. However, construction virtually ceased with the Revolution, as did U.S. investment. Building has only recently resumed, and new high-rises are being constructed off the beach. Development plans for Varadero include an underwater marine park emphasizing ecological order.

Prior to the Revolution, virtually the entire length of the beach was in private hands. On March 17, 1959, the beaches of Cuba were declared open to the public, and many Cubans who had lived within sight of Varadero Beach for years walked on it for the first time. Some of the beachfront homes remain private, but since most owners left Cuba after the Revolution, the villas have been converted into hotel complexes where tourists and Cubans can rent rooms or entire houses at moderate prices.

Varadero remained active as a resort all through the years when U.S. citizens were forbidden to travel to Cuba, and Canadian tourists have constituted the majority of foreign guests. Aside from the beach, there are numerous recreation possibilities, sports and restaurants, plus a town which in itself offers interesting side activities. Varadero Beach is truly a self-contained resort excellent for family vacations, and surely Cuba's greatest tourism asset.

THE LAY OF THE LAND

Cubatur. All activities at Varadero are coordinated through Cubatur, which maintains a representative in every hotel and villa complex. The main office is located on Via Blanca, near the Darsenas boat docks (tel. 061-580 or 2506).

Street Pattern. Cross streets perpendicular to the beach begin at Kawama suburb in the west and are consecutively numbered from 1 to 69, where they end at La Torre suburb in the east. Thereafter the cross streets are lettered from A to L until Las Americas suburb, where they disappear. First Avenue parallels the beach between 11th and L streets, with Playa Avenue cutting in closer to the beach between 30th and 54th streets, and Camino del Mar from 3rd to 15th street. Maps are usually available in the hotels.

Useful Varadero addresses. The following may prove helpful during an extended stay:

Polyclinic, First Avenue at 60th Street
Police, First Avenue at 38th Street
Shoe Repair, First Avenue at 50th Street
Pharmacy, First Avenue at 42nd Street
Varadero Bookstore, First Avenue at 41st Street (Because Varadero is so clearly a resort, many more foreign language books are available here.)
Coppelia, First Avenue at 46th Street
Public Lockers, Calle 44 on First Avenue (8,000 lockers built since 1959 for visitors to Varadero who are not hotel guests)

CULTURAL EVENTS

Varadero Amphitheater, Via Blanca and South Autopista, is the scene of dramatic performances, dance performances, and political rallies.

Varadero Exposition Gallery, First Avenue at 46th Street, rotates art and photo exhibits. The bookstore sells political posters and books in foreign languages, otherwise difficult to find. Open daily 4 p.m.–10 p.m.; closed Mon.

Culture Week is usually Dec. 7–14 and offers a series of special events. Varadero's Ministry of Culture office sponsors numerous concerts, dances, poetry readings, and other events for the citizens of Varadero to which the tourist is enthusiastically welcome. If a schedule of events is not available from Cubatur, contact the Ministry of Culture directly (tel. 2793, First Avenue at 23rd Street).

HOTELS

Usually, hotels have been preselected and booked to travel wholesalers on a package basis. However, individual travelers can make their own reservations through Cubatur.

Deluxe

Varadero International, Las Americas Avenue and 70th Street (tel. 553-260 or 3011). A full service modern resort hotel, with sweeping driveway and manicured lawns, considered Varadero's best. 160 large rooms, all with air conditioning, balcony, hot water, private bath. Swimming pool and spectacular beach. The cabaret here is Varadero's star nightlife attraction. Ask for sea view, second floor. Rates: twin, 24 pesos; single 19.

First-CLass

Oasis Hotel, at the east entrance of Varadero, Avenue A (tel. 540-290 or 2902 or 2946). Accommodation arranged in two-story bungalows around pool. Smallish, quiet, and removed from central city. 126 rooms, each with private bath, terrace, air conditioning, radio, and telephone. Rates: triple, 25 pesos; twin, 20; single, 15.

Hotel Kawama, Camino del Mar and 1st Street, in Kawama suburb (tel. 3113 or 218-317). Varadero's most elegant, if one prefers timeless Spanish wood and stone construction. Built in 1934 and subsequently expanded. Main "hacienda" hotel with individual houses adjacent. Lovely beach. 46 rooms in houses; 63 in main hotel, all with private bath, air conditioning, and hot water. Beach cabanas are very pleasant, scattered among uva caleta and pine trees. No pool. Rates: triple, 29 pesos; twin, 24; single, 19.

Villas Tortuga, Barlovento and Sotavento; First Avenue and 4th Street, 11th Street and 13th streets respectively. Pleasant villa complexes with same rates and atmosphere as Kawama. Phone Cubatur for reservations.

Villa Los Cocos, First Avenue at 22nd Street (tel. 2552). A small villa complex near the beach; no pool. Rates not available.

Hotel La Caribbean (formerly Vapi Apartments), First Avenue at 30th Street (tel. 3310 or 3319). A several-story modern construction with 117 rooms, all with air conditioning, hot water, but no phones in rooms; pool, cafeteria, and restaurant. Rates: twin, 14 pesos; no singles or triples.

Granma Complex, First Avenue between 24th and 34th streets. To be completed by 1980; a tourist "city" with 25 buildings and capacity for 3,000 persons; 2 pools, dock, recreation area.

Hotel Imperial (formerly Villa Delfines) and Derovera Apartments, Playa Avenue and 39th Street (tel. 3305 or 3230). Joint administration. Spanish-style stone construction, 39 rooms with air conditioning, but no phones; no pool; restaurant, bar, shops. Rates available from Cubatur.

Arenas Blancas, First Avenue between 64th and 67th streets (tel. 2638 or 148-338). Pleasant white stone buildings; includes entire houses for rent and individual rooms. 75 rooms, air conditioning. Rates: twin, 14 pesos.

Marazul Hotel, Las Americas Avenue at 69th Street, same administration as International Hotel (tel. 2217 at Marazul or 3011 at International). 32 cabanas, pool, air conditioning, apartment complex with restaurant privileges at International Hotel. Ideal for families; most units have stove and refrigerator. Rates: 3 bedrooms, 30 pesos; 2 bedrooms, 22; 1 bedroom, 15.

Cabanas del Sol, Las Americas Avenue at 67th Street (tel. 2828). Low-rise stone cabanas. 139 rooms, no pool; air conditioning, restaurant, bar, telephone in rooms, hot water. Rates: twin, 22 pesos; single, 19.

Villa Cuba, First Avenue and C Streets (tel. 2975). Lovely tree-shaded house complex, no pool, 106 rooms, restaurant, bar, hot water, no phones in room, right on the beach. Rates: twin room, 12 pesos; 3-room house, 23.

Pullman Hotel, First Avenue at 69th Street, not open to tourists but interesting to see, since it was one of Varadero's earliest. A fine old stone construction.

Tourist-Class

Cabanas Tainos, Avenida Las Americas at extreme east end of Varadero. Rustic wood cabins scattered through the woods. No hot water. For those who like to rough it and be far from the crowd. Mosquito repellent recommended. 27 cabins and 78 rooms. Book through Cubatur.

Hotel Leto, Playa at 43rd Street. Youth hotel with simple amenities, no hot water. Rates: 12 pesos per person.

Hotel Playa Azul, Playa at 34th Street, similar to Hotel Leto.

RESTAURANTS

All the hotels or villas either have their own restaurants or provide dining exchange privileges at a nearby facility, which is specified when you check in. If you choose to eat in a hotel or villa other than your own, advance reservations are required. Restaurants in Varadero range from snack bars to deluxe. Among the best are:

Las Americas, Avenida Las Americas, about 10 minutes east of International Hotel (tel. 3415). The magnificent former Du Pont estate. Lunch or dinner impeccably served in the first-floor former library. The food is among the best in Cuba. Expensive (about 10 dollars per person with glass of wine, for lunch). Reservations imperative. Closed Monday. (D)

Albacora, Playa at 59th Street (tel. 3111). Often used by tour groups for "seafood fiestas." An exceptionally lovely restaurant with large outdoor terrace facing the sea. It specializes in fish and shellfish. (FC)

Restaurant Caleton, First Avenue and A, near Cabanas del Sol (tel. 448). Cuban and continental food. (M)

Castel Nuevo, First Avenue and 11th Street. Italian food and pizza. (M)

RECREATION AND SPORTS

Boating. At Darsenas boat basin, all types of craft can be rented. Speedboats cost 3 pesos per hour per person. Fishing safaris via large schooner are organized regularly, for a minimum of 15 persons. The entire day, with lunch, costs 15 pesos and can be booked through Cubatur at your hotel.

Scuba diving. All the major hotels have a scuba instructor in residence. Check with Cubatur for schedule of classes and status of the planned marine park. The rates are 6 pesos per class, 8 pesos per 30 minutes of diving. French equipment for rent.

Snorkeling. It's best to bring your own snorkel and mask, although some equipment is available. The best snorkeling is at the western extreme of the beach, heading toward Matanzas. Be sure to check with resident diver, since entry to the snorkeling areas is tricky due to changing sea conditions.

Tennis. There are courts at the International Hotel, Kawama Hotel, and Villa Cuba, with dirt surfaces. The cost is 1 peso per hour with equipment, 50 centavos without. (Guests of other hotels may use the facilities.)

Horseback riding. Horses are corraled at the Villa Cuba or Hotel Oasis, though Cubatur at your own hotel can make the arrangements. 3 pesos per hour.

Golf. There is a 9-hole regulation course at Las Americas Estate. Clubs are available for rent. The cost is 6 pesos per round. There are few handcarts, no motorized carts. Caddies are available with advance notice, booked through Cubatur.

Bicycling. This is an excellent way to see Varadero, best in late afternoon when the heat of the day has broken. Rent through Villa Cuba, Hotel Oasis, or Cabanas del Sol at 50 centavos per hour. Many tandems are available.

Mini-Golf (Golfito), First Avenue and 42nd Street.

Cinema, Playa Avenue at 43rd Street.

NIGHTLIFE

Varadero has constant nightlife. Each hotel sponsors a weekly *Noche Cubana* ("Cuban Night") on rotating days, featuring outdoor dining and dancing, usually roast pig with full trappings, all you can eat. The most outstanding cabaret shows are *Varadero International,* a mini-Tropicana, reservations required (tel. 553-260), dinner served in the nightclub, casual dress not permitted; *Oasis Cabaret*, Oasis Hotel, reservations required; and *La Rada*, Villa Blanca near Darsenas boat basin.

BARS

Every hotel and villa has its own bar. In addition, there is *La Cueva del Pirata* on the south highway. This deep, dark cave, dimly lit and romantic, is a favorite with lovers of privacy. It has dancing and a cabaret show. Book through Cubatur, and be sure to request return transportation in advance. There is no phone in the cave to call a cab. The 3-peso-per-person minimum includes 2 drinks. Open 9 p.m.–2:15 a.m.; closed Tuesdays. Also try the *Club Kastellito*, Playa between 49th and 50th Streets.

WHAT TO DO

It will be hard to tear yourself away from the exquisite beach, and indeed Varadero is primarily a sun-and-fun resort. However, the town itself and the nearby city excursions add immeasurably to Varadero's tourist possibilities. One can easily spend a full week here.

Walking. An extremely pleasant activity here. Varadero offers superb examples of the ornately carved wooden "balloon frame" houses which were built in Cuba during the late 19th century. Best examples are on First Avenue in the lower 20s blocks.

INIT train. A jitney-style open-air train that tours the resort area regularly. It makes stops at all the major hotels, and the nearest Cubatur representative will have the accurate schedule.

Varadero Archaeological Museum, Las Americas road. The Ambrosio cave where pre-Columbian Indian pictographs were discovered. The museum was in preparation in 1978. Cubatur can provide up-to-date information.

EXCURSIONS FROM VARADERO

Cubatur offers the following optional excursions from Varadero, with guide and deluxe motor-coach transportation provided (see the alphabetical index for information about each location): *Matanzas*, half-day tour including the museums; *Guama*, full-day tour; *Havana*, one-day trip or overnight excursion; *Cienfuegos and Trinidad*, one-day trip; *The Triunvirato genetic plan*, half-day trip. Obtain a schedule and book through the Cubatur representative in your hotel.

In addition, the cities of *Matanzas* and *Cardenas* are within a few pesos by taxi and public bus. Each city offers a full day of sightseeing possibilities. The *Varadero Bus Station* is located at 2nd Avenue at 14th Street.

During the sugar havest, December—June, Canadian tour operators have sponsored weekly *cane-cutting excursions* (usually on Sunday mornings) for tourists who want to watch, or participate in, the cutting process. These tours were successful and will be expanded in 1979–80. Contact the Cubatur representative at your hotel for details.

VEDADO. Section of Havana (see "Havana").

VICTORIA DE LAS TUNAS. Est. 1759; pop. 99,604; 76 km (45 mi) W of Holguín, 123 km (73 mi) E of Camagüey; Las Tunas prov.

The town begins (or ends, depending on the direction you are traveling) the great plains of Cuba. Originally it was called simply Las Tunas, but a Spanish governor renamed it to commemorate an 1869 military victory against the Cubans. The city changed hands twice thereafter, but finally in 1895 the Cubans won it, and the honor of the name, back again. Today, the city is a hub of the cane and cattle land around it, a commercial center similar to Ciego de Ávila. It straddles the road for about a mile and then dissolves into open pasture land.

The El Cornito hotel and restaurant complex is located about seven miles west of the tow center, in itself not worth an overnight, but handy to know about for a refreshment stop after lots of driving.

VIÑALES. Est. 1895; pop. 15,000; 25 km (15 mi) N of Pinar del Río, 200 km (120 mi) W of Havana; Pinar del Río prov.

BACKGROUND

The approach to this region from the southern highway—via curving, climbing, two-lane road—wends its way through verdant landscape to reach one of Cuba's most scenic spots.

The area's fame derives from the strange rock formations which interrupt Viñales valley as though the earth had bubbled up, burst into flat-top ridges, and then subsided. Actually, these limestone hills, called *mogotes*, date from the Jurassic Period (160 million years ago), when the valley was roofed. Eventually the roof collapsed, and what remained were the column "supports."

The area is worth a visit, not only for its scenery but for its country lifestyle. Small cottages and farms dot the valley; patches of tobacco, malanga, and some citrus are the main source of income. Most of the farmers used to rent the land and receive approximately 2½ pesos for a quintal of tobacco. Today the state guarantees them market price—36 pesos in 1977. In addition, the valley has schools, polyclinics, and other installations which did not exist before the Revolution.

WHAT TO SEE

The valley. For nature lovers, a walk or horseback ride through the valley celebrates the philharmonia of the earth. Like a vast sheet of litmus paper, Vinales seems to take on shades of green before your eyes. Occasionally egrets lift off, white specks against the valley; ponies roam. Walks are best in the afternoon, when the valley fills with the sights and sounds of the day's ending.

The town. Viñales is a thriving, cowboy-style mountain town with a church plaza, bookstore, and workers' social club. One of its oldest houses, on the main street, is a wooden gingerbread structure still in private hands. An arbor leads to it, the house itself is vine covered, and in winter the bright orange flowers of the *jubia d'oro* drape over the entrance like royal mantle.

The mural. Approximately 2.5 miles north of the town, there is an unpaved turnoff leading into the hills. About 1 km (.6 miles) from the turnoff, the Cuban National Academy of Sciences painted a gigantic mural intended to depict the geological and anthropological evolution of the area. The mural itself has been weather-damaged and needs restoration, but the trail is interesting and worthwhile for hikers or riders.

Cave of the Indians (Cuevo de los Indios). This cave, about 3 miles from town near Rancho San Vincente Hotel, was discovered in the 1920s. It contained a number of pre-Columbian artifacts that have been moved to the Academy of Sciences. You can walk the full length of the cave, about ¾ of a mile, and then take a rowboat along an underground stream, emerging at the cave's back end. Open Tues.–Sun. 9 a.m.–5 p.m.; closed Mon.

Cave of San Miguel. About 2.4 miles from town, in the mouth of this cave, a small bar does a bustling business, on Saturday nights especially. San Miguel is interesting, but not comparable to the Cave of the Indians.

Republica de Chile. A taxi or car is necessary to visit this new rural community, about 3 miles from the town of Vinales.

HOTELS IN VINALES

Los Jazmines, overlooking the valley at the entrance to the region from the south, about 1.2 miles from town (tel. 93114). This charming Spanish-style inn is the best in the area, with very comfortable rooms. 14 rooms, each with TV, private bath, telephone, hot water, and radio. Ask for a valley view, and don't miss the sunrise and sunset. Large pool, bar, and restaurant. Also 16 cabana units with no hot water. Rates: twin in hotel, 12 pesos; in cabana, 8; no single rates.

La Ermita Motel, at the opposite end of the valley from Los Jazmines (tel. 93120). This low-rise hotel, arranged around a swimming pool, has a less dramatic view than Jazmines but a more intimate atmosphere and accommodations. The lobby is beautifully furnished with authentic Spanish period pieces. 17 rooms, each with private bath and kitchenette, some TV, no hot water. No restaurant in hotel. Rates: twin, 7 pesos.

Rancho San Vincente, 5 miles north of the town of Vinales (tel. 93113). This remodeled extension of a building originally completed in 1940 is located across the road from the sulphur springs of San Vincente, used to treat arthritis, dermatitis, and rheumatism. It's a pleasant motel-style low-rise. 30 rooms, each with hot water and private bath; 14 triangular cabins scattered through the woods for use at the springs. Swimming pool and excellent restaurant. Rates: twin, 7 pesos; triple, 8.50.

RESTAURANTS IN VINALES

The best food to be had is at either the dining room at Las Jazmines or Rancho San Vincente, both moderately priced. The Rumayor at Pinar del Río is the nearest worthwhile restaurant outside Vinales (see "Pinar del Río").

THE DRIVE TO HAVANA

If you arrived at Viñales via the southerly route, opt to return via the north coast, (or v.v) a 109-mile trip almost all of which is sweepingly lovely. The landscape mixes vast cane fields with palm forests sprayed on hills with young pine reforestation projects. This route takes you through Las Cadenas, Cabanas, and Mariel. See "Driving Around Cuba."

APPENDIX

English	Spanish
Good morning (afternoon, evening).	Buenos días (tardes, noches).
How are you?	Cómo está usted?
Very well (not very well).	Muy bien (no muy bien).
Thank you.	Gracias.
Please.	Por favor.
You are welcome.	No hay de que; de nada.
I speak only English.	Sólo hablo inglés.
I am from the United States.	Soy de los Estados Unidos.
Yes, no.	Sí, no.
Do you speak English?	Habla usted inglés?
How much?	Cuanto?
Why?	Por qué?
When?	Cuándo?
Where is ?	Dónde está ?
I am looking for .	Busco .
What time is it?	Qué hora es?
Hour	Hora
Minute	Minuto, momento
Wait a minute, please.	Un momentico, por favor.
Today	Hoy
Tomorrow	Mañana
Yesterday	Ayer
Tonight	Esta noche.
Airport	El aeropuerto
Bus station (train station)	La estacion de autobuses (ferrocarriles)
Ticket	Un billete
What time does it leave (arrive)?	A qué hora sale (llegará)?
I want to reserve a room (table).	Quiero reservar una habitación (mesa).
Left, right	La izquierda, la derecha

North, south, east, west	Norte, sur, este, oeste
What street is this?	Qué calle es ésta?
Please tell me where to get off.	Por favor, avíseme dónde me bajo.
What bus do I take for ?	Qué autobus tomo para ?
Baggage	El equipaje
I want to call .	Deseo hacer una llamada a .
May I speak to ?	Deseo hablar con ?

DAYS OF THE WEEK

Monday	Lunes
Tuesday	Martes
Wednesday	Miércoles
Thursday	Jueves
Friday	Viernes
Saturday	Sábado
Sunday	Domingo
Open, closed	Abierto, cerrado

MONTHS

January	Enero
February	Febrero
March	Marzo
April	Abril
May	Mayo
June	Junio
July	Julio
August	Agosto
September	Septiembre
October	Octubre
November	Noviembre
December	Diciembre

RESTAURANT AND FOOD

Meat/beef/veal	Carne/carne de res/ternera
Steak	Bistec
Soup	Sopa
Fish	Pescado
Shellfish/shrimp/lobster	Mariscos/camarón/langosta
Pork	Cerdo
Chicken	Pollo
Salad	Ensalada
Dessert	Postre
Cheese	Queso
Drinks	Bebidas
Wine/beer	Vino/Cerveza
Breakfast/lunch/dinner	Desayuno/almuerzo/comida, cena
A little of	Un poquito de
More of	Mas de
Coffee	Café
Sugar	El azúcar
Milk	La leche
Tea	El té
Hot/cold	Caliente/Frio
Toast	Tostadas
Eggs/fried/scrambled	Huevos/fritos/revueltos
Plate	Un plato
Knife/fork/large spoon	Un cuchillo/tenedor/cuchara
Teaspoon	Una cucharita
Bread/butter	El pan/la mantequilla
The check please.	La cuenta, por favor.
Well done/rare/medium	Bien cocida/bien cruda/termino medio

NUMBERS

One/eleven	Uno/once
Two/twelve	Dos/doce
Three/thirteen	Tres/trece
Four/fourteen	Cuatro/catorce
Five/fifteen	Cinco/quince
six/sixteen	Seis/diez y seis
Seven/seventeen	Siete/diez y siete
Eight/eighteen	Ocho/diez y ocho
Nine/nineteen	Nueve/díez y nueve
Ten	Diez
Twenty	Veinte
Thirty	Treinta
Forty	Cuarenta
Fifty	Cincuenta
Sixty	Sesenta
Seventy	Setenta
Eighty	Ochenta
Ninety	Noventa
One hundred	Cien
One thousand	Mil

DISTANCE AND MEASUREMENT

Cuba follows the metric system:

One kilometer	=	0.62 mile
One meter	=	39.37 inches
One kilogram	=	2.2046 pounds
One centimeter	=	0.39 inch

Caballería	A measure of land equal to about 33 acres. Derives from old Spanish. Initial land grants were made to nobles who were willing to use the land to support one "soldier-at-arms and his horse" (caballo).
Arroba	A measure of weight equal to 25 pounds
Hectare	A measure of land equal to 2.5 acres.
Quintal	A measure of weight equal to 220 pounds approximately.

SOME INDISPENSABLE CUBAN TERMINOLOGY

Before/after/the Revolution	Antes/despues/la Revolucion
Campanero/companera (Cro. / cra.)	Preferred form of address, used for everyone (friend, officials, waiters, porters); means "comrade-partner" and has gradually replaced "señor, señora, señorita"
Norteamericano/a	North American, used to distinguish between Canadians or U. S. Citizens and Latin Americans

ADDRESSES

Calle	Street
Avenida	Avenue
Between	Entre
And	Y

An address written *Calle 31, e/A y B,* means "31st Street, between A and B." Often this is the best address available, since buildings are not always obviously numbered.

INDEX

NOTES